PROVE MY SOUL

Another Side to the Vietnam War

D1601641

BRIAN M. BIGGS

Hellgate Press   Ashland, Oregon

PROVE MY SOUL
Another Side to the Vietnam War

Published by Hellgate Press
(An imprint of L&R Publishing, LLC)
Hellgate Press
PO Box 3531
Ashland, OR 97520
email: info@hellgatepress.com

Interior & Cover Design: L. Redding
Cover photo by George K. Myrus, May 4, 1966 (our first day in Vietnam)

Cataloging In Publication Data is available from the publisher upon request.
ISBN: 978-1-55571-952-4

Printed and bound in the United States of America
First edition 10 9 8 7 6 5 4 3 2 1

For everyone who was touched by the Vietnam War and the American War (how the war is known in Việt Nam).

What Others Are Saying about *Prove My Soul:*

"In PROVE MY SOUL, *Marine Lieutenant Brian M. Biggs takes us to the front lines, not of a shooting war, but of the battle for the hearts and minds of the Vietnamese people. The story that Biggs pieces together straddles decades, and it is full of wry humor and unintended consequences. It is the story of Biggs' persistent effort to breach the barriers of language and cultural differences, and to understand what really happened inside the fog of war. Biggs is an honest narrator with a big heart, his prose marches smartly along, and* PROVE MY SOUL *gives us a remarkable look at a seldom seen side of the Vietnam War."*

—Stevan Allred, author of *The Alehouse at the End of the World*

*"*PROVE MY SOUL *is a vivid new look at an American veteran's relationship with Vietnam and the war he was swept up in more than 50 years ago. This is not a tale about mighty global forces clashing in a jungle. Rather it is the story about one man determined to make sense of it all—a half-baked war, unlikely friendships, and a lifelong enchantment with Vietnam and all its complexities. Come for the soul-searching and stay for the food. You can't read this book without wanting to finish it off with a big bowl of noodles!"*

—Wendy Willis is a poet and essayist living in Portland, Oregon. Her second book of poems, *A Long Late Pledge*, won the DorothyBrunsman Poetry Prize. Her first book of poems, *Blood Sisters of the Republic*, was published by *Press 53* in 2012. Her latest book is *These Are Strange Times My Dear: Field Notes from the Republic*.

"Marine Lieutenant Brian M. Biggs served in Vietnam as a motor transport officer, and ran his unit's Civic Action Program. He built additional classrooms for an over-crowded school, taught English, and made Vietnamese friends who would welcome him back into their lives 34 years later. This is the story of those friendships, and of the richly rewarding return trips that revealed the dark complications for the villagers that came from having a friend in the US Marines. There are many memoirs of the Vietnam war; PROVE MY SOUL *is a tender and illuminating story of healing and connection."*

—Joanna Rose is the author of *Little Miss Strange*

CONTENTS

Author's Note

WHEN I BEGAN writing this memoir in 2001, some of the events had taken place over thirty years in the past. Many of them were still in my memory bank but there were others that needed clarity. After my first trip back to Vietnam in October, 2001, the memoir began to take shape. Much of my information came from the Super 8 movies I took during my tour of duty in Vietnam, May 1966 to May 1967, my letters home, the University of California at Berkeley Writing Correspondence Course I took while in Vietnam, and conversations with those Marines who were stationed with me at MASS-2 in Danang.

Once I completed three trips back to Vietnam, the second, for the Tet celebration in January/February 2004, and the third in May 2006, I had enough information to put together a story. There were dozens of photos, tape recordings, diaries for each trip, and conversations with my Vietnam friends. Mr. Hoan and Miss Xuan provided many stories about my Civic Action work at Hoa My Elementary School.

Three of Mr. Hoan's grandchildren have given me tremendous support answering questions and providing information about Vietnamese culture. In 2001 they each spoke fluent English. Song Ha, who was in high school that year, is now a Lecturer at the University of Science and Technology in Danang. Hanh Quyen who was also in High School in 2001 now works as the Sales

Manager for Ba Na Golf Course in Danang. She is fluent in Chinese, English, and Vietnamese. Hanh Dung was a Freshman in College in 2001 and is now working at Danang University.

It has been a long journey with its ups and downs but the journey had wonderful highlights: Reading events where I could share some of my poems about the experiences I had in Vietnam, or prose stories taken right out of my memoir. But it is indeed an honor to have the memoir published so I can now share my entire story with you.

Prologue

...win the hearts and minds of the Vietnamese people.

—President Lyndon Johnson

FINALLY, I WAS leaving Vietnam. The war could go on without me.

A stewardess with that Bridget Bardot pout posed on top of the portable platform positioned next to the plane's open door. My heart beat double time when I reached the top of the stairs, her blue cap askew just enough to make her look even more like Bardot. I paused for a moment while I inhaled her perfume, Tabu. "Welcome to Pan American Airlines," she said then turned to the Marine behind me.

In just a few hours—after being gone 405 days—I would meet my six-month old son for the first time, feel his chubby cheeks, brush his hair, then hug my wife and six-year-old daughter.

I sat on the left side of the Boeing 707, nervous a Viet Cong soldier would mortar the airstrip in broad daylight. Fifteen May 1967. We taxied south and turned around to head back toward the Bay of Danang. We sped past Quonset huts that lined the runway until the plane's nose tilted up and a burst of ac-celeration thrust me back into my seat.

As we dipped to the left and turned to head northwest I saw cars and motorbikes driving on Highway 1. Then I saw Hoa My (whah me) Elementary School, the school I went to twice a week as my squadron's Civic Action Officer to "win the hearts and minds of the Vietnamese people"—a phrase President Lyndon

Johnson borrowed from John Adams or maybe William Shake-speare and used many times. In truth, the Vietnamese people captured my heart and mind.

The previous day I taught my final English Language class at that school and said goodbye to the faculty and students, many of whom had grown to be my friends, especially Miss Xuan (*Soon*), one of the seven teachers in my class.

I saw her for the first time on 4 May 1966, the day I arrived "in-country." She stood on the playground of Hoa My School wearing the traditional dress of Vietnam, an *ao dai*, (ow yai) white and tight to her slender body. Her hair, short and black as crow's feathers, curled around her face accenting a smile that had its own language.

Miss Xuan took to her English lessons, continually repeating, mispronouncing, correcting, testing. Wanting more. She never missed a lesson...except the day before I left Vietnam. It seemed so out of character.

On that last class I had brought in her final assignment to return, an essay on King Quang Trung written in almost perfect English. But no Miss Xuan. I asked Mr. Hoan, one of my other close friends, if he knew why she was absent.

"Miss Xuan cannot be here today," is all he said. He was a man of few words but open to learn and took his English lessons seriously.

I kept her paper, thinking I'd drop it off at the school on my way to the airport. But that didn't happen. I could only guess at her reasons for missing that final class.

Maybe she was Viet Cong. The other two officers in our outfit who helped me teach the English Language classes suspected as much. If she was Viet Cong the South Vietnamese Government would arrest her and put her in prison. A death sentence for sure. Whatever the reason, I had a bad feeling.

It would take thirty-four years and three trips back to Vietnam to find the answer.

ONE

The Road to Vietnam

Lord, we know what we are, but know not what we may be.
—Hamlet, Act 4, Scene 5, William Shakespeare

Vallejo

IN THE TENTH grade, on my walk home after track practice, a black '55 Chevy slowed down beside me with three older guys in it, two of them, one in the front seat, one in the back, held their arm out the window and stared at me. Cigarettes hung out of their mouths and flopped up and down when they growled. This could be bad, I thought, so I looked straight ahead and kept walking but the two started howling and slapping the side of their Chevy trying to get my attention.

Finally, they pulled over to the curb ahead of me, parked the car, and walked over to the sidewalk, slow, like they had nowhere to go but right there ten yards in front of me. They just stood there, blocking the sidewalk with their six-foot frames, cigarettes dangling from their mouths, and identical DA haircuts greased down with a curl combed into the center of their forehead. Their T shirts had cigarette packs rolled up into the shirt sleeves. These guys were big, probably seniors from Floyd Terrace. I should have crossed the street or turned around, but for some reason, I just kept walking even though I knew at that moment I could get my teeth knocked out.

Then the bigger of the three took a drag off his cigarette, pulled it out of his mouth and pointed at me, "Hey, that's Bob Biggs's brother, not a good idea to mess with him." They gave me a sneer, nodded their heads, got back in their Chevy and drove off.

This was Vallejo, California, a small town located at the northeastern edge of San Francisco Bay. A town with a Navy base that employed many of its citizens. Also, a town known for its tough neighborhoods, where growing up you were either an athlete, a car club member, or a fighter. My brother, six years older, was all three. I was a two-sport athlete—football and track.

My brother, tall and thin with bicep muscles that bulged out of his white T shirt, had a reputation in Vallejo for being tough; that is, winning every fight he fought, some he started, most he didn't. That reputation passed down to me. I played football for Vallejo High, the only high school in town and a team that won the North Bay League Football Championship each of the previous four years.

My first encounter with Assistant Football Coach Dick Biama set the stage. Coach Biama was short, five-foot-six or seven, but no one would ever mess with him. He was one tough football coach.

Coach Biama wanted to know if I was as tough as my brother. "Yes," I lied.

Then he related a story to me. He told me my brother came into the coach's office after practice one day and showed him his index finger. A bone stuck out just below his fingernail with blood oozing around the bone turning his finger and fingernail red.

"I got stepped on in practice, Coach."

Coach Biama asked him if it hurt and my brother said, "Not much."

Then he told my brother to put his finger flat on the counter so he could look at it. But instead of looking at the finger, he took a padlock, locked it, wrapped his fingers around the ring, raised it up and swung it down hard on the counter right next to my brother's finger.

Coach Biama looked at me and chuckled, "He didn't flinch or move that finger one iota. Are you that tough?"

"Yes." I lied again.

* * * *

High school had three of my favorite things: football, girls, and Drama. Suzie Schmutz was in my Drama class. She was also a cheerleader for the football team and the most popular girl in school with a big smile and beautiful blue eyes. Maybe I could finagle a date with her.

Tryouts for the Fall play, *I Remember Mama*, came up in November so I tried out. "Hey Brian, you got the part of Uncle Chris," Russ Obee said. Russ Obee was our quarterback on the football team and also in Drama.

"Who's that?" I said.

"He's the lead."

The lead in the school play, how cool was that? I also dated Suzie Schmutz. Took her to a movie, *The Vikings*. It was my third time but she had never seen it. I took my dad's new two-tone '59 Ford Fairlane, orange and white. Only 259 miles on it.

After the movie I parked in front of her house and we talked. "You're a good football player," she said.

"Thanks."

"You're welcome."

"You want to go out again?"

"Yes."

"Good. Maybe another movie."

"That would be okay."

I kissed her. Not long. But long enough. I smiled all the way home driving my dad's new Ford.

One night at a rehearsal of *I Remember Mama*, after I finished a scene with Mama, Miss Dutton, our Drama teacher, said, "Uncle Chris, could you sing some sort of ballad at the end of that scene? You're a little tipsy from the drink so you can slur it a bit. Just some tune, you can even make it up."

I said, "How 'bout the theme from *The Vikings*, this guy's Norwegian isn't he?"

"Try it."

"De DAAAAW da, De DAAAAAW da, de daaw, de daaw, de daaw, de daaaw, de DAAAAAAAW!" I bellowed.

"Great, Brian. Keep it."

Suzie Schmutz stage managed the play, which gave me time to get to know her.

At breaks we talked about high school and college. She wanted to major in Drama at some college. She had her life planned out. College, New York City, an acting career. That's why she wanted to stage manage the play. She wanted to learn all facets of the theater, backstage work, makeup, acting, set construction.

Suzie and I dated most of our senior year. One night after a date I drove my dad's new Ford just outside of town and parked in a clump of eucalyptus trees on American Canyon Road. We talked in the pitch-black dark about pimples, our brothers, and how we might be in college together majoring in Drama. I put my arm around her shoulders. Then we started making out. After a bit, I tried to undo her bra but just then a car drove up behind us. We sat there, frozen, until we heard a *clack, clack, clack* knocking noise on Suzie's window. She screamed, I jumped back.

"Roll down the window please, Highway Patrol." Suzie rolled down her window.

"Everything okay in there?" he said with a flashlight shining in our eyes.

"Yes, sir," I said.

"May I see your driver's license?"

"Yes, sir."

"You okay, Miss?"

"Yes, sir," Suzie said.

After he looked at my license, he handed it to Suzie and said, "You better move on now."

I took her home and walked her to the door where we stared at each other. I said "Goodbye," too scared to kiss her, then drove down Tuolumne Street to Tennessee Street, and as I turned left onto Tennessee I forgot to signal and didn't see the oncoming Ford pickup and crashed head-on into its front end. The police came with flashing red lights that lit up the intersection like a July 4th fireworks show. Some of my friends drove by and stared, some yelled out while I had to stand there. Luckily neither of us were going very fast so there wasn't too much damage, not much at all on the pickup but my dad's new Ford had to be towed down to the Wilson Russel Ford Dealership.

My dad was great about it. Didn't even take my driving privileges away. That came later in the spring, after my second wreck with his '59 Ford.

After graduation, Suzie went to UCLA, majored in Drama, graduated, and moved to New York City. I went to Vallejo Junior College to play football. It was seven years before I saw Suzie Schmutz again. That was in New York on my way back to Camp Lejeune from Naval Justice School in Rhode Island, one day before I received orders to Vietnam.

The University of Washington (UW)

After graduating from Vallejo Junior College (now Solano College) I received a football scholarship to the University of Washington. Bill Siler, one of our quarterbacks on the team, was 5' 9" and 172 pounds. He was a tough little guy at quarterback and a tough little guy off the field. Both being from California, he was from L.A., we quickly became friends. At one time, he'd been a "water-boy" for the UCLA football teams coached by Red Sanders.

The Washington football team lived in the Husky Crew House during the fall. And during winter and spring quarters the Husky Crew took over the facilities. This meant we needed to find other accommodations

Siler, nicknamed "Froggy" because he had a face like a frog, wanted me to move in to the Sigma Alpha Epsilon (SAE) fraternity house with him. We both needed a place to live that provided meals and Charlie Bond was already an SAE. Charlie Bond, a tackle on the Husky Football team, was 6' 4" and 245 pounds, a big guy with a big smile. Charlie and I became fast friends since his family lived in Puyallup and owned the largest blueberry farm west of the Mississippi. Also, his mother cooked a "to die for" blueberry pancake breakfast and a prize-winning blueberry pie whose warm crust would dissolve across my tongue and send the sweet and slightly salty flavor throughout my entire body. One heated piece, with vanilla ice cream, was never enough.

Fraternities, I found out, fostered one thing: drinking. Before weekend parties we would have a pre-party somewhere with a keg of beer. At the party itself, we would drink more beer, and at the post-party we would again, drink more beer. I weighed 160 pounds, even though the football program listed me as 170, and I assumed the beer would add some weight. It didn't.

After football season we drank beer at the Rainbow Tavern on 45th. Husky football players had the back room, an alcove large enough for six or eight of us. After we emptied a pitcher of beer, it was three hard slaps on the table by each one of us, *BANG, BANG, BANG*, and then we yelled, "MORE BEER!" as loudly as we could. The other patrons in the tavern sometimes clapped and sometimes yelled obscenities, depending on our level of obnoxious behavior.

One early January evening the assembled crowd included Bill Siler; Johnny O'Brien (O.B.), a guard; Dave Kopay, later a running back for the 49'ers and the first professional football player to come out as gay; Charlie Bond; and me. After we finished our third pitcher of beer and did our "More Beer" chant, Siler, impatient because the next pitcher hadn't arrived, bit off the top half of his empty glass.

I winced at the thought of the damage to his teeth or lips or gums. O.B. tried it and spit out little pieces of glass onto the table.

Siler said, "Come on Weasel try it." ("Weasel" was my nickname since my back stretched out like a weasel when I ran.)

"No, I'll pass." I was fairly drunk and didn't want my teeth any more damaged than they already were. In Junior High during a pickup football game in the park, I fell onto the sidewalk mouth-first after being tackled and the collision onto concrete left me with a chipped upper front tooth. When my mom saw me, she screamed "Brian, Brian, what happened?! Your tooth is chipped! You know that's a permanent tooth. A permanent tooth!" She shook me by the shoulders yelling, "It won't grow back! It won't grow back!!"

After our waitress brought Siler his beer, I realized I was too drunk to have any more and did not want to find myself biting off the top of beer glasses, so I decided to leave the group. Kopay asked for a ride to his BETA fraternity just down the street from the SAE House so Dave and I left in my black, '56 convertible V.W. Beetle. While going up the hill on 47th I figured, in my drunken state, that I could run the stop sign on 16th even though it was a blind corner. I didn't stop.

Luckily, no cars came, but it was the most stupid thing I had done in my entire life. My little V.W. Bug would have been crushed and both Kopay and I would have been seriously hurt or killed. I turned right onto 17th and stopped to let Kopay off at the Beta house, then drove down to the SAE house and parked in back.

When I wobbled down the hall to the sleeping porch another SAE, Tom, I think his name was, said, "Brian you're 'shitfaced.'"

"Yeah," I said and zig-zagged down the hall.

"Whoa, there big boy." He was a chubby 5' 5". "You're really blasted, you need some coffee."

"No, I'm just going to bed."

"No, really buddy, you need some coffee."

"Okay."

He drove me to the Hasty Tasty. I'd never been there but we parked and went inside. As I walked in I happened to stumble into someone sitting at the bar.

"Hey, shithead. Watch what you're doing."

I'm not sure what I said if anything.

"You want to take this outside?" he said.

I remember saying, "Sure."

We walked back to the front door and out to the parking lot with a clamoring crowd following. I stood in front of this tall guy who looked like Clark Kent and said, "I'm going to take off my watch," which I did, and then I used both hands to put the watch in my pocket. And at this point, Clark Kent hit me right in the mouth. I went out, unconscious.

I woke up lying on the pavement with some woman holding my head and yelling. She gave me a hanky or cloth to wipe the blood from my mouth and then "SAE Tom" came over to help me up. Off we went to his car with blood spilling out of my mouth. Back at the SAE House I realized I did not have my four upper front teeth. I was drunk but I knew that was not good.

It took time to heal, but fortunately the football team dentist built a partial denture and I was normal within a month. And no more chipped tooth.

* * * *

After football season I tried out for one of the Theatre Department's winter plays, *The Trickeries of Scapino* by Molière. I got the part of Silvestro, Scapino's sidekick who assists in many of his "trickeries."

My partial denture was ready about halfway through our rehearsal period of *Scapino*. This was fortunate since one cannot say words beginning with Vs or Fs without upper front teeth. However, in the scene where Scapino asks my character, Sylvestro, to scare the bejesus out of the rich Argante, Vanick Galstaun, our director, thought it would add a menacing flavor and some extra humor if I came on stage without any upper front teeth. It worked, I also added a black eye patch.

My next theater experience, included the part of Barnadine in Shakespeare's *Measure For Measure,* directed by Duncan Ross and staged in the Showboat Theatre moored below the UW campus on Lake Union. The Showboat designed by John Ashby Conway and built by the Works Progress Administration (WPA) opened in September 1938. Some of the actors that played on the Showboat stage included Lillian Gish, Robert Culp, and Chet Huntley, who later switched from acting to broadcasting the evening news with David Brinkley.

Duncan Ross wanted me to have a full beard as Barnadine which I enjoyed growing. And, of course, no front teeth would be perfect for this prisoner, so I removed my partial plate for that role also.

Seattle Times Theatre Critic Tom Robbins wrote in his review of *Measure for Measure*:

If Brian Biggs would growl like a Tasmanian devil instead of bellowing like a bison, he would succeed in an otherwise perfect characterization of the most interesting figure in the play: Barnadine, a drunken condemned criminal, a symbol of those who took the savageries of Elizabethan justice for granted and went unconcernedly, or with crude jest, to the ax.

Journalist George Burley had this to say:

Brian Biggs, portraying the "independent" prisoner, Barnadine, deserves an "o-le" as probably the play's best comic actor—by doing almost nothing. It is rather unfortunate that his stage time is so short.

We toured the show all over the state of Washington during Spring Break, then returned to the Showboat for three more shows on April 4-6. On Friday, April 5, 1963, Coach Owens called a meeting of the football team to prepare for our spring practice. At the end of the meeting we lined up to collect our playbooks at the front table. When I reached for my book, Coach Owens said, "Biggs, you better get rid of that beard and get rid of it quick."

"Yes, sir," I said. "It's for the Shakespeare play I'm in and it ends tomorrow night. It will be gone right after the play."

"See to it."

In 1963 there were very few beards on the University of Washington campus and I can't remember any shoulder length hair on the men. But change was a'comin.

* * * *

Siler and I went to the Montlake Tavern the Friday before Spring Break. School was done and we wanted to celebrate. Charlie Bond, who was now my roommate in an apartment, had gone home to Puyallup. It wasn't crowded so we sat at the bar and ordered our beer. The man next to Siler said to the bartender, "The Huskies sure had a shitty season last year," not realizing we both played on the team. Siler could snap pretty quick when taunted into an argument or disagreement. He turned to the man not much older than us and asked where he was from. He said Seattle and Siler jumped off his stool, shoved the guy's shoulder hard enough to knock his beer all over the bar, and yelled, "You wanna see what a Husky football player can do?"

He reared back to throw a punch and I grabbed his arm, "Come on Froggy, let's get out of here." The guy stood up and towered over Siler, saying, "You want to lose some teeth, shit bird?"

That did not deter Siler from the fight he was anticipating but by that time, the bartender had come around to help me escort Siler out of the tavern.

"I don't give a shit how tall your are, ass hole," Siler yelled as he fought to free himself from my hold as I wrestled him out the front door. "You're the shit bird!"

Once outside I escorted Siler to his car and made sure he got in and then walked around to the passenger side. "Shit bird," he yelled again and again as he took out his keys, started the car, and took off with the gas pedal down to the floorboard and slammed into a telephone pole.

No seat belts back then, so I hit the dashboard mouth-first and broke my partial plate. The teeth weren't damaged, they just snapped off the plate.

Our bus for the theater tour was scheduled to load at 2:00 p.m. the next day and then head down Highway 99 to Olympia for our first showing of *Measure For Measure* on our state tour.

Our team dentist came in to the office on that Saturday just to glue my front upper teeth back on to the plate. My character didn't need his teeth but I didn't want to spend all our free time without upper front teeth. I had a crush on Bridget Hanley, who played Marianna in the show, and missing my upper front teeth changed the way I talked besides looking weird.

* * * *

During my senior year, the fall of 1963, my third year at Washington, I made second team, enjoyed some playing time, and proved myself to the coaches. Then, in a Monday evening shop class for the Theatre Department, we worked on the set of *The Fantasticks*. Marcie, a woman I had dated twice and someone I would have liked to continue dating, started cleaning up just before the 10:00 p.m. quitting time. I needed to make one more cut on the table saw but wanted to walk Marcie back to her sorority. It was an easy cut, taking a quarter-inch off a six-foot piece of molding, and I rushed to do it before she left the shop. I adjusted the blade's height, measured out the width of the cut, lay the molding on the table, turned on the saw, and began to push the wood through, putting slight pressure on the molding so it would slide against the fence. However, I didn't pick up a push stick to use for such a close cut, too interested in Marcie since she had finished her sweeping job. When I moved the molding near the rotating blade, *WHACK! WHACK! WHACK!* All the fingers on my right hand were sucked into the whirling razor-sharp points while the molding flapped up and down and blood splattered all over the saw and me.

Marcie screamed and other students ran to the see what happened, but Tyke Lounsbury, the instructor, calmly brought out a clean towel and wrapped it around my hand and then organized a team of two students to take me to the Hull Health Center. Marcie left the shop at the same time I did but we went our separate ways.

The nurses at the Health Center said they couldn't handle something that serious so they sent the two students and me to the University Hospital. Those nurses cleaned and wrapped the wounds on all five digits then knocked me out with a pain killer.

The next morning, Dr. Blue operated on my hand and left me with sixty-three stitches, a hard cast from the tips of my fingers to my elbow, and some more pain pills. When he came in to see me later that day, he said, "Brian, you are a very lucky man. You won't lose any fingers."

"Good," I said, "I have a game against Stanford this week."

"A game?"

"Yes, I'm on the Husky football team."

"Brian, you won't be playing any more football, not this season at least."

He was wrong on that point. I was getting some playing time, bumped up to second team, and at this point in the season I was playing my best football as we prepared for Stanford at Stanford.

I sent tickets to my Vallejo buddies and my mom and dad. I was sure we would beat Stanford on Saturday, October 19th, and I might score touchdown.

But that Monday night, October 14th, my right hand got sucked into that table saw blade and I missed the Stanford game. And it looked like I would miss other games. My fingers took a long time to heal, but once the cast came off I started going to practices and running with the team. I still couldn't catch the football or scrimmage.

Eventually, I could endure a full practice again with a wrap around the two middle fingers as they had the deepest cuts. The season came down to a must win at Washington State in Pullman on November 23rd to go to the Rose Bowl. My two fingers were still tender but I didn't tell any of the coaches. I wanted to play in that Washington State game and I was ready.

However, the assassination of President Kennedy on Friday, November 22nd delayed most college football games that weekend. The Kennedy tragedy gave me two additional weeks of practice and I was fully recovered for the Washington State game on December 7th. We beat them 16 to 0 and were on our way to play Illinois in the Rose Bowl!

The Rose Bowl was a special time for all of us—a trip to Disneyland, dinner at Lawry's Prime Rib Restaurant, reporters asking questions and a luxury hotel. There was an article on me by Dave Beronio, the Sports Editor for the *Vallejo Times Herald* and an article written in the *Seattle Times* about my conquest at Lawry's Prime Rib Restaurant:

> *Regarding those dinners, Brian Biggs, a 170-pound back, is the champion eater on the Washington squad. He consumed three large servings of meat, potatoes and vegetables. That was in addition to bread, salad, milk and dessert. As one teammate described Biggs' efforts: "He destroys everything in sight."*

We lost the Rose Bowl game 17 to 7, to Dick Butkus and crowd. At our year-end banquet Charlie Bond received the Flaherty Inspirational Award, Dave Kopay was a co-captain along with John Stupey, and I received the Most Inspirational Player award for a non-letterman, an award honoring Brian Stapp who died in a diving accident at the beginning of his junior year. Coach Owens, however, gave me a letter so I could join the Big W Club. It was an honor for me to receive the Stapp award at our banquet, although I couldn't go up to receive it, nor did I get my picture in the *Seattle Times* with Charlie Bond and the other players honored as I was staring in another play at the Showboat Theatre that night and needed to leave the banquet early. My father accepted the award for me.

That spring I graduated with a degree in Drama and planned to go to Hollywood to find work as an actor. A friend of my brother's, Joe D'Agusta, was casting director for Paramount and had TV shows like *Mission Impossible, Star Trek*, and *Rawhide*. I figured he could help me find an agent and hook me up with the right people.

But two days after graduation I received a letter that opened with, "Greetings: You are hereby ordered for induction into the Armed Forces of the United States."

Drafted into the Army! But that news did not alter my plans for Hollywood. I was twenty-two years old and in excellent shape. My father was a Marine and my older brother was a paratrooper in the Army. Hollywood could wait.

However, since I had a college degree, it made no sense for me to be a private in the Army, so I signed up to attend the Marine Corps Officer Candidate School in Quantico, Virginia.

On 11 December 1964, after ten weeks of leg lifts, pushups, pullups, and wind sprints, plus forced marches with sixty-pound backpacks, crawling in mud under a barbed wire screen, pugil-stick fights, and mental harassment from our Drill Instructors, none of which bothered me, nor most of my fellow Officer Candidates, I stood at attention in Quantico, Virginia, as a Marine Second Lieutenant.

On that date, I had never heard of Vietnam.

TBS: The Basic School

Our Marine Corps Basic School Class, 4-65, billeted (lived) in O' Bannon Hall. Two weeks into the six-month TBS program, my roommate George Bocock, gave me a note that was taped onto our door: "Report to Captain Hancock, ASAP."

With note in hand and field jacket collar up, my shined black boots crunched across the green and white snow specked lawn that sloped a hundred yards down to Heywood Hall, TBS Headquarters building.

Once inside Heywood Hall, I walked halfway down the hall to a woman with short hair, red finger nails, and a sweater over her shoulders. She sat at her desk typing, her red-tipped fingers in constant motion like keys on a player piano.

She did not look up. Just stared at the typewriter paper.

I knocked on the counter. Nothing. "Excuse me," I said.

She looked up with a start. "Oh, I'm sorry, Lieutenant. What can I do for you?"

"Can you tell me where the ASAP office is, Ma'am?"

Her eyebrows wrinkled in to each other, almost touching. "I beg your pardon."

"I need to report to the ASAP office."

She pushed her chair back and looked into an adjoining office. Then back at me for a moment. She rose from her chair and walked to the doorway. There was a sign above the adjoining office door that read, "Commanding Officer." My heart raced. This was Colonel Platt's office, the Commanding Officer (CO) of Basic School.

"Now, Lieutenant, what is it exactly you're looking for?"

"I've got this note here that says to report to Captain Hancock at the ASAP office."

She walked to me, "May I see the note?"

"Yes."

"Lieutenant, the note says for you to report to Captain Hancock, A-S-A-P." She pronounced each letter individually like I hadn't learned the alphabet. Then she continued, "A.S.A.P.—As Soon As Possible?"

I looked at her, back at the note, and then over to Colonel Platt's door. "ASAP. Really. I've never heard that."

"Captain Hancock's office is just down that hallway, Lieutenant, she said."

"Yes, I know where it is. Thank you. I'm on my way." In the hall I muttered, "ASAP."

I knocked on Captain Hancock's door. "Lieutenant Biggs requests permission to enter, sir."

"Come in Lieutenant Biggs." Captain Hancock rose from his chair and looked at me. His olive drab utility uniform, starched as always, seemed extra crisp like he'd just put it on. And his belt buckle, Brassoed to a mirror-like sheen, seemed fake, way too bright for a belt buckle.

Captain Hancock was quiet for a moment and then said, "Have a seat Lieutenant Biggs." I sat down in front of his desk and he sat back down. It was a small office with no windows. The Captain had some plaques on the wall but I couldn't read them. His file cabinet sat in a corner. He was a career Marine.

"Your mother called headquarters a while ago. She wanted you to know your grandmother passed away yesterday morning. In her sleep."

That was news I hadn't expected. Captain Hancock was silent. I was silent. My grandmother had moved to Portland, Oregon, after my grandfather died. She lived with my uncle. I saw her during the Christmas break on my way up to Seattle to see Charlie Bond. She had a strong influence on my life, reading to me when I was younger, picking flowers and vegetables out of her garden.

She came from Scotland and spoke with a Scottish brogue. She often stayed weekends with us in Vallejo and when I introduced her to my teenage friends, she would stick out her firm hand and say, "Howjadoo." They'd crack up when she left the room. I laughed sometimes, but "howjadoo" sounded normal to me.

"Should I call my mom?" I said.

Captain Hancock said, "Your mother wants you to call her. Wants to let you know about the funeral."

He walked out of the office to let me use his phone. I called my mom collect and after I talked to her, decided not to go to the funeral. It was going to be a small service and my mom didn't think it would be important for me to attend.

Captain Hancock was in the hall when I left the office. "I'm sorry to hear about your grandmother, Lieutenant Biggs. If you need leave time, come and see me."

"Thank you, sir. Thanks for letting me use your phone. I won't need any leave, sir."

I nodded to the woman outside Colonel Platt's office. She looked at me and nodded back with that wrinkled up forehead. She must have thought, *How is he ever going to make it through Basic School?*

The lawn was all white now and large snowflakes filled the air. My middle name, Murray, is my grandmother's maiden name. All the officers at TBS were in the process of turning information in for our calling cards. It was a big deal to have a card we could hand out to friends or a business. I hadn't decided how to have my name printed. "Brian Biggs" was my first choice. I liked the simplicity. I was not going to use "B.M. Biggs." But on that walk across the snow toward O'Bannon Hall, "Brian M. Biggs" popped into my head.

Brian M. Biggs
2nd Lieutenant USMC

That would be my card. And anytime I used my name professionally, for writing books or poems or plays I would direct, the "M" in "Brian M. Biggs" would remind me of my grandmother.

I smiled and laughed out loud at ASAP.

* * * *

After dating East Coast women for about six months, I had had enough of them and their odd names for pop, their starched shirts, and the fact that none of them wore jeans. So, I wrote Colleen, the woman I dated my last year at Washington, and asked her to marry me. She loved camping and clam digging and pheasant hunting and all the things I did and had a great smile.

Colleen and her daughter, Kaye, were to arrive any minute. She used AAA Trip Tiks to drive from Seattle, Washington, to Quantico, Virginia, and I watched from my dorm window for her 1962 white Mercury Comet. Our wedding was in two days, Sunday, 4 April 1965, at 1400.

And there she was heading up the hill, right on schedule. I ran downstairs and out to the parking lot to greet them. Kaye was sleepy as she stepped out of the car but still the cutest little four-year-old girl there ever was. We hugged and kissed and all talked at once about their trip across country and what they saw, and they said they both needed to go to the bathroom so we went into O' Bannon Hall where I would live for just two more nights.

Charlie Bond came downstairs and hugged Colleen, and I introduced him to Kaye, who was shy and hid behind her mom's legs. Colleen and Charlie Bond met while I dated her my last six months in Seattle.

Captain Hancock ordered everyone in our platoon to attend the wedding, so the church was full. Several of us went to the Officer's Club to celebrate. Charlie Bond, who stood up as my best man, gave a little speech that ended with, "Brian may be a bit odd, but he can sure choose a woman." Eric Barnes and his wife, Noreen, were there, and Eric stood up to say, "You'll be happy to move out of O' Bannon Hall, Brian, Colleen is a hell of lot better roommate than George Bocock. And since you'll now live next door to us, we can make sure you take good care of her." Everyone shouted and drank beer and sent us off to our new quarters, while Kaye spent the weekend with Colleen's aunt who lived in Falls Church, Virginia.

Eric helped me put together a new bicycle for Kaye, one that had training wheels. "What the heck is this bolt for?" I said when trying to put on the training wheels? It was a comedy of errors reading and following the directions but we finally finished the job. I put her on the seat and let her get used to the feel since she had those training wheels. And when it came time for a solo ride down the sidewalk to the next apartment building, I gave her a pat on the back, a gentle shove, and off she went gaining speed on the slope down toward some garbage cans.

"Put on the breaks!" I yelled.

"Did you show her how to use the breaks?" Eric asked as he ran past me.

"I don't think so. No, I didn't. Push the peddle backwards!" I screamed.

She crashed into the garbage cans with a clatter that brought out all the neighbors, including the owner of the garbage cans, a captain who gave me a lecture on how a child's trust can easily disintegrate.

* * * *

At the end of Basic School, Eric Barnes, one of the top ten Marines in our class, asked for an Infantry MOS (Military Occupational Specialty) and his wish came true. They gave him 0301, the most sought after MOS given to the best Marine officers, the ones who would lead a platoon in combat. They gave me 3501, Motor Transport. Not one of my three choices.

Both Eric and I were sent to Camp Lejeune, North Carolina, me for the one-month Motor Transport School and Eric for playing war games. I didn't learn too much about Motor Transport in one month: What was the load capacity of the various military vehicles? How do you organize a convoy? What is the driver's maintenance program? How does a Military Motor Pool operate? Nothing about any of those fairly important concerns, but by August 1965 I did know that the Marines had landed in Vietnam in March of that year and secured the Danang airbase so our planes could land and takeoff without incurring enemy fire.

After Motor Transport School, my first assignment came in for Company C, 2nd Motor Transport Battalion, 2nd Marine Division, right there at Camp Lejeune. However, that fall I was given TDA, "Temporary Duty Assignment," to the football team and played halfback for Camp Lejeune. I literally only had one cup of coffee with the Motor Transport Officer, Captain Hutzler.

After football season, the Marines sent me to Naval Justice School in Newport, Rhode Island, and after that school I volunteered for duty in Vietnam. While drinking my second cup of coffee in Captain Hutzler's office, I received orders to the 1st Marine Air Wing in Danang. On 17 January 1966, with little training and no practical experience in a motor pool, I had my chance to help the people of South Vietnam stave off the onslaught of communism.

TWO

"Hello Vietnam!"

The scented obscurity of the shore was grouped into vast masses, a density of colossal clumps of vegetation, probably—mute and fantastic shapes. And at their foot the semicircle of a beach gleamed faintly, like an illusion. The mysterious East faced me, perfumed like a flower, silent like death, dark like a grave.

—From *Youth*, Joseph Conrad

I N SAN DIEGO, California, at "O Dark Thirty" on the morning of 16 April 1966, I joined three thousand other Marines aboard the troop transport ship, USNS *William Weigel*, bound for Vietnam. At lunch on our first day, somewhere off the coast of Southern California, while eating *Filets de Flet a la Moutrarde* in the Officer's Mess, I started to feel nauseous and walked outside for some fresh air. I stared down at the ocean waves breaking against the ship's hull but that didn't help so I went into the nearest head and vomited. Seasick.

When I returned to the table I realized with unimaginable consequences, that I didn't have the partial denture that held my four upper front teeth. My cabinmate aboard this ship, George Myrus, who was in Boot Camp with me at Quantico said, "What's wrong Brian, you look like you saw a ghost."

"I threw up in the head and lost my front teeth. They're with my lunch on the way to the bottom of the ocean."

He laughed but knew it wasn't funny. "That's the ship's dentist sitting next to you, he can fix you up."

Unfortunately, not. "I'm sorry, Lieutenant, we don't have the equipment on board to make a partial denture. They'll take care of you in Danang. It's a fully equipped dentist facility"

For the three weeks aboard ship I settled into the fact I had four missing front teeth, however there were no visitors, other than the albatross that floated in the wind at the ships stern for several days, and no parties, other than the ceremony for crossing the International Dateline.

George Myrus, a short and stocky guy, and one tough Marine, had not crossed it, nor had I so we were initiated into the "Royal Domain of the Golden Dragon." We were called on deck shortly after breakfast and told to take off our shirts and boots and sit down on a bench with about twenty other Marines.

After they blindfolded us, we sat there while they screamed out bird calls and dog yelps and announced they would rub a potion on us to eat off our skin. They rasped a gooey liquid that smelled like rotten shrimp across my chest and stomach.

Then a thick, syrup-like liquid ran down my face and around my lips. It was difficult to breathe without ingesting some of that not-so-sweet syrup. Then the shouting and dog barking began again while we were helped up and taken over to King Neptune who wanted us to kiss his belly. The belly belonged to a chubby sailor who had some odious concoction plastered onto his belly. And that was it for crossing the International Dateline.

The days on board ship were boring and monotonous. We ate meals, watched movies, read, showered, inspected the troops on occasion, jogged, watched more movies, and read more books.

On 4 May 1966 Myrus woke me up at 0400 to watch the ship and its contingent of 3,000 Marines sail into Danang Bay. Myrus and I were in the same Officer Candidate School class, which was the officer's version of boot camp, but we were in different companies at TBS. During that five-and-a-half-month school, we learned how to be an "Officer and a Gentleman." Myrus, an artillery officer, thought he would go north. I would stay near Danang.

The lights of Danang City shimmered below a ridge of mountains until the sun revealed a khaki-colored beach that circled the bay below a line of gnarled pine trees. The sun also revealed a flotilla of Navy and commercial ships that covered the bay.

The landscape looked serene and peaceful and reminded me of the San Juan Islands in Washington State, the landscape all forested and green and canopied down to the water's edge. The only sound was the drone of our ship's engines. But then I heard the explosions of artillery fire that made me realize they were explosions that killed people.

Splashes of cold mist washed over my face as I rode the landing craft across Danang Bay and up the River Han but the sense of anything cold vanished when we docked at Museum Beach where the humidity, like a vacuum, sucked away the air. My sea bag thunked onto the ramp when I stepped out of the boat with thirty other Marines. My T-shirt, utility jacket, face, arms, and crotch were soaked with sweat and the air smelled musty, like festered seaweed, russet and dry and lifeless on a beach.

Dust from trucks and motorbikes and rickshaws swirled up from the road and floated in a thick, brown cloud. The air was stagnant and still, like a grainy photograph. The Vietnamese people, under their pointed bamboo hats, walked expressionless, through the haze. They were all short, like junior high school children on a playground.

A woman shuffled by with blackened teeth. She carried a long bamboo pole across her shoulders, a pole that bent low at each end from the weight of cookpots that nestled into a hanging wicker basket. She didn't walk, she shuffled in sync with her load so each basket bounced within an inch of the ground but never touched.

Horns honked, hawkers hawked and the putter sound of motorbike engines filled the air as we walked across the street to a park lined with yellow-blossomed trees. A four-foot wall boarded the park with a sidewalk below. We threw our sea bags down and tried to keep cool but the heat was too oppressive. Some sat on their sea bags, most stood waiting for the truck or jeep to come by and take them to their duty stations. The heat was bad enough but then bees attacked a group of Marines that jumped up on the wall to lie down in the grass. They jumped back down waving their arms to drive them off.

A sergeant drove up in a jeep and yelled out my name. With the troops aboard our ship the total number of Americans serving in Vietnam rose to 254,000. Roughly 8,000 Americans had already lost their lives in the war and at that moment another 50,178 would be killed before this war ended, including my future son's namesake and his godfather.

* * * *

My duty station, a Marine Air Support Squadron known as MASS-2, sat halfway up a hill, six kilometers north of Danang and overlooked the bay and surrounding villages. The area looked like a mining camp nestled into the Sierra-Nevada foothills, a gathering of tents and wooden walkways and corrugated metal roofed hooches that shined in the bright sun.

The Commanding Officer, Lieutenant Colonel Sheppe, shook my hand and sat back down at his desk. Two fans whirled in his screened in office at the center of the MASS-2 compound as I stood there without my four upper front teeth. I caught myself covering my mouth while I talked so I decided to explain what happened.

"Not a good idea for a Marine to get seasick, Lieutenant," he said with a slight chuckle.

"No, sir." I didn't know if he disliked Marines who were prone to becoming seasick or thought I was just a weak link in his outfit but he seemed cordial enough with that added "chuckle."

"We haven't had a motor transport officer for the last six months," he said, "but the NCOs (Non-Commisioned Officers) down there have been doing a fine job. They're good people. They'll appreciate your guidance and leadership.

"I'm also giving you the Civic Action job. Most Marine units have a Civic Action Officer who goes into a particular village to help them improve their lives. Ours is heading back to the States next week, Lieutenant Lloyd, so you can take over his job. He'll show you around down there. He goes into an Elementary School in the Village of Hoa My."

"Thank you, sir. I would enjoy that assignment."

"If you need anything, just ask. I'm not saying I can approve it but please ask. Lieutenant Lloyd has taken our corpsman down there to check out the kids. President Johnson says we need to 'Win the hearts and minds of the Vietnamese people.'"

When I turned to leave he said, "We have a good dentist at 3rd MAF Headquarters, Lieutenant, I'll get you in touch with him."

My memory of Lieutenant Colonel Sheppe is vague. He finished his tour in Vietnam just a month after our initial meeting but his last sentence endeared me to him for life. That 3rd MAF dentist he suggested made a partial plate better than the one I fed to the fish and lasted until I replaced it with a permanent bridge.

As Lieutenant Lloyd, the tall and lean short-timer, drove me to the supply building, he told me that he worked in a cubicle up on top of the mountain and called in air strikes. "This Civic Action job has been nice though," he added. "Gave me a chance to meet the Vietnamese people. You'll like the job."

On our way to the village of Hoa My, about halfway down the hill, a crack of thunder slapped the ground to our left. The noise jerked me up in my seat and Lieutenant Lloyd stepped on the gas. It wasn't thunder it was an explosion that sent a plume of white smoke thirty meters into the air. Mortar attack I thought. Rocks tumbled back down to the ground and I looked for signs of enemy fire. My helmet sat on the gear back at my hooch. My feet pushed down on the jeep's floorboard to help accelerate the vehicle forward but Lieutenant Lloyd remained calm, almost oblivious of the explosion.

My whole body pressed down on the floorboard, "What was that?"

"Blasting in the rock quarry. It goes on all hours of the day. Sometimes at night. You'll get used to it."

"Ah," I said, trying to act nonchalant. But he had to hear the Taiko drumming in my chest.

Hoa My Elementary School sat far enough back from Highway 1 to accommodate a playground that held over a hundred students. We ambled through the yard amongst the children as if they were animals in a petting zoo. We had holsters with .45 caliber pistols strapped to our sides and wore dark glasses, imposing figures for a grade school playground but these children took little notice.

Some waited their turn on the four sets of teeter-totters, some gathered around the four swing sets to push a friend or wait their turn, and others sat in circles around diagrams drawn in the dirt where students played a game. They sat, squatted, with their feet flat and their knees bent so their butt almost touched the ground, a common rest position for the Vietnamese.

Dark glasses must have been mandatory in the air wing at least for the officers. Maybe to let people know you were air wing I don't remember but when I received my orders to Vietnam someone explained that "MarAirFor" meant "Marine Air Forces," which also meant good duty and dark glasses. So, I bought a cheap pair before we left the States and thought I looked cool wearing them.

Two Vietnamese teachers walked out to the playground and Lieutenant Lloyd introduced me. I again met someone for the first time without my four front teeth but they didn't seem to notice. When I shook their hands they each greeted me with the same expression, "I am pleased to meet you, Lieutenant Brian."

"Lieutenant Brian" sounded strange but I let it go.

Miss Xuan only came up to my shirt pockets but her smile gave the impression that she enjoyed life and enjoyed her work.

Mr. Hoan, a little taller than Miss Xuan and a little older, had thick black hair with a wayward curl that curved down onto the middle of his honey colored forehead. He wore a white short sleeved shirt with pencils in his shirt pockets and invited us into his sixth-grade classroom lined with narrow wooden tables on each side of an isle down the middle of the room. The room was cooled by a breeze from the one window. Each table could sit five students and the room's pale green walls were empty, no portraits of government leaders, no pictures or posters or calendars or samples of student work.

When we sat down, students served tea in white porcelain cups without handles and we decided that I should teach English to the school's faculty since Mr. Hoan had the books.

After our tea we walked out of Mr. Hoan's classroom and into a heat that pressed against my uniform wet from the humidity. We joined four other teachers and Miss Xuan asked if I would take a picture of Lieutenant Lloyd and the school's faculty.

Lieutenant Lloyd nudged me and said, "My last day down here."

Once I took the picture, Miss Xuan asked Lieutenant Lloyd to take a picture of me with the faculty and I felt honored to be included.

When we walked off the playground a small convoy of two-and-a-half ton trucks drove north past the school on Highway 1. In the back of each truck, under a canvas tarp, Marines sat on benches in the dark, mannequin-like, in rumpled camo uniforms with their rifles held between their legs. The scene made me realize we were at war, a war where the enemy looked no different than the school teachers with whom I would spend the next twelve months.

* * * *

After dinner that day, Sergeant Greene greeted me when I assumed the Officer of the Day duties. My first day in Vietnam and assigned to be O.D., a job junior officers are assigned that included walking or driving around the compound to check on security.

Sergeant Greene was also the MASS-2 Truck Master, the one who made sure drivers arrived on time for their deliveries or pickups. He looked like a linebacker for the Oakland Raiders, six-foot-four, probably two-hundred and thirty pounds with massive biceps and a neck as thick as a watermelon. He looked like the Marine on recruiting posters.

"Let me give you a tour of MASS-2 Lieutenant," Sergeant Greene said, "and I'll explain what the O.D. generally does. It's not too bad. You'll be in your rack by midnight."

We drove up to the top of our ridge in his jeep to check on our radar controllers and the Marines guarding MASS-2 in bunkers with M60 machine guns. Sergeant Greene parked behind one of the bunkers and stepped out. The valley floor on the other side of our ridge looked about two kilometers wide and stretched out to the horizon's twilight in the eest and disappeared in the darkened hills to the wast. Just enough light slipped through the clouds so I could make out the gray shapes and contours.

"Happy Valley, sir," Sergeant Greene said. "Beaucoup VC down there. When they attack the airfield at Danang, they'll come up this hill and overrun our entire area on their way." That bit of information made me feel a little uncomfortable.

(The Viet Cong, aka "VC," or in the military alphabet, "Victor Charlie," but commonly known as "Charlie," were officially designated as the People's Liberation Armed Forces or PLAF.)

We walked to a small bunker dug into the Happy Valley side of the ridge where Sergeant Greene slapped the sandbags on the roof and yelled into the bunker, "Sergeant Greene coming in."

He then turned to me and said, "Lieutenant, MASS-2 has two

bunkers for security up here, this one and that one down there by the Com shack. Two guards in each one."

Sergeant Greene and I stepped into the bunker to a damp smell of mud and moss and mold. Cobwebs dangled in my face from the four-by-four roof supports and roots poked out from the dirt walls where spiders had weaved their webs from one root to the other. An M-60 machine gun sat in a horizontal window pointed toward Happy Valley and I could see that the brush in front of the bunker had been cleared for thirty meters or so but beyond that it was nothing but a wall of colorless night. The two guards were just shadows.

"This here's Lieutenant Biggs," Sergeant Greene said. "That's Lance Corporal Bishop. And this is PFC Knight, Sheldon Knight."

"Nice to meet you guys. How's it goin' up here?"

"OK, Lieutenant." PFC Knight said. "Spooky sometimes. You a controller, sir?"

"No. I'm the new motor transport officer."

"I'm a mechanic, Lieutenant."

"And a damn good one, sir," Sergeant Greene said.

"I'm looking forward to working with you guys," I said.

The brush down the hill moved with a light wind and there were muffled explosions in the distance.

"Trip flares ever go off?"

"Haven't seen 'em yet, sir," PFC Knight said.

"Me neither, sir," said Lance Corporal Bishop. "I wanted to send a flare up last week sir. Heard some weird noises and called the OD, Lieutenant King. He said he'd come on up if they continued. It was weird, sir. I called him back and he came right up. But shit."

"What happened?"

"It was the fuckin' rain, sir. Drippin' off our roof makin' weird noises. I thought sure we was dead."

"Well, you take care. It's not raining tonight. Nice meeting you guys," I said.

We walked up to what looked like half a railroad boxcar that sat inside three walls of sandbags on the MASS-2 side of the ridge. Sergeant Greene put his hand on the door handle and said, "The controllers in here actually contact the aircraft to carry out missions." He opened the metal door and cold air washed over us like he had opened a freezer.

Inside this cubicle, two Marines, their faces lit by the glow of a large Plexiglas map, looked over at us. I recognized the map, lit with bright green, red, and yellow markers, as the area from just south of Danang up to the DMZ that separates North and South Vietnam.

The two men turned back to the map and one talked into his headphone. Sergeant Greene whispered into my ear, "That's the crew chief and the other Marine is the controller. They receive targets early in the evening and then work all night on bombing runs. They lock onto planes with our radar gear and tell the pilot when to drop his payload."

The controller spoke into his headphone, "Five thousand meters, arm all ordnance." There was a pause and some static on the radio. "Two thousand meters, stand by. Stand by. Mark. Mark."

The crew chief stood up from the bench. "Another one down." He turned to me and said, "Hi, I'm Lieutenant Baker, that's Staff Sergeant Johnson. You the new Motor T man?"

"Yeah, Brian Biggs, nice to meet you."

"Next time we'll serve some drinks," Lieutenant Baker said. "See you around campus."

Sergeant Greene and I stepped out of the TPQ-10 into the heat. "The radar equipment in there," Sergeant Greene said, "is run by our generators. There's two here, the backup and the one making all that noise behind those sandbags. They're Steward Stevenson 52300s. We have two at each site."

"How many sites do we have?"

"Several. Here at Danang, Quang Ngai, Marble Mountain, Phu Bai, Dong Ha and others. Mostly from here north.

"Was he talking to a pilot in there?"

"Yes, sir. When the lieutenant said 'mark' the second time, the pilot hit the pickle and released his payload."

"Pickle?"

"A term for the bomb release on the aircraft, sir. Probably took out a bridge or a VC position."

* * * *

Back at my hooch I untucked my mosquito net from the mattress and crawled into my rack. Roommates, whom I hadn't met, lay snoring in their own mosquito net cocoons. The day started aboard ship at 0400 and it was now a little past midnight. It was a long day but I'd made it through and looked forward to my work both at the motor pool and in the village of Hoa My.

I was lucky to have traveled by ship to Vietnam. Those three weeks at sea counted as part of my thirteen-month tour of duty. *On my first day I'm down to twelve months and one week, and I'll have a new baby when I go home,* I thought. My wife, Colleen, was pregnant and due in November.

THREE

Vietnam, 2001

A new generation, freed from the bitterness of war and brought up in an environment of peace and growing freedom, are starting to make their mark and have started to challenge the fixed notions of their elders.

—From *Shadows and Wind*, Robert Templer

A FTER MY TOUR of duty in Vietnam I became the Operations Officer for the Marine Corps motor pool at the huge base in Twentynine Palms, California. During that year I tried to contact Miss Xuan and Mr. Hoan. However, a Vietnamese man who worked at the base told me not to contact friends in Vietnam because it could send them to a reeducation camp or worse, especially if the contact came from a U.S. Marine or even a former Marine. So, I made a vow to contact both these friends when it was safe to make contact. In 1998, after I retired from teaching, I decided to return to Vietnam and visit my friends.

The impetus came in April 2000 when I heard Robert Templer talk about his book *Shadows and Wind: A View of Modern Vietnam* on American Radio Works. After that interview I read Mr. Templer's book, contacted him where he taught at the University of California in Berkeley, and sat down with him at the Caracas Café on University Avenue to discuss locating my friends and my return to Vietnam.

He suggested I send photos of Mr. Hoan and Miss Xuan to Hoa

My Elementary School and ask if they were still in the village. In June 2000, my Vietnamese language teacher that tutored me sent my letter and the two photos to her uncle, a Catholic priest in Danang.

On the day after Christmas, December 26, 2000, I received an e-mail from Mr. Hoan that began: "I recently met someone who informed me that you would like to know about what happened to me and Miss Xuan. I am very happy that you still remember us."

Mr. Hoan located Miss Xuan who had moved from Danang to a small village south of Ho Chi Minh City, and on February 27, 2001, I received an e-mail from Miss Xuan:

> *I'm very happy and emotional to know that you still remember us. It was your whole-hearted teaching, that now I can use a little bit of English. Now I make a sketchy exposition of my life: After teaching at Hoa My School I left my family and took part in the people's liberation army until 1975. I now live on a cashew farm in Hac Dich.*

I booked a flight to Vietnam to reconnect with these two friends.

* * * *

Expressionless faces were pressed against the glass window on either side of the Danang airport exit doors as Vietnamese watched for friends and loved ones, but I did not see Mr. Hoan among the crowd. *What if he didn't come? I didn't have his phone number.* A pain tried to drill its way into my stomach.

Next to the door, just to the right and above the pressed faces, a yellow sign taped to the glass read, "Welcome, Brian M. Biggs."

Someone is here to greet me. Before the plane landed I reviewed the procedure for greeting friends in Vietnam. Hanh

Quyen, Mr. Hoan's granddaughter, explained in an email that the Vietnamese prefer to shake hands rather than hug. *But where was Mr. Hoan?*

As soon as I walked through the double doors the heat and humidity wrapped around my body like a blanket. People rushed toward my cart as it wobbled to the left. A young woman, thin, with long black hair and tall for most Vietnamese, said "Welcome to Danang City, Mr. Brian." She came up to my chin. "I am Hanh Quyen, granddaughter of Mr. Hoan." She held out her hand for me to shake.

My voice quavered. "Hello, Hanh Quyen." My hands wrapped around both her hands. "Thank you for your letters."

A woman behind Hanh Quyen said, "Welcome, Mr. Brian."

"This is my mother, Mrs. Hanh," Hanh Quyen said. "She is the daughter of my grandfather, Mr. Hoan." Mother and daughter looked alike, same height, same narrow face. Both had high foreheads and a wide smile with large white teeth.

Mrs. Hanh and I shook hands as my brain mustered the Vietnamese phrase for greeting a married woman. Others approached and smiled. A portly man took my luggage cart and pushed it across the street, it still wobbling to the left.

And then Mr. Hoan appeared in the crowd with a faint smile when we made eye contact.

Hanh Quyen took my arm and led me to her grandfather.

"Hello, Mr. Brian." His smile grew as he shook my hand. "Welcome to Danang City." Mr. Hoan looked like he did in the recent photo he sent—serious, lips straight across and wearing glasses now. He put his hand on a woman's shoulder and said, "This is my wife, Mrs. Co." Mrs. Co was shorter than her husband but about the same height as the masses of people who milled around outside the airport dressed as the people from Portland, Oregon, dress—jeans, skirts, and shirts with the same textures and colors found in any American mall. And from my twelve-inch height advantage I saw all that black hair, nothing dyed red or blond, just natural black hair bouncing and blowing in the wind.

Mrs. Co handed me a bouquet of yellow Asiatic Lilies and shook my hand.

"*Cam on,*" I said.

Khong co chi," Mrs. Co said.

"My grandmother says, 'You are welcome,'" Hanh Quyen explained.

Mr. Hoan held my arm with both hands and said, "We must go to the taxi."

As he maneuvered us across the street around taxis and motor-bikes that sped by I thought, how lucky to finally reconnect with this friend.

"My granddaughter, Hanh Quyen," Mr. Hoan said, "is the one who translated my letters for you."

Hanh Quyen had contacted me for the first time in an e-mail on June 10, 2001:

Ong Brian kinh men,

You may be very surprise when receiving this letter. May I introduce myself? My name is Hanh Quyen. I am Mr. Hoan's niece. I'm seventeen years old. My grandfather, Mr. Hoan, told me about you. I am the one who helped him for sending, receiving and printing your e-mail. So I know you will arrive to Viet Nam. I'm very happy because my grandfather will be meeting his friend after 30 years. Do you permit me to contact with you as frequently? I'm studying Toefl Course so I need practicing more English. I know that I will make some mistakes. Would you please show me and help me to correct it? I stop here. I will talk more at the next letter. Best wishes to you and your family.

—Hanh Quyen

I corrected her English in that e-mail and explained the difference between "niece" and "granddaughter," and began a correspondence with Hanh Quyen that has continued to this day.

I slid into the taxi's back seat that was crowded with just Mr. Hoan and me. His wife sat in the front seat and we drove out of the parking lot while the relatives stood in a group and waved from the sidewalk. We sat in silence, no dispatcher calls or radio static, no conversation, just a few tinny motorbike horns heard through the opened windows.

As we drove the darkened streets of Danang, I saw no familiar buildings or landmarks but the sensation of being back in Vietnam caused my throat to plug up. I couldn't swallow, but no one knew. I just watched the groups of Vietnamese on the sidewalk, squatted around charcoal fires in front of their homes, their faces lit by an orange glow.

I could smell the Vietnamese spices through the taxi window and I saw, not these Vietnamese, but the Vietnamese men and women and children I saw during the war, squatted around platters of exotic dishes, this one pealing and eating dragon fruit, that one holding a bowl next to her lips so she could shovel rice into her mouth with chopsticks, called *dua* in Vietnam.

Maybe it was the heat or just seeing Mr. Hoan again but those Vietnamese were as real and clear as if they were there outside the taxi's window laughing and eating and raising their hands to make some gesture as rice dribbled down their chins.

Mr. Hoan looked youthful at sixty-seven, no wrinkles on his face, only two slight depressions from his nose to mouth. I was now fifty-nine about to turn sixty, but I remembered that year from May 1966 to May 1967 through the Super-8 movies I took, letters home, and the U.C. Berkeley Creative Writing correspondence course assignments I wrote during my tour of duty in Vietnam.

Amidst the irony of a war that divided both our countries into two hateful factions, we struggled to understand each other's cultures and formed a friendship. To renew that friendship, I had to return to Vietnam, to bring myself to this moment, to this taxi, and be with my friend without the horrors of war.

FOUR

The MASS-2
Motor Pool, 1966

The M35 cargo truck is used to transport equipment, materials, and/or personnel. Since it has permanent steel-welded sides, it is the preferred vehicle for use in transporting bulky payloads that may shift during transit. The truck body provides 270 cubic feet of cargo space. Side racks have built-in troop seats for troop transport operations.

—Operator's manual for the 2 ½ ton, 6X6 truck

S ERGEANT GREENE'S EBONY biceps stretched out the sleeves of his white T-shirt when we shook hands and his baritone voice bellowed, "Welcome to the MASS-2 motor pool, Lieutenant." He introduced me to one of our dispatchers, Sergeant Wix, a barrel-chested man with a thick neck and Southern accent. The two sergeants lived in the motor pool and guarded the equipment.

Sergeant Wix suggested we take a walk around the motor pool. One forklift, three 2 ½ ton trucks, and a few jeeps were backed up cattywampus next to a fence on one side of the lot, half the size of a football field, and some generators mounted on trailers sat on the other side.

"What's that structure out there?" I said as I pointed to a covered area in back of the lot.

"That's our shop," Sergeant Greene said.

It had a corrugated metal roof that was twenty feet in the air and supported by four-by-fours spaced around the structure like telephone poles. There were no sides on the shop, just the flat roof that sloped a bit to let the rain drain off one end. The shop had enough space so mechanics could work on three vehicles, but there wasn't much protection from the wind without any sides.

One end of the shop had shelves of old carburetors, head gaskets, spark plugs, brake shoes, oil pan covers, and an engine block that sat on a tool bench blackened with grease. Even in the open air, the shop had that familiar smell of gasoline, oil, grease, and gunk.

"It's hard to keep parts clean because of the dust and dirt floor, Lieutenant," Sergeant Greene said.

"And when it rains," Sergeant Wix said, "the water runs out here where our mechanics work on vehicles."

"The good thing," Sergeant Greene said, "is the roof don't leak. The bad thing is the rain comes in sideways," he said with a laugh. Sergeant Greene's laugh was a series of guttural "heh, heh's" with the last one held.

I pointed to the rice paddies beyond our motor pool, "What's out there?"

Sergeant Greene looked through the shop to a row of trees beyond the paddies. "Friendlies." Then he looked over at Sergeant Wix with that big smile of his and winked, "Mostly."

The two sergeants and I passed a line of generators on our way back to the dispatcher's tent. "These generators, Lieutenant," Sergeant Greene said, "power the TPQ-10s, the radar equipment you saw last night on the hill. Two generators are offline right now, waiting parts. That one next to the fence over there is what we use to cannibalize parts off to make sure we got a running generator and a backup at each of our sites."

"Are there any other vehicles?"

Sergeant Greene walked out to the center of the lot. He moved slow and determined, like a train leaving the station, then stopped. He put his hands on his hips, looked over the lot, and boomed back to me, "Our tractor and trailer rig is out right now. Haulin' lumber over to the Marine chopper base across the river and Sergeant Walker took the Cerlist to pick up some parts. But every other vehicle you see completes our inventory."

"What's a Cerlist?"

Sergeant Greene walked back toward me, "The Cerlist is basically a jeep but it looks like a pickup with a canopy. The one we have anyway. It's an M676 Diesel, smooth running but temperamental."

With all this information I realized my responsibility came down to supervising the maintenance and operation of several trucks and jeeps, one tractor and trailer, one 6,000 pound forklift, and all the generators. Since I didn't know the equipment, not from the one-month motor transport school, and I didn't have any experience working on vehicles, I had to make sure the NCOs had the time and proper equipment so they could do their jobs.

Sergeant Greene assured me that our mechanics could keep our equipment running. "The CO," said Sergeant Greene "wants generators operating at each of our sites twenty-four hours a day. And each site has a backup generator. We're responsible for running the MASS-2 radar equipment and keeping the electricity on in the MASS-2 Headquarters area."

"Our CO, Lieutenant," said Sergeant Wix, "also needs to know the status of every generator and vehicle. We'll give you a report each morning when you come in."

In other words, make sure the MASS-2 vehicles and generators are up and running or 2nd Lieutenant Brian M. Biggs, 090784, will be standing at attention in front of the CO.'s desk.

FIVE

Mal Interpréter, 2001

One, two! One, two! And through and through
The vorpal blade went snicker-snack!
He left it dead, and with its head
He went galumphing back.

—From "Jabberwocky," in *Through the Looking Glass,*
and What Alice Found There, Lewis Carroll, 1871

M R. HOAN'S RELATIVES, transported from the airport en masse, stood unaltered, like a billboard ad, and waved from the hotel steps as we walked into the lobby. Mr. Hoan curled his fingers to wave me to the front desk. He had not said more than ten words since we met at the airport but he was always reticent and most likely didn't have the opportunity to practice much English after I left Vietnam in 1967.

The woman at the front desk, Miss Hong, took my passport and said, "Please sign your name here, Mr. Bigg." She gave me my key and room number and when we stepped toward the lift Mr. Hoan's relatives, like a school of fish, seemed to float through the lobby on their way to the elevator with my suitcases floating along with them.

Our bodies pressed together with little space to turn around. "Fourth floor," I said over the murmur of words, some high pitched, some low pitched, some held, some staccato—a melodic jumble of voices that sounded like a tape recorder on fast forward. But for that brief upward lift I soaked in the music, the physical and emotional closeness, and the realization that I was back in Vietnam, a Vietnam at peace, a Vietnam that finally reached out for Americans to visit.

A young woman squeezed past the portly man who wheeled my cart away from the airport and grabbed my hand, "Hello, Mr. Brian. Welcome to Danang City. I am Hanh Dung." She emphasized the pronunciation of her name, "*Yoom*," and spoke in a high-pitched voice. Hanh Dung looked at the world as if it were a never-ending joy of new experiences. "I am the older sister of Hanh Quyen." Hanh Dung explained she was in college and took English classes.

When we filed into my room, Mr. Hoan's relatives sat on the bed or around the room on the few chairs available, or stood. There were nine of us in the room. I opened one of my two suitcases and pulled out a coffee table book with scenery from the state of Oregon. "Mr. Hoan, this is for your family. My home state."

Hanh Dung translated.

Mr. Hoan turned the pages in the book and admired the Columbia River Gorge, snowcapped Mount Hood, the wheat fields of Eastern Oregon, and the Oregon Coast.

"Thank you, Mr. Brian," said Mr. Hoan, a man of few words.

"*Khong co chi* (You're welcome)," I said, then gave Mr. Hoan a framed photo of the soccer team I organized at Hoa My School. It was a picture of the team with Mr. Hoan and the Marine from MASS-2 who coached them.

Hanh Quyen received a purple handbag. She felt its smooth texture, then opened a pocket and screamed when she pulled out a bag of candy. "Thank you." She struggled to rip open the candy wrapper.

"Thank you for translating my letters. Those are Snickers, Miniature Snickers Chocolate Bars."

Hanh Quyen took one and passed the rest to Hanh Dung who

took a candy, opened it and bit off half the bar immediately. She chewed and smiled. With her mouth full she mumbled, "Good chocolate, Mr. Brian. Thank you."

Mr. Hoan said, "We are happy to have you visit Danang City, Mr. Brian. Are you hungry? Do you want the dinner?"

"I'm too full for dinner but I could eat something. A snack maybe. Yes."

"Yes. Yes. Yes. Out for a snack," said Hanh Dung with eyebrows raised.

We left the hotel on motorbikes and I felt safe with my hands around the ample waist of Mr. Thang, the man who wheeled my cart away from the airport. Fishing boats, tied up for the night outside my hotel, bobbed in the River Han and dark mounds of net, dotted with white floats, sat on the pier in piles. The pungent smell of those fish-soaked nets blended with the smell of saltwater, barnacles and kelp—an aroma that permeates the docks of every seaport in the world, and I loved it.

Just upriver from the fishing fleet was a large cargo ship with the letters VINASHIP on the side. That ship stayed in port the entire time I visited Vietnam with dock workers loading cargo from sunup to sundown.

We reached an outdoor restaurant with decks on different levels, each with its own thatched roof and each with a musical chatter from people of all ages. Yellow flames flickered from kerosene pots on top of tilted poles and the black smoke that drifted upward caused shadows to dance on everyone's face. Hanh Quyen reached into her new purse and pulled out some of the miniature Snickers candy bars and passed them around the table.

"Ah, Snickers bars for a snack," I said.

Hanh Dung, who pulled at the hair on my right arm, translated what I said into Vietnamese. Mr. Thang looked at the small wrapped candy in his hand and read the label out loud, "Sneaker." He looked down at me and smiled but seemed puzzled.

"Snicker," corrected Hanh Quyen. She opened her wrapper and put the bite size candy in her mouth. "Mmmm. It is good." She chewed and talked to the others in Vietnamese.

Hanh Dung opened her Snickers wrapper and moaned as she spoke with her mouth full, "What is a Snicker Bar?"

"Snickers is the name of the candy, a candy bar. It means a bar of chocolate," I explained. "A small piece of chocolate shaped in a bar."

Hanh Dung laughed out loud. "I thought you mean a bar. Go to have a drink at a bar. My uncle, Mr. Thang was confused because I told him it's where you buy a drink."

"Ah. No. Same word, different meaning. 'Bar.' It's a small thing, a small chunk of something. A 'bar' of soap. A candy 'bar.' Or a long pole is also a 'bar.' And you can 'bar' someone from coming into your home. It's a confusing word with many meanings. But it is also a place to go for a drink because of the long counter, called a 'bar.' I'm sorry for the confusion, Hanh Dung."

Hanh Quyen and Hanh Dung were the only ones, besides me, who spoke fluent English, but it was Hanh Dung, the eldest granddaughter, who took charge. She talked to her uncle in Vietnamese then asked me, "What do you want to drink? Do you want a beer?"

"Yes, that would be nice," I said

A waitress brought two green Heineken bottles and two glasses. I expected "Tiger" beer, the beer of choice during the war, but Heineken was the beer of choice in Vietnam now.

Mr. Thang held up his glass of beer and the others held up what they were drinking, "*Chuc suc khoe*," they all said. Hanh Dung explained that meant "To your health."

While I listened to the musical chirping of Vietnamese conversation the cold beer relaxed every muscle in my body and I smiled at the assembled table of Mr. Hoan's family.

"What food do you enjoy?" Hanh Dung said.

"I like all kinds of food. Anything you want to order is fine with me."

Hanh Dung spoke to her uncle and he talked with the waitress then Hanh Dung said, "My uncle ordered for you a snack. It is fried squid. Is this okay for you?"

"I love squid." The beer tingled the insides of my stomach. People sat around crowded tables and talked and laughed and ate their meals and drank their Heineken beer.

"What is it that you call this?" asked Hanh Dung. "What you eat before the meal? A snack?"

"We call it an 'appetizer' or an 'hors d'oeuvre."

"You don't call it a 'snack?'"

"Not usually. Snacks are eaten in the afternoon or late evening."

Hanh Dung explained the word *snack* to her uncle.

I looked across the table at Mr. Thang and said, "*Anh Thang, lam nghe gi?*" Everyone stared at me.

Hanh Dung said, "What do you want to ask my uncle?"

"I asked, 'what is his job?' *Anh Thang, lam nghe gi?*"

"No. You don't say any Vietnamese words except, my uncle's name, 'Mr. Thang.' You must say, '*Anh Thang, anh làm nghe gi?*'"

"*Anh Thang, anh làm nghe gi?*" I said.

The group erupted into laughter and Hanh Dung said, "You ask my uncle what kind of buffalo calf he is?"

Mr. Thang who laughed loud and long at the misinterpretation, handed me one of his business cards with English on one side and Vietnamese on the other. It read, *Manager, Import–Export Department. Danang Mechanical & Electrical Equipment Company.*

Mrs. Hanh walked around the table to where I sat. She put her arms on Hanh Dung's shoulders and spoke in Vietnamese.

Hanh Dung looked up at her mother and smiled. "My mother asked if you noticed my back? My short body?"

Mrs. Hanh's eyes drooped on purpose. She wasn't sad, but at this moment, she wanted to indicate sadness to me. She turned

Hanh Dung around so I could see her back then rubbed the hump on her daughter's left side about the position of her shoulder blade. Mrs. Hanh wanted me to see the deformity on Hanh Dung's back.

"It is a birth defect," said Hanh Dung as she pulled again at the hair on my arm. "My mother wants you to know so you don't think I am just a short daughter."

"Yes, I can see, I notice."

SIX

The Hoa My School Facilities, 1966

It's autumn in the orchard. A rosy apple falls to the grass near a cow pat. Friendly and polite, the cow shit says to the apple: "Good morning, Madame la Pomme, how are you feeling?"

She ignores the remark, for she considers such a conversation beneath her dignity.

"It's fine weather, don't you think, Madame la Pomme?"
Silence.

"You'll find the grass here very sweet, Madame la Pomme."
Again, silence.

At this moment a man walks through the orchard, sees the rosy apple, and stoops to pick it up. As he bites into the apple, the cow shit, still irrepressible, says: "See you in a little while, Madame la Pomme!"

—From "A Load of Shit," in *Keeping A Rendezvous*, John Berger

A T THE END of my first week in Vietnam, I finished teaching the English class at Hoa My School and packed up assignments to correct. "Mr. Hoan," I said, "is there a bathroom in the school?" Too many cups of tea.

Mr. Hoan paused a moment. "Ah, we have no bathroom at Hoa My School. You must go in the back."

"Is there an outhouse out back?"

"You can go to the back. I will show you."

We walked around to a large open field I had only seen through the classroom window. There were scattered clumps of weeds and small rocks and chickens that strutted around to peck at pebbles while barefoot boys kicked a soccer ball back and forth. The chickens fluttered up a few inches when the ball came too close.

Up on the ridgeline in the distance I could see metal roofs from the MASS-2 area where I lived but I didn't see an outhouse on the playground.

"Is there an outhouse?" I asked again.

"What is an 'out house?'"

"A small house, a shack. To go to the bathroom. There is a hole dug under the house."

"Ah. No house. You can go there." Mr. Hoan pointed to a bush.

I walked over to the bush. There were homes next to the school where children sat or squatted in that rest position in the scant shade of palm trees while I stood and relieved myself. The children played a game on squares drawn in the dirt and used small rocks to move around the squares. They paid no attention to me.

"Where do the students go to the bathroom?" I asked Mr. Hoan when I finished.

"Bush."

"And the teachers?"

"Bush."

"Our outfit can build you an outhouse back here," I said. "It could be built in a day or two. It's just a small house with a raised seat and a hole in the seat. Or with two holes, ones we call 'two-holers.' The one we use has a fifty-five-gallon drum cut in half that is slid under the seat instead of a hole dug in the ground. When the drum fills up with waste it's burned with diesel oil."

"We use a bush."

"Yes, but an outhouse would give the children privacy and it would be nice for the faculty. We could build two, two two-holers, one for the students and one for the faculty."

Mr. Hoan and I walked back around to the front of the school. He said nothing. But on that day, I visualized an outhouse, a two-holer, at the back of the school. Maybe two of them. Mr. Hoan, I thought, would appreciate its convenience.

As I think back at that conversation, I'm startled by how naïve I was, so determined to build that outhouse. My American values and ideas of privacy, cleanliness, and status cluttered any common sense that might have played a part in my decision. This group of Vietnamese students and teachers were perfectly comfortable relieving themselves next to a bush.

However, with that mentality, I forged ahead and asked Sergeant Wix to scrounge the material to build an outhouse for Hoa My School. Not an elaborate one, a simple two-holer that had a deep pit dug underneath the house. Sergeant Wix suggested we construct an outhouse with a hole in the ground, not one with a fifty-five-gallon drum cut in half and each half slid under the seats. That would require burning out with diesel fuel on a weekly basis. He thought it would be awkward for the school administration to add the burning of human waste to a teacher's duty list. Awkward, and burning feces smelled worse than the rectal zephyrs my uncle John expelled after a dinner of Aunt Evelyn's chili. (I speak from experience. My hooch at MASS-2 Headquarters was ten meters from our head and Marines with latrine duty burned the contents of that drum with diesel fuel once a week.)

We framed the Hoa My outhouse up with two-by-fours and covered it with sheets of corrugated metal. It took two days and when we finished the project, the ever-curious Mr. Hoan went inside to examine the new structure. I went over and opened the door to see how Mr. Hoan liked it and found him squatted above the toilet with his feet on the bench.

"Oh, no," I said. "You don't stand on the bench, you can sit on the toilet seat. Sit, right down on the seat." I climbed up on the other seat to show Mr. Hoan what I meant. "Sit on the seat just like this." Mr. Hoan said nothing all the while. He was not testing the toilet but using it.

"I'm going to wait outside," I said.

SEVEN

Danang City, 2001

It soon became clear that even ten years had not been long enough to break the emotional embrace in which the war held me. I had to go back, whatever the risks. I had to see the war end, even though it looked as if it was going to end in a defeat of the cause I had served as a soldier. I cannot explain the feeling. It just seemed I had a personal responsibility to be there at the end.

—From *A Rumor of War*, Philip Caputo

M R. THANG AND Hanh Quyen drove over the curb and parked near the hotel's front porch. Hanh Quyen swung her long leg over the motorbike and removed her helmet. "My grandfather must rest today," she said. "He has the high blood pressure. What do you want to see in Danang City?"

"A bookstore. I would like a new map of Danang City. And I would like to see where I landed in 1966, where a small boat from our ship docked. Is there a place on the river called 'Museum Beach?' Maybe a dock or beach or boat landing?" I wanted to experience this new Vietnam journey from where it began in 1966.

"You can ride with my uncle, Mr. Thang," said Hanh Quyen. "We can take you to the museum."

Mr. Thang smiled and pointed to the seat of his motorbike. My arms again went around his waist and the three of us merged into traffic.

Hanh Quyen sat up straight on her motorbike with her shoulders erect. Her hair blew in the wind and the new bag from America hung around her neck by the strap. The small red and white store tag, still attached to the bag by a plastic loop, flopped in the wind. Hanh Quyen had an elegant, almost regal, look about her. But when she laughed or even smiled she held back. She didn't lose herself in laughter like her sister, Hanh Dung. She was more reflective.

Up river, just past the River Han Bridge, we parked across the street from the Danang Museum. Hanh Quyen unwrapped a miniature Snickers bar and put it in her mouth. She held up the bag of candy and said with her mouth full, "Do you want a piece of candy, Mr. Brian?"

"No thank you. Save those for yourself." She folded up the bag of candy and put it back in her purse. "You can take that tag off your purse if you want."

"I don't want." She chewed her candy and swirled the chocolate juices around in her mouth before swallowing.

I stood next to one of the fishing boats docked at the brick covered quay and looked across a river that seemed wider now and there was no beach as in Museum Beach.

Hanh Quyen pointed down river, "We can take you to the bookstore, Mr. Brian."

"Thank you, *Cam on*," I said.

The fishing boats began to rock up and down from the waves of a passing ship. "There was a wooden pier along here," I said. "I think it was a pier. I can't remember. No brick walkway or wall like this. And there were more trees. Over there." I pointed across the street. "Nothing looks familiar."

Hanh Quyen and her uncle looked at me from their motorbikes.

There were no 1966 movies that I took of this spot. This place was only in my memory now and it didn't look familiar. I remembered there were trees, but *these* trees were in the wrong place. However, the museum was just across the street. *This must have been the spot where we landed,* I thought, so I determined this would be my starting point for 2001.

Several metal bookshelves no more than five feet high sat in rows throughout the store. Not the dark, wooden shelves of Powell's or other American bookstores that stand floor-to-ceiling on narrow isles with the musty smell of antiquity. These bookshelves, made for easy access, also allowed light to come in through the store's windows. I only found two maps of Danang City. I bought both.

* * * *

My first full day ended with dinner alone at the top of the Thanh Lich Hotel in a restaurant that overlooked Danang with a panoramic view to the north, east, and south. Up river, the lights on the River Han Bridge gave the impression of a golden pyramid. Beyond the bridge the five peaks of Marble Mountain reflected the last streaks of sunlight, and in the other direction, a mountain called Ban dao Son Tra, covered with a canopy of tamarind, eucalyptus, and talauma trees, stood as a sentinel for Danang City. That mountain at the eastern end of Danang Bay became known to Americans during the war as "Monkey Mountain" for its numerous troops of monkeys.

Halfway through my dinner a waiter came to my table. "Mr. Bigg," he said, "you have a phone call. Please, you may take it in the cook."

Who could be calling me? It must be Mr. Hoan I thought. Steam poured out of a half-dozen pots on the stove and the kitchen smelled like fried prawns and dirty ashtrays.

"Hello?" I said.

"Hello, Mr. Brian, this is Mr. Hoan. Are you at the restaurant?"

"Yes. I'm on the top floor."

"I will come to the restaurant to visit you there."

"Ah. Wonderful. Please do. Have you eaten dinner?"

"I will come to your restaurant. To visit. I will not eat dinner."

Mr. Hoan and I had not sat down and talked in over thirty years. I thought again of my Vietnamese language tutor's uncle here in Danang, the Catholic priest whose effort brought me to Mr. Hoan. I should have asked for his address so I could have thanked him in person.

Just as I finished my dinner, Mr. Hoan joined me and looked as healthy as ever. He may have high blood pressure but it didn't curb his evening activities.

When Mr. Hoan started to tell me a story, I opened my notebook of plain white paper to make stick figure drawings when the language didn't work. Sometimes we wrote out the words since we could both read the other's language easier than trying to decipher the sounds.

Mr. Hoan poured our tea. He sat opposite and wore a white, short-sleeved shirt with a pen in the right pocket and papers in the left. "Tomorrow, please come to my house. My granddaughter, Hanh Dung, wants to practice her English."

"Thank you, I would like to visit with Hanh Dung and see your house. Is your house the same house you lived in during the war?"

"No. It is a different house."

"Ah. And can we try to find my old military base? The base where I lived up on the mountain? I want to go back there. And I'm excited to see the school. You said last night that Hoa My School was not an elementary school now. Did you say it was torn down? Taken down. Rebuilt? Was the entire school taken down?"

"What do you say?"

"I'm sorry. The Hoa My School of 1966, *nam sau muoi sau*, is gone?" I wrote the year on a page. "The school is gone?"

"Yes. Hoa My School is gone. No more."

"The entire school, all the buildings? They're all gone?"

"Yes."

"What grades are at the school now? Grade levels. What grade levels are at the school?"

Mr. Hoan wrote the numbers, six, seven, eight, and nine in my notebook and looked up at me. "Four grades at the school. How do you say these numbers? How do you call these grades?"

"Sixth, seventh, eighth, and ninth."

"Ah."

"And there is a new building?"

"Yes. A new building." Mr. Hoan held his handle-less ceramic cup with both hands and took a sip of tea. "The building you started, the classrooms you built are gone."

"I would like to have seen that building. It wasn't finished when I left in 1967."

"It is gone now. Torn down, taken down."

Hearing this again, that the two classrooms I arranged to be constructed were gone, made me feel like I had lost some family relic, something that should have been saved. I knew it wasn't my fault and that a new building, a new modern school would be better for the children and teachers, but I didn't care. Selfish, I know, but I did not like this turn of events. It wasn't even an elementary school any more.

I hoped for the possibility of a photograph that someone may have saved, a student of Mr. Hoan's or a teacher that taught in one of those classrooms.

"My house will be torn down next year," Mr. Hoan said.

"What's that? Your house is what?"

Mr. Hoan filled both our cups with tea. "My daughter, Mrs. Hien, who lives in Canada, will help me pay for the new house. It is to be built on the same land where my house is now."

He drew a house on the pad and then put a line through it.

"Gone."

"That is nice," I said. "You will have a new house."

"A new house. I do not have enough money to build. But my daughter will help me."

"Good," I said. Mr. Hoan wrote down a set of numbers with the dollar sign after the zeros, 10,000$. "What does that mean?" I asked.

"US dollar. My new home will cost this much."

"After you retired what did you do? Do you have a hobby? What is your day like now?"

"I read the newspaper and watch the television." Mr. Hoan turned to look out at the darkened panoramic view of Danang City. The glass window reflected his face and white shirt with the muted city lights in the distance.

EIGHT

Dogpatch, 1966

"Unconquered Fried Dog Indians"
who never surrendered to the USA.
— From the comic strip *Lil' Abner*, Al Capp

"DOGPATCH," A SMALL village on the road to and from the Danang Airport, is a reference to Lil' Abner's shack-filled hometown in Kentucky that featured the famous "Kickapoo Joy Juice." Al Capp's comic strip town bordered "The Badlands," home of the "unconquered Fried Dog Indians" who "never surrendered to the USA." Dogpatch in Vietnam bordered Happy Valley, home of the "unfriendlies": "Charlie," the "Beaucoup VC" that, according to Sergeant Greene, were going to overrun MASS-2 on their way to the Danang Airport.

The Americans gave it this pejorative name due to the shanties, shops, and brothels dotted with flattened out Coca Cola, Budweiser, and Pepsi cartons patched over the holes in their walls and roofs. Most of the Marines who walked through this village had M-16 rifles slung over their shoulders. A few carried .45 caliber pistols. Some rode in on motor bikes, others jumped off six-bys for their hour of liberty. Young prostitutes leaned against door frames wearing miniskirts or tight pants with cleavaged tops and hair that swirled skyward in a black bundle of beads and bows.

Bits of food, trash, and human waste floated in water that filled the ditches on each side of the road. Wooden pallets lay across the ditch so customers could venture into shops without getting their boots wet, and the village thrived because Marines and other servicemen frequented the shops to spend their blue and pink *piasters* on trinkets, haircuts, gedunk, booze, and sex. Most of it on sex.

My promotion to first lieutenant arrived in mid-May 1966, and the 327 PX, just below Hill 327, near Dogpatch, had silver lieutenant's bars to replace my bronze. There was also a Canon Super-8 movie camera in the PX. It was my first big purchase in Vietnam along with a splicer, an editor, and a really cool Duel Elmo Super-8/Regular-8 projector.

Since I planned to act, write, and direct movies in Hollywood after the Marine Corps, I used my movie camera to document all my MASS-2 projects and activities.

There was enough lumber stored in our motor pool for me to build an editing table and cabinet with a twenty-five-watt bulb inside to keep the equipment dry from the humidity.

This was 1966—no digital cameras or smart phones. After I shot five, fifty-foot rolls of film, I sent them home to my wife, Colleen, to have them developed. She watched them with our daughter, Kaye, and sent them back to me. That way my family could see what I did in Vietnam. Once I received the developed rolls of film, usually in three weeks, I watched them at my work station, did some editing, and spliced them onto a 400-foot reel. My first project was titled "Dogpatch":

Exterior, long shot

1. On the corner of Highway 1 and the road through Dogpatch, my movie camera focused across the road onto a Vietnamese family squatted around a pot of soup and a large plate of fruit.

Close-up

2. Green oranges, cherimoya, miniature bananas, grapefruit, and clusters of grapes.

Zoom out

3. The family nibbles on the fruit and uses the *dua* to scoop in bun noodles from a bowl held to their lips. Children, jump in and out of the frame, like sparrows that flutter on and off a picnic table to peck at crumbs.

Close-up

4. A girl, maybe sixteen, picks up some grapes and throws a bunch toward me and laughs with her family. Then she looks directly into the camera lens and rubs her right index finger under her nose. (A gesture meant to provoke anger.)

Zoom out. Pan from girl to hostess. Vehicles rumble by.
Medium shot

5. Hostess wearing red pedal pushers and a black blouse standing in the doorway with streamers draped over her body. A Marine walks up to her. She smiles and shakes his hand. His companion, a corporal whose M-16 rifle hangs upside down from his left shoulder, notices me, and gives his Marine buddy the signal: pecking motions with his index finger that points across the street toward the camera. The buddy continues his conversation with the woman in red pedal pushers and doesn't see the signal. The finger pecks at the air in bigger and more emphatic motions. The corporal with the M-16, motions toward me with his head and says something to his buddy.

The camera keeps rolling. The corporal's eyes get bigger as he tries to convey to his buddy that he's on film. His finger continues to peck at the air: peck, peck, peck, peck, peck.

Zoom in. Close-up

6. The hostess whispers into the buddy's ear and he turns to the corporal and laughs. But the corporal doesn't laugh. He points across the street again to the camera. Finally, his buddy turns and sees the camera. He quits talking to the woman in red pedal pushers and walks out of the frame.

That Marine went back to his base disappointed, unfulfilled, and worried about being documented on film. Not like today, in 2018, when everyone who ventures out of the house or barracks is on film. I was just shooting a roll of film for myself, to document my tour of duty. Having a good time like the two Marines. But how could I let them know that with my eye stuck in the view finder and the film rolling?

NINE

Hanh Dung, 2001

*Children visiting the Saigon Zoo often likened the apes
to Americans, because both had such long, hairy arms.*

—From *Vietnam: An Epic Tragedy: 1945-1975*, Sir Max Hastings

M ISS HONG, THE clerk at the desk of my hotel, called me
on the phone. "Mr. Bigg," she said, "your guest is waiting
for you in the hotel lobby." Mr. Hoan was indeed in the lobby
waiting for me. His blood pressure must have been fine that
morning since he was fifteen minutes early. We hopped onto his
motorbike and headed out of the city.

Hanh Dung and her mother, Mrs. Hanh, stood on Mr. Hoan's
green tiled porch decorated with sculpted bonsai trees. Hanh
Dung waved her hands in the air and wiggled like a puppy when
we drove up. "Come in, Mr. Brian," she said as she reached for
my hand.

Mr. Hoan's wife, Mrs. Co, stood behind a wooden loveseat
that had animals and trees carved into the molding.

"This is a beautiful loveseat," I said.

"Love seat?" said Mr. Hoan.

"Well, it's maybe a bench but we call this size of chair a
'loveseat' because it's only big enough for two people."

Mr. Hoan laughed, "The seat is not a love seat."

"What is this wood?" I asked.

"Wood is *go*. This chair is named *ghe truong ky tram*. No 'love seat.'" Mr. Hoan chuckled again.

Apparently, a "love" seat had other meanings in Vietnam.

A motorbike stopped in front of the house and Mrs. Co walked out to greet the driver. When she returned she handed me an envelope, "For Mr. Brian."

Mr. Hoan echoed, "Ah! Mail for you, Mr. Brian."

The envelope contained a birthday card from my second wife, Vicki. This was amazing, a birthday card arrived from my wife in the States on the day of my birthday, within five minutes of the time I arrived at Mr. Hoan's house. We were married in 1988 and on each of our birthdays we always send a card through the mail besides the card on a present. She knew the hotel's address in both Danang City and Ho Chi Minh City but not Mr. Hoan's address. She must have found it in my file. Vicki wrote, "Happy 60th Birthday. I love you and miss you. Enjoy your visit." And the card had a quote from Thich Nhat Hanh: "Life can be found only in the present moment."

"From my wife, Vicki. A birthday card sent through the mail, this is very special."

All four friends said, "Happy Birthday, Mr. Brian."

"Thank you. *Cam on*. I am sixty years old today. This very day, October 24th."

"It is a very special birthday. Sixty," said Hanh Dung.

"It is?"

"Yes."

Before I sat down on the love seat Hanh Dung took me into an alcove where an altar displayed fresh cut flowers and mementos set in perfect harmony with a young woman's photograph as the centerpiece.

"This is the altar of my aunt."

Mr. Hoan picked up the simple 8x10 frame, "My daughter,

Hoai. She is who died of cancer at thirty-one years. She was a teacher of mathematics in high school."

I didn't know what to say to Mr. Hoan. I could not imagine losing a daughter at such a young age—or at any age. "I'm sorry for your loss," I finally said. "Where did she live?"

"Danang City."

Four curtains made of silk hung side by side as a backdrop for the altar. One of the curtains had a Vietnamese phrase, "*Nhan du Tien canh*," meaning "Free to visit paradise."

Mr. Hoan set the picture frame back on the altar. He looked at it a moment and adjusted it slightly to the right.

Hanh Dung said, "Let's sit down for tea, Mr. Brian." Mrs. Hanh poured tea into three cups while Hanh Dung sat next to me on the love seat and tugged at the hair on my arm. She said, "Vietnamese persons do not have hair on their arm. It is such a strange thing to have this hair."

I felt Dung's arm and she was right, it was smooth with no hair at all. She looked at me and smiled, like it was okay for me to be a little different.

Mrs. Hanh set teacups down on the table and walked to the love seat to speak with her daughter. After a short conversation she turned Hanh Dung around to face away from me so she could raise her daughter's blouse. I saw a bare back with a hump on the left shoulder blade and a long scar that ran down her spine from neck to waist.

Hanh Dung, twenty years old at the time, did not hesitate to have me see her bare back. "My mother wants to show you the scars from my operation."

Mrs. Hanh took my hand and placed it on Hanh Dung's raised hump. The circular hump rose to about an inch in the center and wasn't discolored or wrinkled but smooth, about the size of my outstretched hand. Hanh Dung didn't squirm or turn around; she just sat with her head down and elbows on her knees. Mrs. Hanh gave me the same sad look as she gave me at the restaurant the night I arrived in Vietnam.

Hanh Dung had other scars on her back, smaller scars on both sides of that scar from her neck to waist. Mrs. Hanh spoke and Hanh Dung turned her head toward me. Not all the way around, just halfway. "My mother says that the doctor made two operations on me to fix my back. But it is not yet fixed. The doctor in Vietnam cannot finish. Maybe we will go to the United States, to Arizona for another operation."

Hanh Dung spoke of her deformed back like she might explain a finger or knuckle with an odd shape. Her smile, her attitude and exuberance for life gave no hint of debilitation or embarrassment.

"Hanh Dung is very brave to have the operations," I said. Hanh Dung translated to her mother as she put her blouse down and straightened out the bottom.

"My mother says the operation in Arizona costs sixty thousand US dollars."

"Do you plan to go to Arizona?" I asked.

"We do not know. Maybe we go." Hanh Dung looked at her mother to see if she knew any more about the trip. Mrs. Hanh, again, gave that sad look.

I can't remember ever doing anything similar to touching the raised area on Hanh Dung's back. The privilege of seeing the deformity first hand, to actually touch her skin, made me feel connected to Hanh Dung who enjoyed life, laughed loudly, and always said what she felt.

Her mother may have intended a plea for me to help them reach Arizona, I don't know; but no plea or comment ever followed that encounter.

TEN

"What Do You Think of This War?" – 1966

1957, Communist insurgent activity in South Vietnam begins. Guerrillas assassinate more than 400 South Vietnamese officials. Thirty-seven armed companies are organized along the Mekong Delta.

—From the "Vietnam Online" section of *The American Experience*: *Timeline (1957)**

A FTER MY ENGLISH class in early June, Mr. Hoan and I walked out to the playground where Miss Xuan talked with some older students, she, and each of her former students were dressed in a white *ao dai*. Besides being the traditional dress for women in Vietnam, the *ao dai* was also worn as a uniform for girls in high school.

"Thank you for the lesson today, Lieutenant Brian," she said, and then added, "I would like to invite you, to dinner."

This request surprised me but I was excited she invited me to dinner. "Yes. That would be nice. When do you want me to come?"

"You can come tomorrow night at 6:00 o'clock p.m."

"Fine. Yes. Do you have directions? Can you draw a map? Directions to your house on a piece of paper?"

Mr. Hoan said it wasn't far and went into his classroom to draw a map.

"It will be nice to meet your family," I said.

"My family wants to meet you. They want you to come to dinner at my home."

"I'm looking forward to it." Miss Xuan was silent for a long time. The shade of the large *kien kien* tree cooled both of us. The *kien kien* tree, common in Vietnamese school yards, produces the valuable teak wood.

Trucks rolled past Hoa My School. Big guns, 105 howitzers, bounced on trailers behind the six-bys. Trucks with Marines, trucks with supplies. All going north. Miss Xuan watched the convoy. She was a calm woman with a smile on her face, delicate and porcelain in her white *ao dai*.

Some school boys walked past us and onto Highway 1, Mr. Hoan's sixth grade students. They laughed and joked and shoved each other and tried to look tough like most twelve-year old boys do. The convoy drowned out their laughter as they left the school yard to walk down the highway and wave at trucks. "Number ten, number ten," a boy yelled at a Marine driver. Brave boys. Maybe scared too. They will be in this war before long. Miss Xuan kept her eyes on the boys. Anxious about them so near the big trucks on the narrow highway.

I knew Miss Xuan to be firm with her third-grade students, firm and loving at the same time. She had polite students who showed their teacher respect. I filmed her classroom often. Her students appeared on my editing screen over and over and over. Smiling, happy, eight-year old boys and girls. They never looked scared on film. Miss Xuan worried about them. Frightened, at times, for their safety.

"What do you think of this war?" I asked.

"The war." She paused a long time, then said, "I do not think."

The last particles of dust floated in from the highway and settled onto the school yard as the noise and the convoy disappeared.

She looked at Highway 1. "The war, Lieutenant Brian. My country has been at war my entire life."

That phrase immediately embedded itself in my brain, her inflection of each word, the look on her face, and the initial impact these words had on me, or would have on anyone.

I said nothing, just nodded. In Vallejo, California, while in junior high, my friends and I sometimes walked over to Highway 40, the highway that linked the San Francisco Bay Area with the California state capitol in Sacramento. We stood at the side of the highway and watched trucks gather speed to make it up Hunter's Hill. When they drove past we held up our arms and pumped them up and down so drivers would honk their horns.

At twenty-seven years old, Miss Xuan had not experienced a life without war. I remember when they built bomb shelters in the fifties and we practiced crouching under our junior high desks. "If you hear the siren and are not at school, what do you do?" said Miss Price.

"Run to the nearest shelter or basement," a few of us said.

We never heard the siren.

ELEVEN

My Birthday Dinner, 2001

We don't stop laughing because we grow old,
we grow old because we stop laughing.

—Michael Pritchard, bassist and backing vocalist for Green Day

R ELATIVES FILLED MR. Hoan's front room, some I'd met and some I had not. Hanh Quyen and Hanh Dung were there with their parents. I counted nineteen for dinner.

Hanh Dung joined me on the "loveseat" with the other children across from us.

"Mr. Brian," said Hanh Dung, "how many days a week do your children go to school?"

"My children are out of school. They're too old. The youngest is thirty-three. But children in the United States go to school five days a week."

"Not six?"

"No," I said. "Not six, just Monday through Friday. Do you go to school six days a week?"

"Yes."

Mr. Thang's daughter, Bia, who was in high school and wanted to go to college asked, "When did you go to college?"

"After I finished high school, in 1959."

"What college?"

"Well, I went to a junior college in California for two years and then transferred to the University of Washington in Seattle."

Hanh Quyen said, "When did you marry Vicki?"

"Vicki and I were married in 1988."

"How could your children be so old?"

"I was married before to someone else."

"When did you marry someone else?"

"In 1965."

Hanh Dung's mother entered the room with a birthday cake in the shape of a heart. It had a large purple, green, and blue "60" on the side and six candles sparkled above the words "*Mung SINH NHAT, lan thu* 60, MR. BRIAN."

I scrambled to take a picture of the cake before the candles burned down and asked Mr. Hoan to take a picture of me blowing them out. The crowd of nineteen gathered around and sang "Happy Birthday" in Vietnamese and then applauded when I blew out the six candles.

"Thank you. *Cam on*," I said, but thought it was an odd custom to eat cake before dinner.

"What did you wish for Mr. Brian?" said Bia.

"I can't tell you that. It won't come true."

Groans from all the children.

Mr. Hoan said, "Mr. Brian, please. We must go to the dining room for dinner."

What a relief, I thought, *cake tastes much better after dinner,* although I would have eaten a piece.

The men had priority seating for my birthday dinner: Mr. Hoan, three sons-in-law plus Mrs. Hanh, the eldest child, and Hanh Dung, to be my interpreter. All the others, including Mr. Hoan's wife, had to eat in the kitchen.

Candlelight reflected off the white china dishes and crystal wine glasses placed around the dining room table. The large Vietnamese soup spoon that resembles a stovetop spoon holder sat at everyone's place setting along with a bone set of *dua.*

"The dinner today," Mr. Hoan said, "is *Mi Quang*. It is what my wife served you at the 1966 dinner when you come to visit my home."

"Yes, *Mi Quang*. I remember that meal. Delicious."

"*Mi Quang* is a special dish in Central Vietnam," said, Hanh Dung.

"*Cam on*," I said. "I am honored to be served this special dish again."

Mr. Hoan's daughters, Hao and Huyen, set bowls of condiments around the table: chopped cilantro, fresh cut wedges of lime, sliced cloves of garlic, roasted peanuts, banana blossoms, bean sprouts, and rice crackers dotted with black sesame seeds.

Mrs. Hanh set a blackened kettle on a portable propane stove in the middle of the table and lit the burner that came on with a loud pop. Vegetables, chicken, shrimp, and pork bellies began to simmer in the broth as Hao and Huyen set bowls of hot *bun* noodles at each place setting. Steam rose from the noodle as two curious geckos watched from the wall.

My Olympus OM10 camera focused on the scene. "Please wait. Don't move the dishes just yet," I said. The hungry crowd stifled a frown and quickly removed their hands from the table. This meal of *Mi Quang* had to be recorded. Another angle. Four more shots to be safe.

Mrs. Hanh picked up my bowl of *bun* noodles and ladled in the broth from the kettle. My mouth watered in anticipation when she set the bowl down in front of me. I untied the bow around my *dua* anxious to enjoy this meal.

But Hanh Dung held my hand back, "I will show you how to prepare your bowl of *Mi Quang*. First you add the salad." She put some of the chopped cilantro and bean sprouts into her bowl. "Then, you squeeze in this lime." As she did so, she accidentally squirted her father in the face. She screamed. He yelled and jerked back from the table with his eyes shut tight. An eruption of shouts and laughter ensued. Family members ran in from the kitchen to see what happened. But her father smiled, quick to forgive his daughter.

After the commotion settled down, Hanh Dung continued, "What was I doing? Oh, squeezing the lime." She did so again. "The lime is too, what do you say, too unpredictable! Enough lime. Now, you sprinkle on roasted peanuts." She did so, then said, "Do you like garlic?"

"Yes."

"So do I."

She added the garlic, then raised a square of the sesame rice crackers and broke it into pieces. "What do you call 'em, 'flakes?'"

"Yes."

"Break this rice cracker into flakes, and finally," she held up a banana blossom, "top it off with this flower."

After I put in the ingredients, I brought the bowl to my nose and took in the lime-flavored fragrance of ocean fresh shrimp and cilantro. The others watched. Now for the taste.

I dipped my spoon holder spoon into the broth with my left hand, brought it up to my mouth, and swallowed. The nectar flowed over my tongue and its kingdom of sensations stimulated the taste of chicken and pepper and shrimp. My right hand used the *dua* to shovel in a cluster of *bun* noodles, dripping with broth and infused with pork and shrimp and chicken and all those spices.

I smiled, no, laughed out loud, as I savored each flavor. The memories of that 1966 meal came flooding back. *Mi Quang*. My favorite meal of all time.

We laughed and ate and talked around the table and then ate some more. There was no shortage of *Mi Quang*.

* * * *

After dinner we went into the front room for the birthday cake and according to Hanh Quyen I had a job. "You must cut the cake and point to a child," she said. "That child must sing you a song. They sing a song before they can take their cake."

"Please say that again."

"You must choose someone to sing for you. That is your present. You choose the children to do this. The children must sing to you before he or she takes the cake."

I looked around the room and began the ceremony of cake cutting. There was a hush as I carefully cut the cake and placed a piece on one of the china plates. As I scanned each set of eyes, the children pleaded with their whole bodies, shaking like puppies at dinner time, to be chosen.

Finally, I pointed to Hanh Quyen's youngest sister Hanh Thy (Tee) who sat directly across the table from me. She looked to her mom as if to say "Do I have to sing?" But she belted out a song in Vietnamese that shook the furniture. She smiled and reached for her cake. I chose Hanh Quyen next, then the youngest cousin, Houng, and all the other children until each one had a piece of cake which left the last three pieces for Mr. Hoan, his wife, and me.

After cake the children wanted to sing again and many took turns to sing me a song. Hanh Quyen sang the Beatles' *Yesterday* in a gorgeous soprano voice.

"I must take a photo of the group before everyone leaves," I said. This evening had to be recorded. It would also be nice to send Mr. Hoan a copy since most of his family gathered for this occasion. My camera needed to sit somewhere. "Can I move this chair?"

Hanh Quyen said, "Yes, yes. That is fine."

The chair from the bedroom served as a base. I set a box on the chair. The camera had to be raised just a bit. "Can I use these books?"

"Yes."

The books went on the box and the camera went on the books. It was a little wobbly but would hold long enough for the picture.

Everyone assembled themselves into a group on or behind the loveseat. They moved into position as though they had done this many times. I focused the camera and looked for a spot in the group. "OK, everyone ready?" I pushed the button and ran to my spot. Everyone smiled.

The camera had a red light that blinked twenty-four times before the shutter snapped. At about blink number ten, the stack of books started to topple. I ran to the camera and caught it just as it fell off the books.

The children screamed. Others gave a sigh of relief. The group, huddled around the "loveseat," tried to hold their composure but couldn't keep it. Some bent down and laughed, others bent back and laughed. They all laughed with their mouths wide open and their faces contorted in some odd shape or other. And at that moment, with the rescued camera pointed directly at the group, the red light blinked for the twenty-fourth time and *FLASH*!

The group realized their picture had just been taken and they all laughed or screamed or fell on the floor—or all three at once. What a great shot, a photo that could never be staged.

I stacked the books on the box and set the camera on top of the books. Take two. It worked that time and just to be safe I took another.

After the photo session Mr. Hoan drove me to my hotel on his motorbike. The warm air and taste of *Mi Quang* flavored a bit with birthday cake made me realize this experience, this connection with Mr. Hoan and his family, had brought me new friends. Friends from another culture, a culture radically different from my own.

How lucky to be in Vietnam again. Not just to be with Mr. Hoan but to interact with his children and grandchildren, grandchildren who listened to him, as an elder in the family, and respected him for his knowledge and experience and influence. Something I don't often see in America.

At my hotel I walked past my room on the fourth floor and stepped onto the fire escape landing to look at the lights of Danang City. The moon allowed me to see the old location of MASS-2 on those silhouetted hills to the southwest. I looked forward to driving up there with Mr. Hoan and seeing where I spent a year of my life. Maybe, even after thirty-four years, I would see some remnants of our hooches and tents, or Club Vagabond, our officer's and NCO's club where I spent the evening of my twenty-fifth birthday.

When I turned twenty-five we ate dinner at Club Vagabond, I don't remember eating, I just remember the drinking and the singing. We had a long table almost the length of the club filled with MASS-2 Marines and Hoa, our Vietnamese waitress, kept bringing pitchers of beer. We sang the Marine Corps Hymm at least four times. "From the Halls of Mon-ta-zuuuu-AH-mah to the shores of Trip-ooooh-Lee..." But no one sang for a piece of cake.

Back in my room I opened my journal to notes that dated back to the spring of 2000:

May 24, 2000. Met with Robert Templer in Berkeley, California. 3:00 PM, Caracus Café on University Avenue.

That cup of tea with Robert Templer and his suggestion to send a letter with photos led to my reconnection with Mr. Hoan here in Danang and Miss Xuan the next week in Hac Dich. Luckily, I could make still photographs of Mr. Hoan and Miss Xuan from the Super 8 movies I took in 1966.

Robert Templer also advised me not to mention in the letter that I was a Marine during the war. I suppose because the Communist government could be suspicious of former military personnel who return to Vietnam. But I've read about how the trips back to Vietnam by former Marines gives them a sense of forgiveness, to themselves, their enemy, and the American government.

According to David Lamb in his book, *Vietnam, NOW: A Reporter Returns*, Bobby Muller, a paraplegic former Marine who served in Vietnam, said, "You could probably shut down a lot of VA psychiatric clinics in the States simply by bringing the vets back to Vietnam. It's better than any medication, and the angrier the veteran is, the more powerful the experience seems to be."

TWELVE

Miss Xuan's Family, 1966

*I have yet to meet a tradition that wasn't
enhanced by interacting with others.*

—Yo Yo Ma

ORANGE FLAMES FROM kerosene lamps danced across
the floor and onto books and knickknacks that filled the
shelves along one wall. A wooden pepper mill with a curved
wrought iron handle sat on one of the shelves and its dark wood
had several notches from years of use. It was the most unusual
pepper mill I had ever seen.

When Miss Xuan asked me if I would like to sit down, I un-
buckled my pistol belt and looked for a place to set it down.

"I will put it on this shelf," she said and took the pistol and
web belt with the barrel pointed up and set it on a bookshelf next
to a table fashioned like an altar. Two burning candles sat in front
of picture frames, a Vietnamese man in one frame and a woman
in the other. A bunch of miniature bananas, each one not much
longer than a finger, sat in a bowl and a vase of yellow flowers
sat in the middle of the table. Miss Xuan moved her hand toward
the Vietnamese man, "This is my grandfather." Then she picked
up the frame of the women with great care, "My grandmother."

A few envelopes lay on the altar along with some papers, two teacups, and a small bowl that sat in front of each picture frame. The bowls were filled with *sand so* joss sticks, some burning, some not, that stuck up in all directions. The burning incense smelled like honey with a tinge of burnt toast.

"This is the altar of my grandparents," Miss Xuan said. "Vietnamese people keep an altar in the home for those who died."

"It's nice to remember your relatives this way," I said. My folded web belt with pistol and holster suddenly slipped down onto the table that held the shrine. It looked out of place next to the artistic arrangement of fruit and flowers and the picture frames lit by candlelight. I wanted to move it but hesitated to disturb the altar. My hosts took no notice.

Miss Xuan's mother spoke to me in Vietnamese. "My mother asks if you want to wash for dinner."

"Yes, thank you."

The memories of this evening, the first time I left our area at night, are clear in my mind as I write these words.

The mother showed me a room through a breezeway and I remember the door opening was low for an American, so I had to stoop. She pointed to a basin of warm water and a bar of soap in a small flowered dish. A folded white towel, embroidered with yellow and red roses with green stems, lay at its side. Miss Xuan's mother smiled and lifted the towel off the counter to remove a piece of red thread from a rose. She looked at me and nodded her head and smiled then set the towel back down and pressed it smooth to the counter before shutting the door. Interesting how that memory is so clear.

On my return to the dining room I looked into a kitchen, not attached to the main house but across the breezeway. Three women who worked at an open fire pit looked up at me and smiled. Back inside the main house Miss Tam and other relatives moved around the table to set out bowls and plates.

"Please sit, Lieutenant Brian," said Miss Xuan.

Miss Xuan's father who sat next to me put his hand on mine and said something in Vietnamese. Miss Xuan's brother, Mr. Phap, said, "Our father hopes you enjoy the dinner."

Miss Xuan sat on the other side of me and the relatives brought out bowls of condiments. Two women from the kitchen came into the room, one with a blackened pot that she set in the middle of the table, and the other with a bowl of lettuce that she placed in front of me. She looked at me and smiled, folded her leathered hand around mine, and squeezed. Then she lifted my hand off the table to give it a shake and made some comment that drew laughter from everyone.

"She says you are a big, strong man and must eat many bowls of *bun bo*." Miss Xuan's translation brought more laughter. "My mother serves us *bun bo*, *bun* is Vietnamese noodle, *bo* is beef. Beef noodle soup."

Miss Tam took the lid off the blackened pot and steam rose into the air. She placed long green stems of lemongrass into the pot and closed the lid.

"The lemongrass is to flavor the soup," Miss Xuan said as she handed me a bowl of noodles and slices of green onion.

"*Cam on.*"

She held up her *dua*, "Do you know how to use the *dua*?"

Since I'd never heard that Vietnamese term I said, "Chopsticks?"

Everyone laughed. "No," Miss Xuan said, "*dua*."

"Some. I've used them in Chinese restaurants at home."

"Hold them like this," she placed the *dua* into my right hand. It was smooth, made of bone, and sat in the "V" between my thumb and index finger. Mr. Phap picked up his *dua*.

Miss Xuan continued, "You must push the top stick to the bottom stick. Like this." She demonstrated with her *dua* and maneuvered them up and down. The two tips tapped together. Mr. Phap did the same.

"You try."

I made an attempt and was successful on my first try. The family clapped their hands.

"Now I will show you how to prepare and eat your bowl of *bun bo*. You must put in this, this food, this vegetable for *bun bo*. How do you call this vegetable?"

"Bean sprouts," I said.

"Bean sprouts. Yes. Then, this." She pointed to the basil.

I added basil to my bowl.

"And salad." She pointed to the lettuce.

Into my bowl.

"Do you like, hot? Hot pepper?"

"A little." I picked up some slices of green and red pepper with my *dua* and put them in my bowl. Miss Xuan took my bowl and handed it to her sister, Miss Tam, who laid several beef strips over the lettuce and then ladled in the stock. The bowl came back to me and I held it up to my nose. The dominant smell was roast beef with a touch of basil.

Miss Xuan added the ingredients to her bowl. Then said, "You like the fish sauce? *Nuoc mam* and this, *rat mong*?"

"Yes, please."

She spooned a little of each sauce into my bowl, then handed me a small section of lime and said, "You must add the lime." I squeezed in the lime and held my bowl up to my nose again. The sauces and lime added a touch of garlic flavor with a hint of citrus.

Miss Xuan grasped her bowl with her left hand and held it up to her mouth, just in front of her lips so there was a direct link from bowl to lips. Her right hand manipulated the *dua* so fast that I barely saw the *bun* go into her mouth.

Finally, my turn. I picked up my bowl with my left hand as Miss Xuan had done and held it up to my mouth. My right hand held the *dua*. I maneuvered a large helping of *bun*, beef and basil from bowl to mouth. I chewed. I moaned. The taste and smell of cilantro, basil, lime juice, peppery beef, turmeric, and paprika swirled across my taste buds. The crunch of bean sprouts added just the right texture.

The soup was at the perfect temperature: too hot until it was stirred. A second tangle of *bun* into my mouth. Same as the first one. My nose ran. Broth dripped down my chin and onto my utility jacket but Miss Xuan provided me with a cloth napkin.

I kept the bowl on the table so I could scoop up some broth and looked for a spoon in what I thought was a spoon holder. "Miss Xuan, can I have a spoon?

"Lieutenant Brian it is there."

"I don't have one. It's not here."

"Yes." She held up the spoon-holder. "This is a spoon."

"It's so big."

Mr. Phap said, "All the more soup for you, Lieutenant Brian."

I held the large spoon-holder spoon in my left hand to scoop up the broth while my right hand held the *dua* that dipped into the *bun.*

When my bowl emptied Miss Xuan picked it up and passed it down to her sister who filled it with the preliminary ingredients and then added the beef and *bun* and stock. She passed the bowl back to me and I squeezed in some lime and picked up a slice of red pepper with my *dua*. Then the same sensation, a flavor like no other soup I'd tasted, certainly nothing like the soups in America, but a soup that conjured up aromas and textures and flavors from a land of bamboo and lemongrass and ginger. And the flavor cuddled around my taste buds long after the last spoonful.

After dinner Miss Xuan suggested we move to the living room for tea and Miss Xuan's father said something to me. "My father asked me to tell you, 'thank you' for coming to our home for dinner," said Miss Xuan. "Thank you for your work at the school of Hoa My."

"I'm happy to work at the school. It is rewarding." Miss Xuan translated to her father.

"You would like to use the bathroom?" asked Miss Xuan.

"No, thank you. I'm fine, very full, but I'm fine." The Vietnamese, I thought, worried about their guest's personal needs more so than hosts in an American home.

Miss Xuan turned up the kerosene lamps and shadows jiggled on the wall with an orange tint.

"The dinner was delicious. Wonderful," I said to Miss Xuan's mother.

The pepper mill that sat on a shelf next to the altar looked as though it had been retired from the kitchen. When I opened the small drawer at the bottom I saw pepper corns among some cobwebs and when I closed the drawer the tiny wooden knob of a handle stayed in my hand. I had to shove it back into the hole. The wooden knob on its top crank, shaped like an apple core, looked as if it would fall off with its next turn. It was split into two halves and barely attached. Inside the metal cover on top I saw more peppercorns and more cobwebs.

"This is beautiful," I said to Miss Xuan.

She pointed to the pepper mill and said something to her mother who then walked out of the room.

"That is old and not for use now. We keep it on a shelf only," said Miss Xuan.

"But it has character," I said. "And the dark wood is beautiful."

Miss Xuan's mother returned with a newer tan colored pepper mill. No cracks or splits and probably no cobwebs. She handed it to Miss Xuan.

"You take this one, Lieutenant Brian. It is a new French pepper mill."

"Oh no. I couldn't take that one."

"Yes," Miss Xuan insisted. She held the tan pepper mill like it was a crystal ball and opened and closed the drawer at the bottom to show me it worked then put it into my hands.

"I couldn't accept this. It is your new pepper mill." I put myself in an awkward position, I knew I had to accept one of the pepper mills but I might have to accept both of them.

Miss Xuan translated what I said. Mr. Phap said in his high-pitched voice, "Lieutenant Brian, we insist you take this French pepper mill. Please you must take it. You would be happy with the French pepper mill." The others spoke and nodded their heads. I did not want the French pepper mill.

"I'm sorry," I said. "If you must give me a pepper mill, I would really like to have this old pepper mill." Mr. Phap looked at it and turned down the edges of his mouth.

"The charm, the joy of this old pepper mill is just that, it's old. It has a history with your family. I don't want to use it but keep it as a memento from my visit to your home. I'll place it on a shelf as you have done."

Miss Xuan translated. Mr. Phap nodded his head like he understood and there were nods of approval from the others. Miss Xuan handed me the old pepper mill.

"Thank you, *cam on*," I said, happy to find myself with the old pepper mill.

(That pepper mill stayed with me until the early nineties when the bottom drawer facing finally broke off. In 1992, Vicki and I placed it in a garage sale where a Vietnamese couple bought it for fifty cents.)

"I should return to my base," I said.

Miss Xuan reached for my pistol. She held the holster, again with the barrel pointed up, and brought it to me. "This was a wonderful meal of *Bun bo*." I attempted the Vietnamese name of the meal and caused much laughter with my poor accent. I shook the hands of everyone. Miss Xuan's father smiled and held my hand tight with his two hands. He looked into my eyes again for a long time but said nothing.

Miss Xuan and Mr. Phap walked me out to my jeep. I waved goodbye and drove toward MASS-2. *I will write a letter to my wife, Colleen*, I thought to myself while I kept an eye out for any-thing unusual at the dark edges of the road. *I'll explain the meal and each flavorful detail of the evening. I'll send the pepper mill home. Colleen and Kaye will enjoy hearing about the meal, the books on the shelves, the orangey-brown color of the walls, the subdued lighting, the photos and miniature bananas on the altar, the out of place pistol, the dishes on the table, the celadon teacups, and the smiling inquisitive honey colored faces of my hosts.*

The visit to the house of Miss Xuan was a gift, like the broken and cobweb-strewn pepper mill that I held in my lap.

THIRTEEN

The Wrong Road, 2001

"Now then! Show your ticket, child!" the Guard went on, looking angrily at Alice.

"I'm afraid I haven't got one," Alice said in a frightened tone: "There wasn't a ticket-office where I came from."

All this time the Guard was looking at her, first through a telescope, then through a microscope, and then through an opera-glass. At last he said, "You're traveling the wrong way."

—From *Through the Looking-Glass, And What Alice Found There,* Lewis Carroll

A T 9:00 A.M. the day after my sixtieth birthday celebration with Mr. Hoan's family, a taxi arrived at his house. It was a white, Suzuki minivan, a "mini-minivan" built just for the Vietnamese and one that could easily lift onto the porch for safe keeping. Hanh Quyen and I squeezed into the backseat and the engine whirred like a model airplane as we merged into the flow of traffic. My feet did not fit in the floor space and my knees gouged into the back of the front seat that held Mr. Hoan, but we were on our way to find the old MASS-2 Headquarters area.

At Highway 1 we turned south toward Dogpatch and the terrain looked familiar. "We will turn to the right up here. Not too far," I said.

I clicked on my microcassette tape recorder: "Thursday, Octo-

ber twenty-fifth, 2001. We're on our way to the MASS-2 Headquarters area where I lived during the war. The railroad tracks
have moved from the west side of Highway 1 to a median strip.
But the area looks the same. Dogpatch should be right up here."

And there it was, the village Americans named Dogpatch, the
pejorative name for the shanties, shops, and brothels dotted with
flattened-out Coca Cola, Budweiser, or Pepsi cartons used to
patch the holes in their roofs and walls.

"Please stop," I yelled up to the driver but he paid no attention.
"STOP, STOP!"

Hanh Quyen spoke to the driver in Vietnamese and he pulled
over immediately.

"Mr. Brian, our driver does not know the word, 'stop.' He said
he is sorry he did not stop the taxi for you."

"I'm sorry, yes, of course he wouldn't know that word. What
is the Vietnamese word for stop?"

"*Dung lai.*"

"Please tell the driver I will use *dung lai* from now on when I
need him to stop."

I struggled to pull myself out of the taxi, built strictly for the
Vietnamese body type. The temperature and humidity made my
shirt cling to sweat, and Vietnam in 2001 still smelled of exhaust
fumes, raw sewage, and fresh baked French bread.

As I stood on the corner, a small boy, maybe ten years old,
jumped over the sewage ditch on the other side of the road and
walked toward me. He wore a polo shirt with Shaquille O'Neal's
picture on the front. "*Chao chau,*" I said.

"Hello," he said in perfect English.

I took the lens cap off my Olympus 35-millimeter camera, focused, and snapped his picture. I smiled at the boy, born decades
after I stood on this corner to take movies.

I walked across the street to take a shot of a Vietnamese family
who stood just outside the door of a market to examine the veg-

etables displayed in precise color coordinated rows. As I focused my camera they all turned around and posed.

In 1966 this market was a brothel. I took movies of young prostitutes who leaned against that same door wearing miniskirts and cleavaged tops. Their hair swirled skyward in a black bundle of beads and bows.

I squeezed my legs back into the Suzuki. "It looks almost the same," I said. The taxi driver turned the corner and drove down the road now called Le Trong Tan, after the commander of military campaigns that took Saigon in 1975.

I put my camera back in its case, happy to have two shots of Dogpatch. The street still consisted of shanties, markets, and shoppers who crowded the walkways on each side of the road. But no Marines looking for sex.

At the end of the village we wound around the base of Hill 327 where the road disintegrated into a quagmire of ruts and potholes. Our driver slowed down and stopped.

"I believe this is the correct way," I said from the back seat. I wasn't exactly sure, it had been over thirty years.

Hanh Quyen translated and our driver looked to Mr. Hoan for a signal to continue or turn around. Mr. Hoan, however, sat still with no indication as to what to do, so the driver shifted into gear and we continued on our journey.

Some of the ruts were as deep as the Suzuki itself but the driver swerved around them as though dodging land mines and then slammed on his brakes. Hanh Quyen screamed when we were both thrust into the back of the front seats.

The Suzuki sat at the edge of a rain-filled rivulet that poured out of the hills and cut a stream across the road fifteen meters wide. Three men stood outside a small building on the hill to our left so Mr. Hoan walked up to them and pointed to the Suzuki. The men became animated and pointed to the hills and pointed to the road and pointed to the stream that cut across the road then they all began to nod their heads up and down.

Mr. Hoan walked back to the Suzuki but had to wait before crossing the road, a five-ton dump truck with tires taller than our taxi, drove past and splashed mud onto the windows that left a coat of brown sludge. When Mr. Hoan slid into his seat, he said, "The road becomes 'more-flat' on the other side of this water."

The stream looked to be about a foot deep with a strong current that grasped branches, twigs, even rocks—anything in its path. Our driver backed up about ten meters, stopped, and drove forward to the right-hand side of the road where he lowered his van into the rivulet. The Suzuki bounced and pitched in the water while moving forward until it clunked against a rock and stopped. The driver stepped on the gas but his Suzuki did not move. Water rushed against the doors on his side and the minivan rocked with the water's thrust.

The driver looked out the back window, put it in reverse, and hit the gas. The wheels spun and debris gurgled out from under tires. The Suzuki shifted from side to side as we bounced backwards over rocks and into holes and then stopped. Water again splashed against the doors, stones clanked onto metal, our feet vibrated and the Suzuki started to slide off the road with the current. Hanh Quyen's eyes doubled in size as the driver shifted into gear and fishtailed forward. He drove around the rock that stopped us and gunned his Suzuki out of the rivulet and onto the road.

"*CAM ON!*" I yelled. "Very good driving!" I patted the driver on the shoulder. "*CAM ON!*" The driver turned around and smiled.

The road did become 'more-flat.' We drove by a group of Quonset huts in the trees to our right that resembled a Boy Scout camp. A long, one-story building sat on a knoll up to our left. A red flag with one yellow star hung on a pole in front of the building and a few men in uniform stood outside. Maybe this was a Vietnamese military base now.

When we drove around the bend I saw a road that went up the hill. "*Dung lai, dung lai,*" I said. "That's the road leading up to where I lived." Overgrown foliage almost hid the road but the mountain ridge in the distance looked familiar.

I jumped out of the taxi and yelled, "This is the road that goes up to MASS-2 and my old hooch."

I started to focus my camera but heard the sound of a motorbike. A uniformed soldier drove up and shook his fist at the camera and shouted as he drove right toward me. "No pictures!" I yelled and ran back to the taxi, "I'll take no pictures!"

I climbed in and we took off down the road. But the soldier drove up beside us on the right and another soldier on a motorbike drove up on the left. They wore military uniforms with red patches on their shoulder epaulets. This was a military base.

"Let's leave," I said. "Go toward the village of Hoa My and Highway 1."

But we had to stop at a guard shack. One of the soldiers roared up on his motorbike and yelled through the driver's window. Apparently, a message for Mr. Hoan, since he immediately opened his door and jumped out of the taxi. The driver backed up his Suzuki and parked. That soldier escorted Mr. Hoan to the guard shack.

The other soldier jerked open the door and shouted into the taxi for Hanh Quyen to get out. I started to follow but the soldier slammed the door on me causing dust to puff into the Suzuki.

The driver and I sat there with only the sound of drill bits hammering into granite. We were surrounded by the same rock quarry that filled the valley below the old MASS-2 Headquarters area during the war.

Mr. Hoan and his granddaughter stood behind the van. They had no hats so the sun beat down on their foreheads while the two soldiers sat in the shade of the guard shack. Mr. Hoan was sixty-nine years old, they should let him sit down in the shade.

Our taxi driver said something. "Excuse me?" I said. "*Xin loi chu?*" No response, he just looked around his Suzuki like he was looking for something, checking some piece of equipment inside the vehicle. He bent down under the dashboard and sweat dripped from his forehead onto the floor. Then he jumped out of the Suzuki, slammed the door shut, and mumbled to himself as he walked around his taxi to poke at the mud caked on each fender. On his second trip around he stopped at the left front fender and looked down. He put his hands flat on the hood and shook his head, just moved it from side to side for a moment, then opened the driver's door and looked in.

He pushed the driver's seat forward to reveal a motor no bigger than a toaster. No wonder the Suzuki sounded like a model airplane.

The driver rolled up his sleeves, pulled out a lug wrench and miniature tire jack from the clamps next to the motor, then slammed the door shut with his foot.

We had a flat tire.

Another soldier, this one with two silver stars on each shoulder, drove his motorbike down to the gate area and parked. His stars flashed in the sun as he strolled over to Mr. Hoan. The two spoke briefly and then walked to the Suzuki. Mr. Hoan opened my door and bent down, beads of sweat covered his forehead. "Two-star" stood behind and tilted his head back so his eyes could focus on me.

"Mr. Brian," Mr. Hoan said, "do you have your passport?" He held out his hand. My mouth opened to speak but nothing came out. I didn't have it. I stuck it in my waist pouch and put the waist pouch in my dirty clothes bag and put the dirty clothes bag in my suitcase. I knew my passport would be safe in my suitcase.

"No, I don't. I'm afraid it's at my hotel."

Mr. Hoan withdrew his hand and relayed the message to the officer. The officer narrowed his eyes and spoke to Mr. Hoan— and spoke fast, an entire Vietnamese sentence spewed out of his mouth as one long word. Mr. Hoan came back to me and looked right into my eyes and said with determination, "Do you have a picture? An identification with your picture?"

"Yes." I reached into my backpack, pulled out my driver's license, and handed it to Mr. Hoan.

He handed my license to the officer who studied the photo then slapped it up and down on his open palm as he looked, again, at my face. He bent down into the van for a closer look and his smell, like an ashtray full of cigarette butts, made me wince. His skin was moist, his eyes squinted, and when he raised his upper lip he exposed a few decayed teeth. He slapped my license up and down on his hand three more times, but now in slow motion, while he scrutinized each line on my face.

Another motorbike came down the road driven by an older man who wore a white, short-sleeved shirt with black polka dots. More dust floated into the Suzuki. "Two-star," "Polka Dot," and Mr. Hoan talked briefly then "Two-star" handed my license to the man in the black polka dot shirt. Mr. Hoan climbed onto the back of "Polka Dot's" motorbike, "Two Star" climbed onto his motorbike, and I watched the three men drive away until Mr. Hoan disappeared behind a grove of eucalyptus trees.

I could see Hanh Quyen on the bench next to the guard booth. I waved but she couldn't see me.

The front of the van started to rise up. Our driver rotated the handle of his jack and the van's left front rose to a position higher than the rear. I couldn't find a comfortable way to sit. My feet didn't fit in the floor space and my knees ached. My legs needed to stretch, if only for a moment. I tried to lift my butt by pushing my hands down into the seat but there was no way to gain leverage. Gritty dust covered the seat. The dust on my arms dissolved in the sweat and created a film of brown goo. Hanh Dung would not be anxious to pull at my sludgy arm hair. I leaned back in the seat and set my feet on the other side of the taxi but there wasn't enough room for my legs to lie flat. Some knob or handle gouged into my upper back.

I turned around to see Hanh Quyen. She now shared a story with the guard of the gate and they laughed out loud. She waved her hand at flies while she talked. Two flies buzzed into the Suzuki and out in an instant, probably because of the heat. That heat and humidity stifled my breath and the taxi's open windows did not provide a breeze, only dust and the two flies. The taxi turned into a sauna.

The front of the van dropped back to the ground and bounced up and down. After our driver put on the hubcap, he opened the door, put the tools back by the miniature motor, and slammed the front seat back into place. When he washed the grease off his hands at the guard shack the stream of water splashed onto the dirt and formed a muddy puddle that gave an illusion of cool. The driver held the hose up to his mouth to drink and Hanh Quyen watched his actions from her bench. Eleven thirty, Mr. Hoan had been gone an hour.

A five-ton truck full of granite rocks the size of a Volkswagen Beetle bounced down the road to the entrance gate and stopped. More dust drifted over to the Suzuki's open windows. The young guard of the gate who laughed with Hanh Quyen looked at the truck and shook his head like he couldn't remember his job but did manage, after a moment of hesitation, to rise off the bench, walk to the truck three times taller than he was, step up onto the running board, and reach for a piece of paper from the driver. The guard didn't look at the paper he just walked to the three-inch diameter pole that barred the five-ton truck and tapped on its weighted end. The driver revved up the engine and took off down the road well before the pole stopped at vertical and vibrated.

The air inside the taxi did not move. Sweat dripped from my armpits, my trousers stuck to my thighs, and heat radiated onto my bald head from the Suzuki's roof. Just when I thought about opening the door to stretch my legs the sounds of drilling and trucks and blasts of dynamite stopped as if someone hit the mute button. Twelve noon, lunch time. Quiet.

Mr. Hoan had been gone way too long, an hour-and-a-half. He just needed to explain how we wandered on to this base. There were no signs or gates for heaven's sake, nothing that suggested a military base.

This trip to find MASS-2 with Mr. Hoan, should not have caused such turmoil. I knew I would return to visit Mr. Hoan someday, but now, just my fourth day back in Vietnam, I caused him to be carted off by the military police.

I heard the faint sound of a motorbike. The man in the white shirt with black polka dots drove his motorbike down the road with Mr. Hoan and parked. Mr. Hoan opened my door. "We can go." He pointed in the direction of the military building with the red flag, "But we must go back the same road."

"On that bad road?" his granddaughter said.

"Yes." Mr. Hoan did not change his expression nor look at his granddaughter. "We must go back the same way."

I was just happy to see him, happy to have him return.

Mr. Hoan looked back toward the man with the polka dot shirt. "You must give them the film from your camera."

"What?"

Mr. Hoan took a breath and lifted up his shoulders. "You must give them the film from your camera."

Hanh Quyen slid into the back seat. "How are you?" I asked.

"I am okay."

I bent down to unsnap my camera case. *What pictures had I taken?* I took one picture of the boy in Dogpatch and one shot of the old brothel building, but I didn't take the shot of the road leading up to MASS-2 because the soldier on the motorbike yelled at me. There were no shots of this base!

The counter read "14." *Fourteen? Where else did I take a picture?* My 60th birthday party.

I'll lose that shot of Mr. Hoan's family where they were falling down and laughing. It was hilarious, and the shot of his family and the birthday dinner of *Mi Quang.* But there was nothing I could do. I had to turn my film over to these officers. Mr. Hoan was safe and we could leave, that was the important thing.

I wound up the film, took it out of the camera, put it in its little round container, and stepped out of the taxi for the first time in over two hours. I stretched until I again felt the blood move through my veins. When I handed the container to the guard, Mr. Hoan blocked my hand and pointed to polka dot, "No! You must give your film to *him*."

I walked toward the man who sat with his shoulders erect and his black high-top boots planted on each side of his motorbike. There were no shots of his base. He didn't know. He didn't care. He'll throw the container of film in a drawer where it will sit until someone remembers that one day, long ago, a crazy American tried to take pictures of their base.

He wanted this mess over with. He took the film with one hand and reached into his polka dot shirt pocket with the other to pull out my driver's license.

"*Cam on*," I said. He did not smile.

At the taxi I squeezed into the back seat, thankful for at least a short stretch. Mr. Hoan climbed into the front passenger seat, the driver slid into his seat, and they both simultaneously slammed their doors shut. More dust puffed into the Suzuki. The driver started the engine and we were off in the direction from whence we came.

It was not fair for us to have to return the way we came in, on that road full of mud, potholes, and rivulets a five-ton truck could negotiate but not Suzuki minivans. I knew that Highway 1 was just a mile or so past this guard station but we had no choice. We drove on. Silent.

We passed the headquarters building with the red flag where soldiers still stood out front and looked down at us. No one waved or nodded, they just stared.

We passed the Quonset Huts and looked for signs that suggested a military base but there were none. There was no gate, no transition of any kind from military to civilian property. The military base simply vanished. Like Brigadoon, gone for a hundred years.

"Mr. Hoan," I said. "What did they ask you? Were you okay? What did you tell them?" Hanh Quyen translated my questions but Mr. Hoan said nothing, he just sat in the front seat and looked straight ahead.

We bounced through the rivulet and swerved around the ruts, then blended into civilization. People drove past without a clue as to what happened to us.

In front of Mr. Hoan's house I said, "Can I buy lunch?"

Hanh Quyen translated but Mr. Hoan again was silent.

Why was Mr. Hoan silent? Was he mad, I wondered. *Did the officers grill him about me?* I thought he might have had to pay some money to get out of that situation. *How could I repay him? Maybe I should ask him again what they said or did.* But the driver ran around and opened his door. Mr. Hoan pulled himself up by the ledge of the window, stepped out of the taxi, and walked toward his house. He took the small step onto his green tiled porch and walked to the opened doorway. He held onto the door frame to kick off his sandals, the right, then the left, then disappeared into his home.

FOURTEEN

Another Movie, 1966

Through the region roared the flames of war.
Gray phantoms, fumes of slaughter leapt the skies
As sharks roved streams and armored men prowled roads.
—From *The Tale of Kieu*, Nguyen Du, 1807

W HEN I DROVE into Danang or across the river to the helicopter base at Marble Mountain, I had to drive by the US airbase just past Dogpatch. I often saw Marine F-4 Phantom jets waiting to takeoff. One day the movie camera was at my side, so I parked the jeep and walked up to the fence that surrounded the airbase. Two gray jets with white tipped noses sat, one just ahead of the other, poised for takeoff. The roar of their engines, even a hundred meters away, hurt my eardrums. The one nearest me started to roll down the Danang runway and gathered speed as it raced south until it left the tarmac and disappeared into the clouds.

The second Phantom took off and within seconds the red circle of flame at its tail also disappeared into the clouds. The end of the runway, where I stood at the fence, was quiet. Down the runway, about a kilometer from where I stood, there were airport hangers and a cluster of Quonset huts that acted as the terminal for the huge Danang airbase. Military personnel moved in and out of the buildings, jeeps and six-by-six trucks drove past Quonset huts, and a staff car with a red flag attached to each front fender drove out onto the tarmac, all in a mad scramble to conduct the business of war.

After my lens cap snapped in place I put the camera into its black leather case and walked back to my jeep. There were no security guards along the fence and no one came up to question me. In fact, there were no security guards anywhere to be seen. That didn't strike me as out of the ordinary in 1966 but it does seem odd to me now as I write this in the winter of 2018. Security is visible everywhere in America: airports, border crossings, docks, apartment buildings, court houses, city streets. And there is, after Benghazi in 2012, enormous security to protect our military personnel and diplomats around the world. But these are different times. Suicide bombers, deranged shooters, or radicalized terrorists can slip, unnoticed, even into "green-zones" and often into crowded cafés or airports or theaters or schools or outdoor markets to detonate themselves or just start shooting to kill dozens of innocent civilians. And we can watch all this on our smart phones.

FIFTEEN

Revelations, 2001

We make ourselves a place apart
Behind light words that tease and flout,
But oh, the agitated heart
Till someone really find us out.

'Tis pity if the case require
(Or so we say) that in the end
We speak the literal to inspire
The understanding of a friend.

But so with all, from babes that play
At hide-and-seek to God afar,
So all who hide too well away
Must speak and tell us where they are.

—"Revelation," Robert Frost

L ATER THAT AFTERNOON Hanh Dung called and said Mr. Hoan invited me to dinner at his house that evening. It was a relief to learn he wanted me back into his home for dinner. *Maybe he will talk about what happened while he was detained. Or maybe Mr. Hoan wanted to tell me that I needed to leave Vietnam.*

After dinner, Mr. Hoan and I went into the living room to have tea and Hanh Dung came in to help translate.

"I'm sorry you were taken away today by the military, Mr. Hoan, I should have suggested another route into my old base," I said. Mr. Hoan just smiled.

"Outside of you being interrogated for almost two hours, I've enjoyed my visit with you and your family, Mr. Hoan."

Mr. Hoan poured tea into our handle-less cups. "Thank you. Mr. Brian. We enjoy to have you here and visit us." He took a sip of tea. "Mr. Brian, please, you do not need to worry about me."

I took a sip of tea. But I did worry about him and I hoped I didn't get him in trouble with the military or the government. Mr. Hoan looked relaxed. I'm sure he had a nap that afternoon. I did.

"When do you go to Miss Xuan's home?" Mr. Hoan said.

"Saturday," I said, "the 27th. Then I'll be back here on Wednesday, the 31st."

"Good," he said. "It will be good for you to visit with Miss Xuan."

"Mr. Hoan, you mentioned that you taught in a high school in Danang City after I left Vietnam in 1967. What did Miss Xuan do? Did she stay at Hoa My School?"

Mr. Hoan took another sip of his tea and nodded his head. "Miss Xuan left Hoa My village after you were gone home because she was afraid the South Vietnamese government would arrest her."

He put his cup down on the coffee table. It was still half full but he picked up the teapot and filled his cup.

"Why would Miss Xuan be arrested?"

Mr. Hoan looked at me and moved the teapot toward my cup. "No thank you."

He set the teapot down and leaned back in his chair. "The students and teachers at Hoa My School were afraid because you was a spy for the South Vietnamese government."

Mr. Hoan's misuse of grammar had not made an impact on me prior to the sentence I just heard. His voice and language had such melodic, such poetic phrasing that the grammar was immaterial. But I knew the phrase, "you was" instead of "you were" had to be wrong. The phrase tumbled around my brain for a moment until I realized the word "spy" was attached to the errant verb.

An acidic pain burned into the left side of my stomach, "A spy?"

"Yes," Mr. Hoan said. "A picture you took of Miss Xuan was given to the South Vietnamese police. She would be arrested if she stayed in the village of Hoa My. She asked me to take her to the mountains to escape arrest."

A gecko scampered up the wall in front of us and stopped in his tracks to stare at Mr. Hoan. Hanh Dung smiled at me across the coffee table. I moved off the loveseat and into a chair next to Mr. Hoan. "I was not a spy for the South Vietnamese government."

"It is okay," he said. "You must do what you were ordered to do. We do not worry about that. The Hoa My students were nervous when you took pictures but you must do it if they tell you."

Hanh Dung sat in the loveseat and smiled but she did not attempt to translate my words. I spoke directly to her, "I took movies at the school because I liked to take movies. It was my hobby. I wanted a record of what I was doing in Vietnam." Hanh Dung nodded at me and I nodded back but no translation.

I turned to Mr. Hoan, "I took movies all the time. No one *told* me to take movies."

Mr. Hoan held his hands together in his lap, "It was your job," he said with no expression. "It is okay. We know you are a friend and you must do it at that time. That was a long time since now."

I shook my head back and forth. I would not have spied on these teachers, these friends, even if it was an order. "I could not have done that, Mr. Hoan. Be a spy. Even if I was told to do it."

"We know it was your job," Mr. Hoan said again. "Miss Xuan knows that when you come to her house for dinner you looked for clues at her house. You looked into a drawer of a peppermill and then you take the old peppermill away. And when you left Vietnam the picture you took of Miss Xuan was given to the Saigon government."

"Miss Xuan's peppermill, Mr. Hoan, that peppermill was a memento, a gift from Miss Xuan's family."

Hanh Dung sat in her chair and looked at her grandfather and smiled at me. I pointed my hands to Hanh Dung and motioned for her to speak, to say something but she was silent.

"The camera I had was a movie camera, Mr. Hoan. It only took movies. Moving pictures." I moved my hands around in a circle. "So I could not give anyone a still photo from the movies I took."

Hanh Dung must understand the difference between movies and a photo. "I would not spy on my friends." I put my hand on Mr. Hoan's arm. "I would not pretend to teach you English just to spy on you. I couldn't do that."

Mr. Hoan smiled and nodded his head. He believed the enlarged photos I brought on this trip were still photos I took in 1966. But those photos were transferred from my movies just a year-and-a-half ago, in June 2000. There are four of them: the shot of six Hoa My teachers next to the *kien kien* tree, the 1966 soccer team photo, and the two close-up shots of Miss Xuan and Mr. Hoan that I sent to the Catholic priest in Danang so he could locate them.

It began to rain. It rained so loud and powerful that it sounded as if Mr. Hoan's porch roof would collapse. He said he would take me to my hotel in a few minutes when the rain stopped and true to his word, in a few minutes, the rain stopped. It was suddenly quiet.

We rode through the narrow streets of Danang

My arms were around Mr. Hoan, who thought my job in the Marines was to spy on students and teachers at Hoa My School. There had to be an explanation I could give to convince him I was not a spy. Maybe show him my fitness reports. Especially the one that said I didn't have the technical knowledge necessary for the motor transport assignment, but as far as the Civic Action assignment, it read: "He relates well with people and conveys a genuine interest in them."

From the day I returned to the States in May 1967 I've worried about these two friends, worried that something might happen to them either from an experience related to the war or an accident or illness before I made contact with them.

But all these years they thought I was a spy. I taught them English and visited their homes, but Miss Xuan had to flee Danang to escape arrest because, as she thought, I turned her photo over to the South Vietnamese government. Now, in 2001, they invited me into their homes, allowed me to take their grandchildren and nieces and nephews on tours and out to lunch; welcomed me as though a close family friend even though they thought I spied on them and turned a photograph of Miss Xuan in to the South Vietnamese government. It didn't make sense.

Mr. Hoan drove his motorbike up Bach Dang Street past the lights on the River Han Bridge that shimmered like a golden pyramid while a warm wind blew around his shirt and onto my face. The pavement steamed from the rain. It was dark and quiet with little traffic on the ride back to my hotel. The smell of wet pavement after a rain blended with the smell of fish from the fleet of boats tied together on the River Han.

We pulled up to the front porch of my hotel. A bell atop the mast of a boat clanged and a lone motorbike drove past the hotel with a young couple meshed together as one.

I shook Mr. Hoan's hand a long time. Both my hands wrapped around his. "Thank you for this evening, for your kindness and your friendship." He turned his motorbike around, pushed his foot down on the starter and drove onto the empty street. I watched him disappear in the dark. His white shirt vanishing along with the putter sound of his motorbike.

SIXTEEN

Danger in Dong Ha, 1966

And we are here as on a darkling plain
Swept with confused alarms of struggle and flight,
Where ignorant armies clash by night.

—From *Dover Beach*, Matthew Arnold

"SERGEANT GREENE," I said in the early summer of 1966, "why don't we pour a twenty-by thirty-foot concrete slab out here so our mechanics don't have to work on vehicles in the dirt or in the mud when it rains? I've done some concrete work and this job can't be too difficult."

"Yes, sir, Lieutenant. That's good. That's good."

"Does anyone know where we can scrounge some concrete?" I asked.

Sergeant Wix laughed, "No problem gettin' concrete, Lieutenant. Me and TV can take care of that."

"TV?" I said.

"TV, sir. For Thomas Virgial Greene." Sergeant Wix smiled.

"Virgial?" I said.

"Let's not spread that around, sir."

"Well, my middle name is 'Murray,' how would you like BM for a handle?"

"Your secret is safe with us, Lieutenant."

By that time, I had built an editing station in my hooch to work on my movies and also a space where I could write or design projects. I designed the concrete slab and gave a list of the equipment we needed to Sergeant Wix. He knew how to scrounge.

After work, the drivers, mechanics, Sergeants Wix and Greene, and I dug out the space for a concrete shop floor. We put in 2 X 6 boards around the edges, leveled them with a slight slant so the water would run out the back of the shop, staked them, put in the kickers, laid the wire down, and unloaded wheelbarrows full of gravel into the area.

Early on a Saturday morning, a cement truck rolled in and poured the concrete while Sergeant Greene and I troweled the slab and edges since we had the most experience with concrete.

Sunday morning, I drove down to the motor pool to admire our work. The concrete slab that filled the area under our shop roof still had a green tinge to it and that distinct smell of lime from wet concrete.

Sergeant Wix walked out of his tent. "Whooeeee!" he said and slapped his thigh and whooped another big holler. "We had us some fireworks down here last night, Lieutenant."

"What happened?"

"We was drinkin' some beer out here in the motor pool around sunset and old TV started hankerin' to visit some of his Vietnamese friends. So, he ups and heads across that rice paddy out to the village on the other side of them trees. Well, after I take a shower at the water buffalo [water tank on a trailer], I was shootin' the breeze with some Tenth Engineers who was guardin' our perimeter. And pretty soon we see TV, barely visible in the dark, creepin' back across the rice paddy. All of a sudden, the sky lights up just like daylight. Old TV had set off a trip flare. So, one of the guards yells, "Shoot 'em, *shoot 'em!*" And TV starts thrashin' around and yellin', 'Don't shoot, don't shoot! It's me!' I 'bout died laughin'."

Sergeant Wix and Sergeant Greene gave me an education on

how to bring out the best in people. I learned from them, praised them, encouraged them, trusted them, and rewarded them. And I was in contact with Sergeant Wix until he died in 2017.

* * * *

Another MASS-2 generator broke down at our base in Dong Ha and Sergeant Stuck, the generator expert, needed to stay in Danang to finish work on a down generator at Headquarters. So Sergeant Greene picked up the part and the two of us hitched a ride on a CH-46 transport helicopter to deliver it. We had to shout to hear each other.

"Sergeant Greene, how far north is Dong Ha?" I yelled.

"Way up north, sir. Fifteen clicks [kilometers] from the DMZ."

When we approached the Dong Ha Airstrip Sergeant Greene yelled through the clatter of rotating blades, "Lieutenant, that's a lot o' Marines down there. There's something up. Yes, sir. Something up."

"What do you think it is?"

"Dunno, sir. Could be drill. Could be Charlie actin' up. Maybe they lobbed a few mortar rounds last night. Lot o' Marines. Lot o' Marines gathered down there."

The big helicopter descended down to the tarmac at Dong Ha where Marines gathered at one end of the runway.

We walked to the MASS-2 tent and Sergeant Greene bellowed, "Say, Sarge. How's it goin'?" in that deep baritone voice.

The sergeant had a bird's beak of a nose and reminded me of an Oklahoma scarecrow, he was so tall and lanky his utility trousers were about to fall off due to his lack of hips. "Up to snuff. TV, how's the man?"

"I'm OK. Good. Yeah, good.

"TV, you and the lieutenant best do your business and git back on that chopper."

"What's up?" I asked.

The sergeant picked up a coffee can and spit out a drool of tobacco. "Viet Cong, sir. Came right up on us 'bout three this mornin'. Mortars fired from out there by that tree line." The sergeant stood at the opening of the tent and pointed to some trees about two-hundred meters away. "No one kilt or injured. But shot the shit out the runway and two choppers. Rooned one, I heard."

"Well, Sarge, we're staying the night," Sergeant Greene said. "We got parts for your broke generator. And we can't leave til' that sucker's up and runnin'. Where we bunkin'? We'll drop off our gear and git the parts out to the mechanic."

"TV, you can stay in my tent. Lieutenant, our officer's quarters is full so you're going to have to sleep in what we like to call, our 'overflow quarters.'"

The sergeant walked me toward the airstrip and showed me my overflow tent then took Sergeant Greene out to the generator shack

The overflow tent sat next to the airstrip with its canvas flaps rolled up. The only "overflow" was the flow of dust through those open screens, covering all the bunks inside the tent. And being so close to the airstrip, I hoped Charlie didn't lob any more mortar shells onto the runway.

I dropped off my gear and walked over to the MASS-2 radar cubicle. Sergeant Greene stood next to one of our generators with two MASS-2 mechanics.

"Good afternoon, sir, that was some shit this morning," said a lance corporal who looked about fifteen. "Some real shit comin' in. We're fifteen clicks from the DMZ and I'm on duty tonight from 0200 to 0600 hours."

Sergeant Greene wiped his hands with a rag and said to me, "The parts we brought should fix the problem, sir. We'll have her up in an hour or two."

"How are your vehicles, Sergeant? Everything running?" I asked.

They're fine, sir. Everything running except this one generator."

"You got the parts you need?"

"We do now, sir."

"I'm going to check in with the OD, I'll meet you at the chow hall later."

"Yes, sir," Sergeant Greene, said.

It looked and felt like the sky could open up any minute. After the MASS-2 Officer-of-the-Day and I chatted a while we walked over to the chow hall for dinner and Sergeant Greene joined us about the time we finished our meal. When I got up to leave there was this loud crack of thunder not far from the tent. Heads and shoulders immediately crouched and the tent went silent. In a moment the heads popped up and scanned the table tops, everyone ready to *hayako* (to go somewhere *fast*) to the nearest foxhole. It rained so hard water dropped off the canvas tent like Niagara Falls.

"I think I'll stay here until the rain stops," I said.

Sergeant Greene and I talked with the MASS-2 people and some other Marines. They retold the story of last night's mortar attack.

"Scuttlebutt is there's gonna be another attack tonight," someone said.

Then a Marine told us about someone in his tent. "This guy was here when I come on board. Listen to this shit. You want to be near this cat when they start lobbin' mortars. A few months ago, I'm playing poker with this guy and some others. But this guy can hear the tubing of a mortar shell."

"He can do what?" Sergeant Greene asked.

"The explosion, you know, when the round hits the firing pin. He hears it. It can be two-hundred meters away. Shit. They say he heard it again last night."

Sergeant Greene cocked his head like he did when he contemplated things. "Say that again."

"When the round hits the firing pin at the bottom of the tube, there's a little explosion. This guy hears it. This is no bullshit.

About three months ago, we're playing poker and all of a sudden, he hears tubing off in the distance and he gets up and crashes through the poker table and our chairs and out the door. We jump up and follow him out to the bunker. When he goes you gotta' be right behind him and sure enough a few rounds were lobbed onto the runway. Charlie just practicin' for that shit this morning."

"Wha'd the guy do this mornin'?" Sergeant Greene asked.

"I didn't wake up until someone yelled 'incoming!' I was sound asleep. But they said he made it to his foxhole before the first round hit. Must have heard it in his sleep."

"That's one advantage I'd like to have," said Sergeant Greene.

The rain finally stopped and I left to find the nearest foxhole to my tent."

"See you in the mornin', Lieutenant," Sergeant Greene said. "I'm goin' to find out jis where the man with them big ears is sleepin' tonight. Heh, heh, heehhh. Yes, sir. I'll follow that Marine to the bunker."

There was a path of wooden planks that led to my tent and rays of sunlight streaked down on Dong Ha through the clouds. The nearest foxhole was out the flap of my tent to the right. A foxhole heavily fortified with sandbags.

I walked over to the portable runway that was made out of green aluminum rectangles connected together like thousands of door mats. A CH-46 helicopter, with towers on each end that supported sixty-foot blades, hovered in the air and began to descend. When its rear wheels touched the runway the craft rolled forward, nose up, like a praying mantis, and finally settled its front wheels down on the tarmac. The noise sounded like a jackhammer thumping at my feet.

Sleep didn't come easy that night. Not only was I nervous about a possible mortar attack, the nocturnal noises were amplified in the empty tent. Mosquitoes screamed outside the net, cockroach legs clacked across the canvas, and muffled mortar explosions rumbled in the distance.

Sometime in the night, loud reports from the mortar fire woke me with repeated blasts. I sat up in my rack ready to *hayako* to that foxhole but heard the pop sound of flares opening up their parachutes. Flares from our own mortars. I could see the bright light outside from the cannisters swinging in the wind on their parachute drop back to earth. Shadows waved across the tent floor to the empty racks and then waved back to my rack. Back and forth until the canister hit the ground. Then, total darkness.

I lay in my rack and thought it would be just my luck to be in Dong Ha when the VC launched a mortar attack on two successive nights. But I finally fell asleep.

In the morning, a CH 46 helicopter revved up its engines to wake me. No incoming. No mortar attack. Just sunshine.

SEVENTEEN

A Walk on China Beach, 2001

While you walk the water's edge,
turning over concepts
I can't envision, the honking buoy
serves notice that at any time
the wind may change,
the reef-bell clatters
its treble monotone, deaf as Cassandra
to any note but warning. The ocean,
cumbered by no business more urgent
than keeping open old accounts
that never balanced,
goes on shuffling its millenniums
of quartz, granite, and basalt.

—From "Beach Glass," Amy Clampitt

H ANH DUNG ARRIVED at my hotel in a cyclo and told me we were going for a ride. The cyclo name comes from the French *cyclo-pousse* or "pedicab," which is *xich lo* in Vietnamese and pronounced, *SEEK low.* This rickshaw style tricycle, or "trishaw" as Graham Greene called them in *The Quiet American,* had two wheels in front with a passenger seat between the two wheels and one wheel in back with a high seat for the driver who steered the front two wheels with a crossbar. This was the most interesting mode of transportation in Vietnam. In Ho Chi Minh City I saw a cyclo driver transport a block of ice the size of a garbage can with a gunny sack on top of the ice. The driver pulled his cyclo over to the curb when a woman waved. He walked around to the dripping hunk of ice and chipped off chunks to fill her bucket.

The most surreal cyclo cargo—one pictured on a Vietnamese postcard, not one that I witnessed—was three huge pink hogs, plopped, one on top of the other, in the front seat.

Hanh Dung and I walked down Bach Dang Street along the River Han and past vendors that held their produce up and asked, "You like this?" or said, "Very good for you." But we ducked into a café and sat down to order lunch.

By the time our order arrived the sky had turned from partly cloudy and blue to one filled with storm clouds, a dusk-like darkness covered the waterfront and a wind whipped off the River Han with such a force that the restaurant curtains blew into a horizontal position straight out from the wall. No one noticed. The owner and wait staff went about their business as though nothing was out of the ordinary.

Hanh Dung had to raise her voice because of the wind. "This is normal weather in October, rain in afternoon, rain at night. Did you bring a raincoat?"

"Yes," I yelled. "I have one in my backpack."

"That is good. I brought one for you in case you don't bring one."

"*Cam on.*"

Hanh Dung took out her cell phone and made a call then said, "You better go now, the storm will come soon. My cousin will drive you back to your hotel."

I finished my soup and, as if some omnipotent overseer took care of me, a motorbike pulled up to the restaurant's open door and the driver, with leather coat and dark glasses, nodded to Hanh Dung like a member of some Asian gang. I paid for the meal and we walked into the powerful Chinook-type wind. No rain yet, just the warm wind. "How will you get home?!" I yelled to Hanh Dung. Someone's hat flew past.

"My cousin will come for me after he takes you!" she yelled back.

The cousin and I took off into the stream of honking and darting motorbikes. The canvas awnings over street vendors flapped in the wind.

My hotel was just two kilometers down Bach Dang Street and we were there in minutes. I hopped off the motorbike and watched the cousin speed away. We never met. My hands were wrapped tight around his muscular frame as we raced through traffic but we never spoke to one another. I only yelled, "*Cam on!*" as he sped away.

No rain yet but the rubbery trunks and branches of the palm trees that lined Bach Dang Street bent over so much it seemed they would snap. The wind whipped and flayed them seaward as though thousands of leaf-like hands warned all boats and ships that a storm approached.

Bicycles, motorbikes, and cyclos drove past the hotel but the drivers and their passengers paid no attention to the weather. From the entrance steps I watched leaves and paper and a few umbrellas whip past the hotel well above the street in a mad frolic to nowhere.

And then the wind subsided. A noticeable calm and sudden portentous drop in visibility. Darkness invaded Bach Dang Street and the east side of the river disappeared into a bank of dark clouds that brought rain in an instant. Bicycles, cyclos, and motorbikes all pulled over to the side of the road in unison as though a fire engine's siren signaled its approach. The drivers and passengers took out clear plastic raincoats and hats, put them on, and returned to the road as though the fire engine had passed and all excitement was gone.

The rain continued for twenty minutes, loud rain that pounded the pavement as though exploded from machine guns concealed in the darkened sky, rain like the rain that pounded the metal roof of my hooch in 1966, my first night in Vietnam.

Hanh Dung gave me a lesson: do not dwell on problems. She was the happiest young woman I know. She was also infectious. People loved to be around her because she enjoyed practically everything she did. *How did she think to bring me a raincoat?* That type of thoughtfulness is rare for a twenty-year old woman.

* * * *

That night Mr. Hoan wanted me to meet his daughter, Mrs. Huy, and her husband, Mr. Son. Mrs. Huy taught 4th grade at an elementary school and Mr. Son worked as a vice principal at a secondary school. They lived in a house across the River Han near China Beach. Mr. Hoan drove me there on his motorbike. The motorbike was the main mode of transportation in Danang. Children, husbands, wives, and friends sat on the backs of most motorbikes.

"Are you French?" a young man on the back of a motorbike asked when we stopped at a stoplight, his face less than a meter away.

"No, American."

"Ah, American. Very good. Do you visit your girlfriend in Vietnam?"

"No." I patted Mr. Hoan on the shoulder, "I visit friends."

"What do you think of my country?" he said.

"I like it very much."

He bobbed his head up and down and smiled, "You will be back." He turned to keep eye contact with me as his driver sped away then held his thumb up high. I did go back, twice.

On the east side of the River Han we drove past acres of pastureland just north of Marble Mountain's five craggy peaks. I smelled cow dung and damp grass but didn't see any cows. We turned onto a dirt road that led toward the beach. It ran along an open field. "That field was part of the 1st Marine Air Wing Helicopter base," I yelled to Mr. Hoan. There were still old American Quonset huts lined up in the distance.

My hernia operation took place in the Naval Hospital across the highway and near the river. The helicopter base was hit with mortar fire just two days before my operation. Needless to say, I was nervous checking in for the operation.

The U.S. discovered years after the war that the Viet Cong and North Vietnamese Army had a vast military complex and large hospital tunneled under Marble Mountain. Marble Mountain, one click south of that helicopter base, was off limits to the US military because of religious reasons.

Mr. Hoan and I entered a residential area and he maneuvered his motorbike around potholes and at one point drove onto the front yard of someone's home. A woman in brown pajamas waved from her open front door and smiled. Her betel nut teeth, the color of eggplant, glittered in the afternoon sun and we were close enough to smell the kitchen's grilled scallops.

We pulled up to a two-story stucco house where chickens clucked and pecked in the front courtyard. This was the home of Mr. Hoan's fifth daughter, Mrs. Huy and Mr. Son.

We were there for dinner but Mr. Son suggested a walk on China Beach before dinner. His daughter, Song Ha, a sophomore in high school and a talented visual artist, came along to translate.

When Mr. Son mentioned China Beach, the memory of diving into waves barely six inches high, drinking beer, and talking to Red Cross nurses came flooding back. R & R without leaving Vietnam. The beer was cold, the sun was hot, and so were the nurses.

Down the street from Mr. Son's house we took a path to the beach that went over sand dunes and around pitch pines with roots that snaked away from the tree in humps above ground. The air smelled of salt and seaweed.

Mr. Son took my hand and crouched beneath one of the pine trees. He pointed to a hole dug beneath the tree that had at one time been fortified with boards but the boards had rotted out, so the hole had caved in a bit. "This is a Vietnamese fighting location," Mr. Son said.

Song Ha said, "My father wants to tell you that this is a Vietnamese fortress. Mr. Brian, what do you call this place?"

"It looks like a foxhole or maybe a bunker."

"Yes, bunker. This is bunker left from the war with the Chinese."

"The Chinese?"

"Yes. The war in 1979."

Mr. Son nodded at his daughter's explanation and as we left the bunker to continue our walk he again held my hand. It is the custom in Vietnam for friends, two males, two females, or a male and female, to hold hands as they walk. Mr. Son walked fast and I hurried to keep up without breaking the hold. We walked through the miniature pines, down dunes, and over clumps of tall sea grass.

The wind blew minute grains of sand onto my skin and my face burned with the sting. My eyes watered from the wind but the fresh air smelled of the sea. Mr. Hoan, ahead of us, held onto his granddaughter's hand. We walked about a kilometer. I felt close to Mr. Son, as if I had known him a long time. I knew he wanted to help me understand his country and by holding my hand, I felt he accepted me into his culture.

The trail ended above a khaki colored beach that stretched out in both directions. Not the white sand I remembered. The sand high on the beach had odd bits of Styrofoam and beach glass strewn among the driftwood, grayed from the sun and sprinkled with sand. The ocean's gentle roar kept time with each wave that tumbled in from the South China Sea and rolled up the beach to a curved ruffle of foam then ebbed with a sigh.

A seagull floated stationary in the wind above our heads as we watched several black circular boats that looked like extra-large beach balls cut in half two hundred meters from shore. The people in them held on tight so the round-bottomed-boat wouldn't tip over. Children held onto the sides like the children on those whirling teacups at Disneyland.

"That boat is called, *thuyen nan*," said Mr. Hoan.

Several of these boats bobbed whimsically toward the north. A guide in each boat, with some mysterious athleticism, maneuvered the craft forward with a set of oars.

We leaned seaward into the wind and looked out at the horizon, marked by a gray sky above a flat, viridian sea. Our shirts flapped and the gull screeched in harmony with the splash of waves.

We took a different route back to Mr. Son's home and he again held my hand. He told me about his job as a vice principal at a high school and we talked about my work as a high school theater teacher. He asked how I could still teach and also be involved with the CIA.

"I'm not with the CIA." I said.

"A friend told me the police think you are CIA," Mr. Son said.

"Well, your friend must have me confused with someone else. I'm not with the CIA."

That little exchange of words lasted ten seconds and was never brought up again. I did not want to find out who the friend was or question Mr. Son any more about a mistaken assumption that I currently worked for the CIA. But this added a bit of tension to my Vietnam visits.

What was it about me, I wondered, that gave the impression I was a CIA agent? My cousin, a "Biggs" from Boston was a CIA agent. I had a student who became a CIA agent, but I was not one.

We arrived back at Mr. Son's house to see other guests in the front yard talking with Mrs. Huy. Mr. Son introduced me to a teacher from his school, Mr. Chot, who taught English. Mr. Chot was there to help translate but Hanh Dung and Mr. Son's daughter Song Ha did fine with the translations.

Song Ha ran to Hanh Quyen and the two cousins sat on a bench and held onto each other as Hanh Quyen relayed stories about the military base fiasco. Song Ha looked at her grandfather and me with eyes opened wide and talked and gestured and bounced on the bench like she was in the small Suzuki taxi until her mother said, "We can go in to the table for dinner."

The girls rose and talked with their heads bent in to each other as they moved toward the door, but then Song Ha turned and asked Mr. Hoan and me if the army officer would come to his house for more questions.

Mr. Hoan shook his head back and forth and put his hand on my arm. He nudged me onto the porch ahead of him as he said, "I don't can know."

* * * *

There is an undeniable redolence, always present in the Vietnamese home at meal time, like the aroma of browned turkey in the American home at Thanksgiving. When Mr. Hoan and I followed the cousins through Mrs. Huy's front door we were greeted with the aroma of fresh prawns, grilled with those secret Vietnamese spices concocted in clandestine vaults located deep beneath the surface of remote mountain villages.

At dinner Mrs. Huy brought in a platter of pink and peppered shrimp for an hors d'oeuvre. She selected one that was extra plump and placed it on a small saucer, "For you, Mr. Brian."

"*Cam on*," I said. I bit the curved morsel in half and juice squirted into all the corners of my mouth. "Delicious." Mrs. Huy smiled. It was tender and juicy with the sweet flavor of basil. The next bite lingered, long after the briny shrimp had dissolved.

Mrs. Huy passed around the platter of grilled shrimp. "Ah, my favorite," said Hanh Quyen.

"They're excellent," I said and took another off the platter. "A meal in itself, sensuous." I chewed and swirled the juices around my mouth. "*Ngon lam*."

"Ahhhhhhhh," from the crowd.

"*Cam on*," said Mrs. Huy. "You speak Vietnamese."

"Not too much. But I know the word *ngon lam* means delicious because the food, the meals on my trip have been so delicious. Beyond delicious."

The faces turned toward Hanh Quyen for the translation. "What is 'beyond delicious?'" she asked me.

"It means that the grilled prawns are *ngon lam*, but better than *ngon lam*. The best. Very, very good."

Hanh Quyen translated and more nods of approval. Mr. Hoan said, "Mr. Brian enjoys the eat." Hanh Quyen translated and the crowd erupted in laughter.

Hanh Quyen said, "When we stayed at the army gate and my grandfather went with the man on a motorbike and you must sit in the hot car alone. No food. I worry for you. But when we come home, you said, 'I will take you to lunch.'" Hanh Quyen and the others laughed.

"Yes, I do enjoy eating. The meals I've had at your homes have been some of the best meals I've had in my life. *Cam on*."

Hanh Quyen translated and there were nods from the group, plus "*khong co chi*" (you're welcome), from Mrs. Huy.

I put my hand on Hanh Quyen's shoulder. "I worried about you and your grandfather in the hot sun and I didn't know where Mr. Hoan was taken."

"My grandfather," Hanh Quyen said, "explained to the officer that we did not know it was a place of military. He said there were no signs of warning on road."

Song Ha said, "I would be scared to drive through the river in that small taxi."

Hanh Quyen said, "I was scared of that river. I thought the taxi was going to go over. What do you call it when the river drops from a mountain?"

"A waterfall," I said.

"Yes, I thought the water would push the small taxi over waterfall." Hanh Quyen's eyes got bigger as she spoke to her family. The group laughed and raised their arms and patted each other on the shoulders while Mr. Hoan just smiled and nodded his head.

We ate dinner and told more stories and then gathered in the living room for a photo. It was a handsome group, but not as large as the family photo taken on my birthday. Several members of Mr. Hoan's family were missing but the military police confiscated my only family photo, so that one had to do.

EIGHTEEN

Mr. Hoan's Daughter, 1966

Advantages to forceps use include avoidance of C-section, reduction of delivery time, general applicability with cephalic presentation. Complications include the possibility of bruising, deformation, [or] nerve damage. —Wikipedia

M R. HOAN ASKED me if I would take his ten-year-old daughter, Hein (Ian with an "H" sound), for a checkup at one of our military hospitals. Hein had short black hair, a round face, and dark brown eyes that looked at me as if to ask, "What are you thinking, Mr. Brian?" She was deaf in her left ear, deaf since birth, and her father thought an American doctor could do something the Vietnamese doctors could not.

I went to the American field hospital near the airbase where a dentist replaced the partial denture I lost at sea, and they were able to schedule an appointment for Mr. Hoan's daughter.

Mrs. Co, Hein, and Miss Xuan rode with me to the appointment. A Red Cross nurse told us the doctor could see us in about ten minutes and ten-year-old Hein reached up to hold my hand when we sat down on a bench. She was fascinated by all the cabinets and medicine bottles and the scale in the corner with weights on the bar across the top.

A Navy doctor, twenty-eight to thirty years old, came in accompanied by a Vietnamese woman dressed in a red *ao di*. I introduced myself to the doctor and explained the situation with Hein.

"I've asked an interpreter to be with us," the doctor said. The interpreter smiled at me.

The doctor knelt down in front of Hein. "What's the girl's name?"

The interpreter spoke to Mrs. Co.

"Hein," Mrs. Co said.

"Can you ask the mother to explain the problem with Hein's ear?"

The interpreter asked Mrs. Co the question and she gave a long answer. The interpreter looked confused and bent down closer to Mrs. Co. "What happened in the hospital? The doctor in the hospital did something?"

Mrs. Co continued to explain the problem in Vietnamese but the interpreter could not quite get the problem.

Miss Xuan spoke to the interpreter in Vietnamese and then began to translate for Mrs. Co. "When Hein was born," Miss Xuan said to the interpreter, "the doctor must take her, must pull her out with..." She paused. "The doctor used a tool," she looked at Mrs. Co and the two spoke in Vietnamese.

Back to the interpreter, "The doctor used a tool. I do not know the correct word." She held out her hand like a crab pincher.

The young doctor who watched this exchange of words said, "Forceps, the doctor used forceps?" He put his hand onto the top of his head like the clamp of a crane, "A clamp on the head?"

"Yes," Miss Xuan said. "Forceps. The forceps damaged the ear of Hein. And she does not hear in that ear." Miss Xuan pointed to Hein's left ear.

The doctor took out an otoscope with a light and knelt down to examine Hein's left ear and Hein, who was curious about the otoscope, sat still throughout this ordeal. After he looked into Hein's ear he asked Miss Xuan to join them in a room across from where we sat.

Mrs. Co leaned forward and watched her daughter disappear into the room, and in twenty minutes, Miss Xuan, the doctor, the interpreter, and Hein walked back to us. "There is a specialist in Saigon," he said and wrote the name of the specialist on a piece of paper, as well as the name of the hospital, and handed it to Mrs. Co. "I'm sorry," he said to Miss Xuan, "we can't do anything here. She needs to see a specialist. How old is she?"

"Hein is ten years old," said Miss Xuan.

The doctor looked at Miss Xuan, "You speak English very well."

"Thank you. This is my teacher of English." Miss Xuan smiled and pointed to me.

NINETEEN

The Road to MASS-2, 2001

*In our Buddhist teachings we learn not
to mourn for the past, nor worry about
the future, but live in the present moment.*

—Nguyen Van Phuc

B ECAUSE MISS XUAN lived in a small village east of Ho Chi Minh City and I was not going to see her until the following week, she asked her nephew, Phuc, who lived in Danang, to provide transportation for me. Phuc not only acted as my chauffeur, but as a translator, historian, guide, entomologist, geologist, botanist, Bodhisattva, and companion for lunch. Phuc was taller than the average Vietnamese male and at five-foot-ten he was almost as tall as me. He had dark hair, broad shoulders, a big smile, and a quick wit in both English and Vietnamese.

He worked for Vietnam Airlines but on his days off offered to be my tour guide, and since Mr. Hoan, his granddaughter, and I were unsuccessful and somewhat traumatized on our quest to find the MASS-2 Headquarters area, I thought Phuc and I should try to find it by going in on the road from Highway 1. That's the road I used going from my motor pool to Hoa My School and back in 1966.

Phuc, who spoke excellent English, asked me not to use "Mr." as in "Mr. Phuc" when I addressed him as he wanted to learn English exactly as the Americans speak the language.

"I appreciate your help in finding my old base," I told Phuc. "After the guards took Mr. Hoan away, I had to stay in the taxi and his granddaughter had to sit outside in the hot sun for over an hour-and-a-half. I worried about him and felt bad about dragging him into that situation. I didn't mind sitting in the car but to have him detained and interrogated and his granddaughter sit out in the sun for that long bothered me. I'm not sure what to do about it."

"You must not worry about that, Brian. In the Buddhist teaching we learn to accept what happens and move on from that. We do not worry about what happened in the past. We only think about the present. You must do this too."

"That's what Mr. Hoan said."

"You see, you don't need to worry about him. He has already forgotten about the time he was detained."

"He also said I shouldn't worry that the faculty at Hoa My School in 1966 believed I was a spy for the South Vietnamese government."

"You must not worry about that, Brian. That was a long time ago and you don't need to worry about it even if it was yesterday. Mr. Hoan is your friend and knows you are a good person."

"A good person wouldn't spy on his friends."

"If you are told to do that in the military, you must do it. But you must forget about that now so long after that time. My father worked for the American military as a translator and his sister was in the North Vietnamese Army. But they are both friendly even during the war when everyone comes home at Tet and at other times. And now we don't even worry about that time. You must do this to be happy, Brian."

Phuc asked questions about my life and the English language, and saw me as a friend, just as I saw him. It was an avuncular relationship that has remained to this day, but I knew I could not be happy knowing Miss Xuan and Mr. Hoan believed I spied on them during the war and worse yet, believed I handed a photo of Miss Xuan over to the Saigon government.

We left Highway 1 and drove the road that led to the mountains and eventually came to a guard station. "Phuc," I said, "I'm not sure we should try to go through that gate."

"It will be okay. Do not worry."

We entered the gate and the guard just motioned us through. So simple. I turned around to make sure he didn't hop on his motorbike, but he just lit a cigarette and waved.

We drove around the base of the mountain where the road leveled off and headed toward the city of Danang. After the first bend we passed a road that went up the hill to the right. "Stop here, Phuc. That's the road up to MASS-2." Phuc slowed and turned his motorbike around. It was a shock to see the road; it looked exactly like it did when I left in 1967. "This is the road. This is the road, drive up here."

The road I saw with Mr. Hoan, the one where I almost took a picture, was the wrong road. During the war I jogged this road, down to the bottom where it widens out to merge with the main road and back up to my hooch, two kilometers, five days a week. I knew each bend, each bush, each low standing palm, and the fork in the road halfway up where it leveled off to give me a breather.

When we passed that fork in the road, I knew we were close and in less than a minute we arrived at the leveled area known as MASS-2 during the war. I remembered the very spot where we watched a nervous Frank Sutton, who played Sergeant Vince Carter on the *Gomer Pyle* show, tell a few jokes.

"This used to be a small city," I said. "The large complex on this hill, built by the US military, was reduced to nothing. It seemed so permanent when I was here, so vital." The CO's shack, S-3 office, hooches, water tanks, and S-1 tent were gone. Only fronds of palm bushes waved in the wind.

"See that flat area over there?"

"Yes," Phuc said.

"We had a butler building there that held all our supplies. And we had a platform, a deck, just below it with a canvas tarp around the sides for our community shower. And our club, Club Vagabond, stood right below where we're standing. That was a wild place. Lots of fun. Birthday parties, I turned twenty-five in Vietnam. There were steak barbeques and after-work parties and when my friends came up to visit I'd take them to Club Vagabond for a beer. Our waitress was Vietnamese, Phuc. Her name was Hoa."

"Her name means 'flower,'" Phuc said.

"Yes, that's right, 'flower.'" My friend Eric Barnes and I spent some evenings in the club and Eric knew that Hoa meant flower. He called her "flower" or "flower child."

"Eric had a band in college called the 'Barn Stormers' so he borrowed a guitar from Henry Lee and entertained us until he had to leave. He had to go down to the airbase right where you work, Phuc, because he needed to catch an R & R flight to Hawaii the next morning. His wife, Noreen, met him there."

"Do you still see Eric Barnes?"

I turned and looked out to the bay when Phuc asked that question. It took me a minute or so before I could turn around and tell Phuc that Eric died shortly after he returned from that R & R. "Killed by a mine on patrol."

Phuc let me have my moment of reflection.

"It's sad really," I said. "He didn't have to go on that patrol since he had made captain, but he volunteered to go."

"I understand," Phuc said. We were both quiet for a long time but Phuc finally added, "All the things in our world are impermanent, so you must think of Eric Barnes with all your sweet memories of the time you had with him. Then you will see the miracle because life does not end after death, Brian. All people need love, so does your Eric Barnes. It's much better if you can send him a thought of love instead of a feeling of sadness. In our

Buddhist teachings we learn not to mourn for the past, nor worry about the future, but live in the present moment."

I didn't know what to say to Phuc. I knew *he* believed that. But I remained silent. I looked at the palm fronds that waved in the wind.

Finally I turned and said, "During the war we lived across this road up on that hill. We lived in hooches. Cabins really."

"I used to play in the American cabins," Phuc said.

"You did? Up here?"

"No. Near my home. Down by the sea. There were many American buildings left in that area. It was not a busy area like now but a rural area. Not much traffic on the roads, only bicycles. It was very rare to see even a motorbike. So we children could run on the streets with no fear. We played the game hiding and finding. Do you know that game?"

"Yes, we call it hide-and-seek."

"That was a fun game. The finder or seeker must face a wall of the cabin and count. Count by five: Five, ten, fifteen, twenty... maybe to one hundred or two hundred. Then the seeker went to seek those who hide. When the seeker finds someone, the two must run fast and touch the wall. At the wall the one who was found must say, '*dap mang*' or in English, I think, 'Prove my soul.'"

"Why did they say, 'Prove my soul'?"

Phuc looked up to the sky as though this childhood memory might materialize from a glimpse of some cloud formation.

"We just said that when we touched the wall. My older cousins taught me the game." Phuc looked down to the bay. "Maybe it happened because the person, or live soul, can save his friend or dead soul. The person who touched the wall can shout out a name of one person who is still hiding. That person's soul is saved and the seeker must continue to search for others who hide."

Phuc took off his coat and placed it in the basket of his motor-bike. "Do you play that game when you were a child?"

"Yes. Often."

Phuc turned his motorbike around and I climbed on and looked back at the MASS-2 area. I remembered that when I left Vietnam in 1967 I thought about returning someday. I wanted to visit my friends but it also had something to do with the beauty of the land. I do remember thinking that these hills with a view of the bay would be covered with homes when I returned. But there were no homes with a view of the bay, million-dollar homes. Maybe someday.

At the fork in the road where it went down to the old French Fort, I tapped Phuc on the shoulder, "Pull over here."

In May 1966, my first day in Vietnam, I practically jumped out of the jeep at that spot when a dynamite blast went off in the rock quarry. And early one night in 1967, on my way home from the motor pool, I pulled my jeep over to pick up Eric Barnes at that same place. Someone dropped him off at the bottom of our hill and he walked up to have dinner with me.

Phuc parked his motorbike and we walked to the edge of the road.

"This is the view in your movie," Phuc said. "It has this same view with the valley and ships in the bay."

"Yes. Some of those Super 8 movie scenes were shot from this spot." That scenic pan showed the rice paddies from above, stitched together in random shapes, each with a pastel color of sage or sorrel or olive green or tan, like pieces of a massive puzzle.

Beyond the valley, Phuc and I could see the sapphire colored Bay of Danang still framed by the two steep mountains, Hai Van Pass to the northwest and Monkey Mountain to the east.

As I stood at the edge of the road with my shirt soaked in sweat, I realized how important it was for me to be back in Vietnam. It was something I had to do— to reconnect with Miss Xuan and Mr. Hoan. And I needed to experience this pain, a pain I didn't realize I had.

* * * *

That fork in the road made an impact on my life. I didn't plan to stop there; I intended to travel the road because it was the only way up to the old MASS-2 Headquarters area. But I didn't know, until right then, that some transformation in my life had taken place. I was a different person for returning to Vietnam. That's understandable, anyone would be a different person for visiting Vietnam, but soldiers in the Vietnam War, certainly the ones involved in battles and even the ones like me who were not involved in the fighting, had to have some form of trauma.

Over 300,000 servicemen and women were wounded in that war and 58,220 were killed. I would guess that every American who served in Vietnam had a friend killed or wounded. But when we returned to the States we were ignored by our fellow Americans. A short haircut meant military because many young civilian men had long hair in the late sixties, the play *Hair* opened on Broadway in 1968, so Americans knew who we were and we were at times vilified. Outside of family, I imagine no one ever said, "Thank you for your service" to a returning Vietnam Vet.

When I returned home from Vietnam I had six months left in the Marines and spent that on the base in Twentynine Palms, California, located in the desert, one-hundred and fifty miles east of Los Angeles and insulated from the general public, so I don't remember any personal vilification. I only heard about harassment of military personnel from friends or on television.

But the veterans returning from Vietnam did not deserve to be ignored. As Mr. Hoan said, we did what we were told to do. There were no "Thank You's" or "Welcome Home" from strangers in airports or on city streets.

When I received my first "Thank you for your service" in 2010, forty-three years after I returned home, I was dumfounded by the remark. I replied something inaudible, then turned around and cried. And some of those veterans now stand at freeway entrances holding a piece of cardboard with the scribbled words, "Vietnam Vet, Anything will help."

* * * *

As I stood at that fork in the road with Phuc in 2001, I remembered Eric Barnes standing next to me in 1967 at the same spot. How we laughed at old stories and how he loved the view. Eric stood at the edge of the road and looked out to the Bay of Danang. He would fly to Hawaii the next morning for R & R to spend a week with Noreen. Phuc was right, so I sent Eric my love from there, where we stood in 1967 and laughed and enjoyed ourselves.

I continued, for a moment, to look out across the bay to the horizon. At the beauty that Eric enjoyed. The horizontal line stretched for miles separating the firmament from the South China Sea.

I finally turned and climbed onto the back of Phuc's motorbike. We drove down the road. It was steep but Phuc was a good driver and took his time.

TWENTY

Movies and Drawings, 1966

He loved to horse around with the Vietnamese in the compound, leaping on them from behind, leaning heavily on them, shoving them around and pulling their ears, sometimes punching them a little hard in the stomach, smiling a stiff small smile that was meant to tell them all that he was just being playful. The Vietnamese would smile too, until he turned to walk away.

—From *Dispatches*, Michael Herr

Movies

T HE NEXT OPPORTUNITY to film came on my way back to MASS-2 from Danang. I stopped my jeep when I saw a woman cutting branches on a hill above the road. She hacked at a large bush with a short-handled scythe but stopped hacking when I walked toward her with my Super 8 camera. There were wicker baskets filled with firewood on the ground around her and when I raised my camera she turned her back to me.

Medium shot:
Back of woman in black silk pajamas and pointed bamboo hat. Left pant leg rolled up high on her thigh. Right pant leg rolled up to her knee. Her right hand down at her side holding a scythe.

Camera moves around to her front:
Woman backs up a few steps and glares at camera.

Zoom in to close up:
Woman's wrinkled face with eggplant-purple teeth from betel nut. She says a few words to the camera and stares. No expression.

"What are you doing here?" she must have thought. "Let me go about my business without your camera in my face."

That scene bothers me every time I watch it even after sixty years. Why did I choose to park my jeep, walk up the hill with my movie camera and film that woman just trying to do her job? What if a turbaned Iraqi walked into a construction site in America and filmed one of the crew.

We Americans don't seem to realize that other cultures have habits and customs different from ours. On my 2004 trip, shortly after I arrived at Mr. Hoan's home for a visit, we sat down for tea and I asked him if the Communist government imposed any restrictions on the people of Danang.

He said, "Mr. Brian we don't talk about that type of conversation just when we sit down to have our tea." I learned later sometimes ordinary pleasantries discussed at tea could last for hours, or even days, before the serious subjects or the real business or important questions are asked and answered. I'm sure some of my comments or actions offended my hosts but they were kind enough, most of the time, not to say anything.

Drawings

After the meal of *bun bo* at the home of Miss Xuan, I wanted to learn how to make the *bun* noodle. I was fascinated with both the taste and texture. I asked Miss Xuan about the noodle and she explained that it was made by a long process of grinding and boiling rice but she wasn't sure exactly how. Miss Xuan said I should go to a house where they made and sold this noodle.

Mr. An, a teacher at Hoa My School who also took my English Language class, went with me to the house where *bun* noodle was made. "Miss Xuan cannot go with you to this place of making the noodle, *bun,*" Mr. An said.

"Is she busy?"

"She cannot go to this house," Mr. An said. And I heard no more about that.

At this house/store, Mr. An translated for the two women who made the *bun* noodle. Rice was soaked overnight and then ground into flour with a stone flour mill. One of these women pushed up and down on one end of a board that was balanced on a fulcrum like a teeter totter. The other end of the board had a weight that dipped into a large stone bowl containing the flour. She pushed up and down for several minutes while the other woman added water to the mixture until a paste formed.

Then they added an adhesive substance to the flour and poured the mixture into a flat stone base or mortar, not a small mortar that sits on a counter but a huge one, three feet in diameter, that sat on the floor. There was a large stone on top of the flat mortar that was turned by a handle. They turned the stone that sat over the flour until the flour was flat like a pancake and pliable. These flour pancakes, very thin and two feet in diameter were folded in half and half again and half again and placed in a trough of boiling water. Then these folded pieces of flour squares went through a screen with small holes. Once the flour pieces passed through the small holes the fresh bun was formed and looked like white angel hair pasta. It was a long and exhausting process.

I drew pictures of the stone flour mill, the mortar and board run by the woman's foot, and the large pot of boiling water with the screen of small holes. When Mr. An and I returned to Hoa My School, I showed Miss Xuan my drawings and she laughed at the odd shapes of the equipment. When she handed back my drawings I asked her why she laughed. She said, "It is impossible for me to understand why an American can take so much interest of how to make the noodle."

"In order for me to understand your way of preparing food, I need to find out what I can." I held up the three pages of drawings. "I want to understand your culture and take these drawings back home with me to keep as a memento, a record of my work with you and Mr. Hoan and Mr. An and the others at Hoa My School. The meal of *bun bo* you served me was delicious and I want a reminder when I get home. Something I can make and share with my family. We don't have *bun* noodles in America. And I want to be sure I have memories, records, like my films, of you and the school, and the children."

To my knowledge, when we had that conversation in 1966 there were very few Vietnamese restaurants in America. No Vietnamese communities, no shops, no markets. How ironic to find that the Vietnam War and its aftermath brought such a vibrant, energetic, and resourceful population to America.

TWENTY-ONE

Hoi An, 2001

Viet Nam's greatest hope for prosperity and success lies in its youth. More than a third of the country's population of seventy-four million is under fifteen years old and has not experienced the horrors that rocked the country during its long, painful civil war.

—From *Chasing the Tigers*, Murray Hiebert

AGAIN, I WAITED outside my hotel for Mr. Hoan to arrive in a hired van, this time for a trip to Hoi An. Our Ford van, filled with Mr. Hoan, two of his daughters, seven granddaughters, and Hanh Dung's college friend, rocked with energy. Thirteen total in the van counting the driver and me. The young women sang songs and waved their hands in the air and moved their shoulders to the music.

They taught me *The Flower Song* with the words, "*Oi ban oi*" ("Oh my friend"). We all sang loud, laughed loud, and swayed to the music. We were on holiday.

Hoi An, twenty kilometers due south of Danang, was filled with artists' studios, tea shops, restaurants, kite shops, card shops, jewelry shops, and others nestled into narrow back streets. It wouldn't be hard to find a gift to take home.

We walked into a wood sculptor's studio that stood on pilings over the River Thu Bon and smelled like a lumberyard. It's barn-like floor had paths of footprints imbedded into the four-by-twelve boards.

The sculptor pulled his two-handled blade along the gunwale of a twenty-foot sampan that ran the length of the studio and wisps of his thin gray beard waved from his chin on each pull. He crouched on the floor, layered thick with curled woodchips to eye his work, then stood for a moment to caress the boat's rim with leathered hands.

Life-size lions and happy Buddhas in the loft peered down at tables of miniature animals carved to perfection.

The sculptor set down his blade, dusted a few wood chips onto the downy floor, and greeted us with a toothless smile. "May I help you?" he said to me in perfect English.

"These animals are amazing. And your boat, how long has it taken you to carve it this smooth?"

"It takes a long time. A very long time." He pointed to the shelves and tables covered with animals carved to life-like quality. "You might like these." There were also caramel and chestnut colored boxes made of teak and smoothed to a glassy finish. One box opened up to reveal a smaller box that opened up to reveal a smaller box that opened up to reveal an even smaller box that contained a water buffalo carved in minute detail.

After I bought the water buffalo box we said goodbye to the sculptor and sat in the shade of a large *phuong* tree on the river bank. The tree, in full bloom with bright red flowers, provided a cool spot to rest. It was quiet and time seemed suspended; the river lapped along the shore as if it wanted to hang there before heading out to sea.

Hanh Quyen sat next to me and picked up some fallen *phuong* flowers to toss into the lazy current. The red petals spun around but went nowhere. "Mr. Brian," she said, "would you become my spirit father?"

She looked at the river for a moment then turned to me with her eyebrows raised.

"Yes, of course," I said. "What would that mean?"

She slapped the *phuong* petals off her hands and said, "I would be your spirit daughter and you could be my spirit father. You could help me with my English when you write. We could think of each other often."

"I would be happy to help you with your English. Yes. That will be fine." I thought, *Did spirit father mean Godfather? Maybe there were other duties besides the English lessons.* The sun filtered through the tree and made me sleepy. I could have taken a nap. But I was Hanh Quyen's spirit father and honored to be asked.

Hanh Quyen and I are still in touch and she has never asked for nor intimated about any extra ordinary favors or tasks or gifts, but I would welcome her or her sisters or cousins into our home anytime.

I did invite Hanh Quyen to visit us during the summer of 2016. She was excited to come to America and went through the process of obtaining a visa for her August vacation, however she was denied a visa since, according to the Consulate General of the United States of America, she did not "demonstrate strong enough ties to make her return to Vietnam." She had no intention of staying in America; she had a job and strong ties to her huge family, but those were the rules. It may be harder to obtain a visa now with a president who seems to disdain foreigners.

We went through the same process in the summer of 2017, this time with a letter from Senator Merkley of Oregon. Again, visa denied, "may not return to Vietnam."

We walked back to the van and took a group photo before we left Hoi An. It rained on our way out of town and I saw families gathered on porches squatted in that rest position to talk and laugh and scratch at the bugs on their ankles. One house had a vegetable garden full of cabbages with a farmer hoeing weeds. He stuck his hoe in the sod, undid his fly, urinated, and washed the mud off his hands in the stream of urine. I stared as long as I could before the farmer went out of view. That was something new to me—

not to see a man pee in his garden, I've seen that, but I'd never seen a man wash his hands in his own urine as though he were at a community fountain.

Once on the highway toward Danang I saw a young boy in a rice paddy slouched forward on the back of a water buffalo, maybe taking a nap. I watched him with my head rested against the seat until he was out of sight. The sun felt warm and the jiggle of the van put me to sleep.

Someone tugged at my arm. "Mr. Brian. Mr. Brian," Hanh Dung said. "Wake up. We are at Marble Mountain."

We parked in front of a shop where two marble lions stood, one on either side of the entrance, each lion five and a half feet tall with eyes and mouth wide open. The lions stood with their front paws on a beach ball made of marble.

Long tables were loaded with marble objects for sale. Small marble tea sets, statues of Vietnamese with conical hats, book-ends, fountains, and ashtrays like the one I bought in 1967 with the words circled around the edge, *DANANG VIETNAM 1967.*

I walked to a flight of marble stairs that led up to the large opening at the base of the Mountain. The cave-like opening was actually the entrance to a complex system of tunnels and rooms used as a hospital during the war by the Viet Cong and North Vietnamese Army. Our enemy lived, worked, and healed their wounded less than a kilometer from a US Marine helicopter base. A base mortared by the enemy on occasion.

TWENTY-TWO

Standing at Attention
in Front of the CO, 1966

Last night I dreamin' dat de sun rose up out of de west, and dat we livin' on de wrong side of de night. I dreamed dat we was dead and did not know it. —From *Far Tortuga*, Peter Matthiessen

O UR GENERATORS BEGAN to wear down with so much use that the mechanics at each of our radar control sites called for parts on a regular basis. We ordered them but it often took a month before they arrived from the States. Sergeant Stuck added another Stewart Stevenson 52300 to the yard so we could cannibalize parts as needed, but our generators often ran twenty-four hours a day and we had trouble keeping ahead of the problems.

"Lieutenant, I need to fly up north to fix a generator in Dong Ha," Sergeant Stuck said.

"Is there a backup generator?"

"The backup generator's on line now, sir. I'm going to pull the parts we need off one of these generators in the yard and catch the next flight to Dong Ha."

Sergeant Stuck pulled the parts and left within the hour but Sergeant Wix got a call from Dong Ha shortly after Sergeant Stuck left. The backup generator went down. Our radar controllers in Dong Ha could not operate and our C.O, Lieutenant Colonel Jones, wanted to see me.

The CO looked up as I stood in front of his desk. "Lieutenant Biggs," he stared at me for a long moment. "Lieutenant Biggs, we can't have those Dong Ha generators down." He got up, walked around to the front of his desk, sat on the edge, and folded his arms.

"You need to anticipate trouble, Lieutenant."

"Yes, sir."

"You should have anticipated the need for parts in Dong Ha. These generators sometimes work twenty-four hours a day. They're not designed for this work, twenty-four hours a day. That's why backup parts are essential. The backup generators need backup parts. Your mechanics need to anticipate!" His eyes narrowed causing his forehead to wrinkle up. "The pilots rely on our radar controllers, Lieutenant. If the radar controller has no radar we can't lock on to the plane. There's no mission. It's that simple."

"Yes, sir."

"Report to me the minute Dong Ha goes back on line. Dismissed."

"Yes sir." Fortunately, he didn't start yelling. That didn't seem to be his style. I thought it was more avuncular advice rather than a chewing out.

Sergeant Stuck does anticipate trouble. He could sense when a generator was about to go down. He called his mechanics and warned them about this generator or that. I had known him for just a little over six weeks but I could tell he was on top this situation.

The Dong Ha generator and the backup generator went on line later that afternoon and Lieutenant Colonel Jones was pleased but still not satisfied with my effort in the motor pool.

That night I had a nightmare about a generator. I was in the ninth grade when we lived in this house but I'm an adult in the dream:

I open the gate and step into my backyard. Out of nowhere, a huge generator with spindly legs and arms and large black-knob-eyes starts to chase me. I panic and run toward the back door of the garage but the yard is filled with two-feet of water and I have trouble running. The generator is close behind and reaches for me with long arms coming out of its side. I turn at the corner of the house but have to strain my legs to move through the water. The generator's thin legs just splash into the water as though it were a mere puddle in the dirt. It's almost on top of me.

I finally reach the garage door and grab the handle. It's locked! I'm horrified! My father is working at the tool bench so I yell at him through the window and bang on the door but he doesn't hear me. I turn around to see the generator's giant hand come crashing down on my head...

...And wake up with a scream!

TWENTY-THREE

Miss Xuan, 2001

"And remember, also," added the Princess of Sweet Rhyme, "that many places you would like to see are just off the map and many things you want to know are just out of sight or a little beyond your reach. But someday you'll reach them all, for what you learn today, for no reason at all, will help you discover all the wonderful secrets of tomorrow." —From The Phantom Tollbooth, Norton Juster

W HEN MR. HOAN first contacted me in December 2000, he wrote that he would try to find Miss Xuan's address. When he found out she lived in the village of Hac Dich, forty kilometers southeast of Ho Chi Minh City, he gave her my e-mail address, and in her first e-mail to me I learned she was happy to know I remembered her and that during the war, she "took part in the People's Liberation Army" (the Viet Cong).

She left Danang shortly after I returned to the States in May of 1967 and lived with the Viet Cong in the mountains until the end of the war in 1975. The news that she joined the Viet Cong did not bother me. Miss Xuan and I have corresponded ever since and her niece, Miss Nguyet Cam, who translated our letters, offered to take me to her aunt's home for our visit.

Miss Nguyet Cam, twenty-five years old, had short black hair that accented her round face and was tall for a Vietnamese woman, as tall as her cousin, Phuc. She lived in Ho Chi Minh

City and told me Hac Dich was an hour's drive toward the coast, so she ordered a van for the trip. Miss Xuan's sister, Miss Tam, and two young girls who lived with her as foster children also came along. Counting the driver there were six in the van.

Miss Xuan owned a cashew farm out a road that took us through agricultural land where crops of cabbage, lettuce, and kale fanned out to the horizon.

When we stopped at a tollbooth, Miss Nguyet Cam paid the first man some Vietnamese *dong*. That man gave it to a second man who put it in a box and poked a third man who slept. Without opening his eyes, the man who slept tapped the butt-end of a lodge pole that floated to vertical so we could pass.

A kilometer after the tollbooth, we passed a truck loaded with brick that had tipped over onto a hay truck parked below the road. Roads are raised in Vietnam so they won't be flooded with water during the monsoon rains. Red bricks lay all around the two vehicles in clumps or all alone clear down to some buildings several meters away. The 2½-ton truck, loaded with the remaining brick, was perched at a forty-five-degree angle onto the hay truck. Rakes and shovels and picks and hoes lay on the ground around the accident as though all the farm hands ran from their field work, dropped their tools and immediately started helping restore order. It was as if this improvised crew had done it every day.

The scene resembled the one in 1966 when Sergeant Wix drove our six-thousand-pound forklift to the Tenth Engineers chow hall to unload pallets of potatoes. However, Tenth Engineers had just oiled their raised road and once those huge forklift tires hit the oil, it slid out of control and overturned into the ditch. Sergeant Wix was okay but called the motor pool for assistance.

Sergeant Greene hopped into one of our 2 ½ ton trucks and drove over to Tenth Engineers. When Sergeant Greene's truck hit the oiled road it also slid out of control and tipped over onto the forklift.

Sergeant Greene called me and I immediately went over with

my movie camera. The oil gave off a purple glare in the midday sun. Sergeant Greene led the recovery operation and his first job was to pull the 2 ½ ton truck off the forklift. He paced back and forth then stopped for a moment to look with his muscled arms folded across his chest. He moved around for this view and that view to note the angle of his overturned truck. He bent down to calculate the placement of each winch and finally told the drivers where to back up their vehicles and park.

When the winches were hooked to Sergeant Greene's truck he yelled "go" and the 2 ½ ton six-by bounced and rocked back to an upright position. Same with the forklift. They pulled it upright and towed it onto the oiled road where Sergeant Wix could ease it back to dry dirt. Both vehicles were fine and no one was hurt. But Sergeants Wix and Greene had to endure a rash of "oil slick" jokes: "Slick driving, Wix" and "That there duce-and-a-half just got Greene broke."

In 2001, three kilometers beyond the overturned truck with bricks, Miss Nguyet Cam and her mother began talking to our driver. He slowed down and both women looked to the left at a one room structure sided with weathered wood. Miss Xuan's home.

When we walked inside I could see Miss Xuan just to our left. She seemed shorter to me, but still only as high as my shirt pockets.

She smiled, "Hello, Mr. Brian."

"*Chao co,* Xuan."

Miss Xuan wore light blue slacks and a checkered long-sleeved blouse, untucked, and had a handkerchief tied around her neck partially covering a series of red sores. Her sister, Miss Tam, pulled down the handkerchief and scolded her sister for the wound.

"It is nothing," Miss Xuan said in Vietnamese.

She looked at me, "It is a spider bite. It does not hurt."

There were purple and red scabs that circled down her neck like a relief map of the Aleutian Islands. They looked infected but I said nothing.

She shook her head and readjusted the handkerchief to cover the discolored scabs then repeated, "It does not hurt."

I also realized that her four upper front teeth were missing. I tried not to stare or seem surprised about her missing front teeth but I couldn't help thinking about the day I met Miss Xuan in May of 1966. It was my first day in Vietnam, and my four upper front teeth were missing.

Besides her missing front teeth, Miss Xuan looked alert. Her hair was still black and short with a few curls that circled down onto the right side of her forehead. At sixty-two years of age she now had indentations, slightly shadowed, under her eyes and a slight depression from just above her nostrils to the corners of her mouth.

She smiled again and I smiled back but felt that we both needed, and wanted, to show something more than a handshake. A hug would have filled that void but Miss Nguyet Cam advised me, as Hanh Quyen had done in Danang, that the Vietnamese prefer to shake hands rather than hug. However, I still felt the need for a hug, some physical connection with my friend after thirty-four years, a woman who I admired and trusted. But the handshake, for now, had to suffice.

Miss Xuan offered to show me her orchard of cashew trees. I had never seen a cashew tree and as soon as we walked out Miss Xuan's back door, Ba, one of the young girls, ran to a tree and climbed onto the lower branch. The branches of a cashew tree are eight to ten inches in diameter and extend straight out from the trunk parallel to the ground a good distance before turning upward to become gnarled and intertwined.

The large bottom branches, only a few feet off the ground, are perfect for a child's horse. The bark peels off so the branch is smooth like a madrone tree. Her friend climbed onto the branch behind her and they both whooped and hollered it up in their make-believe cowgirl world.

The cashew tree stood thirty-five meters tall, and Miss Xuan's orchard consisted of a row of trees on each side of a path that ran about forty meters down to the bottom of her property.

Miss Xuan said, "These are old trees and have been on my farm for many years." She walked off the path where there were no trees and pulled back some tall grass and reached down to the soil. Miss Nguyet Cam and I leaned over to look at a slender two-foot unbranched start of a cashew tree. Miss Xuan folded her hand around the thin limb and leaned it back just a touch. "I must watch over the young tree until it is much bigger growing."

"When will they bear fruit? When will they have cashews on the tree that you can sell and eat?"

"In three years these nine young trees will have the cashew nut to pick."

We went back into the two-room house where it felt like a furnace had run on full strength while we were gone. Miss Xuan invited me to sit down for tea at a marble topped table. "Do you like tea, Mr. Brian?" she said as she sat down.

"Yes. I enjoy tea. You gave me a can of tea when I left Danang in 1967. Do you remember?"

"Yes," she said.

A few months after I returned home from Vietnam, my daughter Kaye showed me the red and yellow can of tea that Miss Xuan gave me. It had Vietnamese writing with a woman washing clothes in a lake. Kaye took apart the two pieces that formed the lid and showed me a logo of Kraft Mayonnaise written in blue letters in a white circle on one of the pieces. We emptied the remaining tea leaves from the can and saw a blue Miracle Whip logo at the bottom.

The Vietnamese scavenged metal and wood from the American buildings that were left in 1975 and apparently took the discarded mayonnaise tins from our military chow halls and crafted them into cans for tea leaves like the one that today sits on a shelf in my office.

Miss Xuan opened a tin on the table and spooned a large portion of dried tea leaves into two glasses then picked up a kettle by its wicker handle and filled each glass with steaming water. The gnarled specks, like blackened blades of dried grass, tumbled in the whirlpool and rotated with the flow until they relaxed and opened into leaves the color of seaweed that waved in the water like a flounder, before settling on the bottom.

She pushed one of the glasses across the table to me. "Your tea." She had calloused fingers. Hands that worked the soil. She held the cup of tea to her nose to smell its aroma as the steam floated past her face. "Tea is called *che* in Vietnam. This is *che hoa nhai*. Jasmine tea."

"Very flavorful," I said. Then I reached into my backpack, "I brought a present for you, Miss Xuan."

"Oh." Miss Xuan's eyes opened wide.

"You mentioned it took you a long time to write letters to me because you didn't have a dictionary. This is an English/Vietnamese Dictionary. Both languages are in this book."

She opened the book and turned to a page, then nodded her head but said nothing.

Why was Miss Xuan silent, I wondered. *She could use this dictionary to help her write letters in English. Maybe she was silent because she didn't have a gift for me. Maybe I shouldn't have brought a gift.* But my family culture would not allow me to visit without bringing something.

My tea smelled like a mixture of honey and loam of the forest. I held up my glass to Miss Xuan and said, "*Chuc suc khoe.*"

She touched her glass to mine, "*Chuc suc khoe.*

A cool breeze with a strong citrus smell from the lime trees out front blew in through the open window and helped cool the room. Miss Xuan turned on a fan behind me and the breeze felt good on my sweat-soaked shirt.

"I have another gift for you Miss Xuan, but it's not really a gift." I took out a folder with a piece of paper in it. "This is your last English lesson in my class at Hoa My School. It was May 1967, you were not in class on my last day and I've kept this for you." I handed Miss Xuan her one-page paper on King Quang Trung and how he won a war with China in 1789. "You received a B+, very good work."

Miss Xuan looked at the paper in her hands and read a few sentences. "You saved my paper a long time. Thank you."

"Yes, thirty-four years."

She emptied the clump of tea leaves from my glass and added a spoonful of dry leaves then poured in more boiling water. Miss Xuan repeated the process for her glass and walked to a mahogany dresser against the back wall. The dresser had glass doors with a picture of a smiling Buddhist monk in a yellow frock taped onto one of the doors. A bunch of the miniature bananas sat in a bowl on top of the dresser as an offering to her ancestors. There were also plastic roses in one vase and fresh yellow-pedaled Asiatic lilies in another. A two-inch marble Buddha sat in the center, fat and green.

Next to the dresser, a darkened television screen mirrored movement in the room and usurped the shrine's stature. She opened the glass door with the smiling Buddhist monk and took a book from the shelf, looked at its cover for a moment, then found one more book and brought them to our table. The books, not large, overwhelmed her hands. "I want to give you these books for your study of my country."

Miss Xuan set the books down in front of me and I picked up *Tuc Ngu, Anh-Viet* or *English Proverbs and Their Vietnamese Equivalent.* There was a strong smell of mildew when I opened the book to a random page. My thumb landed on proverb #747, "*Duc toc bat dat,*" I said, and read the English translation: "Slow and steady wins the race."

"Yes," Miss Xuan said.

"It's 'The Tortoise and the Hare,'" I said.

Miss Xuan looked at my bald head, "Where is your hair?"

"No. The story. The phrase is from a fable called, 'The Tortoise and the Hare.' A hare is a rabbit."

"Hair is on the rabbit?"

"The word 'hare' means 'rabbit.'"

"What is *means*?"

"Means is 'is the same as.' 'Hare' is another name for the word 'rabbit.' Rabbit, hare. The same meaning."

"You like this book?"

"Yes. Thank you, *Cam on*. This is a wonderful gift."

Miss Xuan smiled and covered her mouth. "I am happy to give them to you. She took a drink of her tea, "My teeth were lost because I lived in the mountains a long time. I did not eat healthy at that time and later," she shook her head. "I lost my teeth."

"When were you in the mountains?" I asked.

"I had to leave the city of Danang in April 1967. I asked Mr. Hoan to drive me to Truong Son Mountain where I stayed with soldiers until April 1975. I did not eat healthy food in the Truong Son Mountains."

"What did you do during those seven years?"

"I was a teacher to the young soldiers. I taught reading and writing and the history of our country." She looked at me a few moments. "It was very difficult to live in the mountains. I jumped from a bridge one day when I must escape."

"Escape from the soldiers?" I asked.

"No. American planes."

"This was in 1967?"

"Yes. My love died in 1972. He was in the army of revolution. When I received the news of his sacrifice, I was sad only three days. Then the task of revolution attracted me to follow the tide of war so I forgot everything except for our nation. War always has grief and loss. I hate war and love peace."

Miss Xuan looked at me and cocked her head slightly to the right. Moisture formed in her eyes. She must have loved this man, this communist soldier, very much. *I'm curious why she was sad for only three days. She must still miss this man but I'm not sure how to ask her about this loss and her relationship with him. Was he with her when she jumped off the bridge to escape the gun fire from American planes? Maybe one day I can ask these questions, if the answers are important. But not now.*

Miss Xuan walked to the mahogany dresser again and brought a photo album to our table. There was a cracking noise when she turned the pages. She pointed to two photos, "This is my father and mother." A sepia toned photo of a man and a woman in their late twenties, each photo from the chest up. She, dressed in a pale pink *ao di*, high forehead, her black hair pulled back tight to her head like a ballerina and her lips just starting to form a smile. He, dressed in a dark suit, white shirt, and black tie with white dots and smiling. Dressed exactly like, and even looked a bit like, the yearbook picture of my ninth-grade math teacher.

"Is that their photo on the wall?"

She looked at her wall above us. "Yes."

"Is your family still in that house?"

"No. My family moved from that house."

"Still in Danang?"

"Most of my family. A sister and my brother, Phap, the ones you met in 1966, live in Danang. My eldest sister died from cancer in 1978."

"I'm sorry."

"In 1968 my father was suspected of being Viet Cong by the Saigon government. He was sent to an island prison. Tortured. He became ill and did not recover. Even after he left prison in 1975."

She looked at her father's picture on the page. "His mind was not good when he left prison and he died in 1980. My mother died soon after."

"I'm sorry," I said again. Then remembered what Phuc told me about not sending sad thoughts to the deceased. Her father and mother were a vague memory for me. Neither spoke English and the father mainly stared at me when I had dinner at Miss Xuan's home in 1966. He stared possibly because he was curious. He knew I was a US Marine fighting to save Vietnam from Communism. And he knew, as I would find out in 2004, that his oldest daughter, Nga, was an officer in the North Vietnamese Army. And Phap, Phuc's father, worked for the American military during the war as an interpreter.

Miss Xuan looked again at the picture of her father on the wall and nodded to acknowledge him.

"Maybe I will move back there one day. To Danang. To the house of my brother. But I must sell this farm before."

"It would be nice to be with your family," I said.

"I am the only child in my family who is single." She looked at me and smiled. "You are very lucky to have an ideal helpmate." She paused and stared at her father's photo in the album then pressed her fingers across the plastic to flatten out the wrinkles.

Miss Xuan's father must have sympathized or maybe even associated with the Viet Cong. She said he was released in April 1975 which coincides with the North Vietnamese Army's march into Saigon to take over the country.

My teaching career started in 1969 while Miss Xuan taught communist soldiers in the mountains of Vietnam and an American plane dropped bombs or fired their guns and nearly killed her. Maybe planes that locked onto radar from the MASS-2 TPQ-10 operated by my generators.

I wondered if I was in danger when I worked at Hoa My School. Miss Xuan thought she would be arrested if she stayed in the village and, according to Mr. Hoan, she thought I was the one who gave the photograph of her to the Saigon government, maybe a photograph showing her with the Viet Cong. And she asked Mr. Hoan to drive her to a communist base in the mountains.

I had many questions about all this but felt it was not the time to ask, nor was this my last trip to Vietnam. I knew at this moment there would be other trips and other conversations with Miss Xuan. Slow and steady wins the race.

TWENTY-FOUR

My Typewriter, 1966

Now is the time for all good men to come to the aid of their country.
—Phrase first proposed as a typing drill by instructor Charles E. Weller

E VERY DAY WHEN I returned to the MASS-2 area from my motor pool I passed an American building where several Vietnamese worked. I never went in but on certain days of the week there were four, fifty-five-gallon drums outside this building. Vietnamese from the local village lined up with containers to receive some of the liquid that steamed in the large drums. An elderly woman in black silk pajamas and flip-flops made out of old American tires ladled the thick substance into those containers. A man and young boy often stood in line to receive their portions. The man held the boy's hand and it reminded me of the times my father and I stood in line to board the ferry when he took me to his work on the Mare Island Naval Shipyard in Vallejo, California.

This man, slight of build, wore a conical hat and loose brown pajama-like pants, a brown shirt, and those same flip-flops. His son dressed almost the same. They stood in line during monsoon tropical rain and they stood in line during 110 degree heat.

* * * *

In late August 1966, my father shipped me the portable Royal typewriter I used in college. I opened the box, pulled out the typewriter case, pushed in the two snaps under the handle, and lifted the hinged cover to reveal my old writing companion. No more hand-written letters. The ribbon was still in place: two-colored, blue on the bottom, red on top.

I stuck in a piece of E-Z Erase typing paper and typed: *Now is the time for all good men to come to the aid of their country.*

My desk needed an addition to hold the typewriter, so I built an extension and also another bookshelf to hold typewriter paper and the books my father sent including the four volumes of Churchill's *A History of the English Speaking Peoples.* A wash basin sat on my dresser and a five-gallon can of fresh water sat on the floor. I could wash my face in the morning without walking outside to the water-buffalo. The two-hole shitter was fifteen meters away and our new CO, Lt. Colonel Hunter, put out an order for every hooch to have a foxhole dug immediately outside one of the two doors.

The foxhole was my project. I dug it deep, six-feet, then packed the rim with sandbags and put in a compartment at the bottom that held an ammo can with emergency first aid supplies and water.

* * * *

Once I had my typewriter, I took a Creative Writing Correspondence Course from UC Berkeley: English X3, taught by Gwendolen Perry Cooke. My syllabus arrived in October and my first assignment was to analyze three essays in the syllabus and write an "original composition of some experience remembered over a period of years." The reading that accompanied our first assignment was *Youth* by Joseph Conrad.

Ms. Cooke's comments on that first assignment written in the fall of 1966 were as follows:

This paper is a promising beginning despite the noticeable weakness in spelling which I hope you will improve by constant reference to your dictionary.

This personal note accompanied her comments:

> *Dear Lieutenant Biggs,*
> *Welcome to English X 3. I look forward to papers which will follow this. What does your address stand for? I hope you are neither in Vietnam nor slated for it. Very best wishes,*
> *—Gwendolen P. Cooke.*

My second assignment:

Read and analyze some paragraphs of "description" in the syllabus (by Charles Dickens and Thomas Hardy) then write a "brief artistic description" of approximately one-hundred-and-fifty words.

My description:

Four Garbage Cans
Four garbage cans sat at the side of the road. They were always in the same place and the same Vietnamese were always gathered around. These were not ordinary garbage cans but what seemed to be large kettles of soup. And yet it couldn't have been soup, or anything edible for that matter, because of the offensive odor. The odor didn't bother the Vietnamese. Particles of filth floated carelessly at the top while an older, expressionless woman poured shares into tins or bowls. When the thick substance splashed out indiscriminately no one recoiled in horror. Rather, a tireless and deter-

mined people accomplished one of many daily chores—puzzling to us but a vital necessity to them.

Ms. Cooke's comment: "A gratifyingly successful paper."

1966-1967

MASS-2 Supply Building in background, generator shed below that, and our shower below that.

Our dispatcher, Sergeant Wix (*right*). and me in the motor pool.

Miss Xuan

Mr. Hoan

Lieutenant George K. Myrus *(right)* and me at the door of my hooch.

Lieutenant Scott Bannister *(right)* and me outside my hooch.

Lieutenant Eric Barnes receiving the Silver Star for bravery during action on September 24, 1966.

The Barnstormers performing at Tufts University. *From left*: Paul "Eggbeater" Young, William "Billy Nye, Neil Cowles on drums, Eric Barnes out front, and Dave Schor.

The two school rooms I had built in 1967. Mr. Chau gave me this photo taken in 1993 at a reunion of students who attended Hoa My Elementary School.

Lieutenant George K. Myrus *(right)* congratulating me for my first child, Charles Colin Biggs, born on November 19, 1966.

Sergeant Wix's forklift on its side with Sergeant Greene's 6 X 6 truck on top of it because of those oiled roads. That's me sitting on the tire.

TWENTY-FIVE

Avalokitesvara, 2001

Avalokitesvara,
One who Listens to the Supplications of those in Difficulty
My joy is like spring, so warm
it makes flowers bloom in all walks of life.
My pain is like a river of tears, so full
it fills up the four oceans.

Please call me by my true names,
so I can hear all my cries and my laughs at once,
so I can see that my joy and pain are one.

Please call me by my true names,
so I can wake up,
and so the door of my heart can be left open,
the door of compassion.

—From *Call Me by My True Names*, Thich Nhat Hanh

O N OUR WAY to the coastal town of Vung Tau we stopped at Miss Xuan's Buddhist pagoda so I could meet the monk, Thuong Toa Thich Quang Hanh. In English, *Thuong Toa* means "Superior Monk."

A teenage Buddhist novice with a shaved head and eyes opened wide to focus on me as if he had never seen an American before, invited us into a sanctuary just large enough for two wooden benches on each side of a picnic table. A cabinet sat against the back wall and the air, cold in this concrete structure, smelled of incense. A large bell, like the Liberty Bell, but without the "bell-curve" at the bottom, hung straight down from a metal frame that sat next to the cabinet. A mallet hung to the side.

The novice brought in hot tea and Miss Xuan poured as we sat and shivered. The cup with no handle warmed my hands. Her monk walked in the room dressed in a yellow frock with a matching yellow towel around his neck. It was his picture on the glass door of Miss Xuan's mahogany dresser. After he greeted us he told a story that sounded as though he were singing the words. His eyes focused on me to be sure I understood his Vietnamese. A stubbled trace of black hair curved around the sides of his shaved head and there were no wrinkles on the face of Thuong Toa Thich Quang Hanh.

He included me in his conversation as though I spoke and understood his language and gestured with hands that appeared from the large openings on his sleeves; clear and articulate gestures one would use when signing to the deaf. He laughed often while Miss Xuan and her niece, Nguyet Cam, both Buddhists, asked many questions. He removed the yellow towel from around his neck and neatly folded it when he spoke of a letter he had mailed to Miss Xuan. His eyebrows moved in sync with the words he sang to help me understand what he was saying.

Miss Nguyet Cam interjected some translations of his words but he spoke so fluently, without pause, the translation only hindered the conversation. I knew certain Vietnamese words and phrases and strained to recognize them, but it was not the occasional word or phrase I recognized—it was the manner in which he sang those phrases that allowed me to follow his story. His eyes, hands, forehead, eyebrows, and shoulders showed me what the words could not.

He told us of the many reasons to burn incense: for continuous fragrance in a room, to worship, and to lift the spirit of teachers and students when they read.

After our tea, he took us to an arbor in his garden that smelled of lavender. The sun filtered through the arbor and for a long time no one spoke, we just enjoyed the scents, the quiet, and the purple and white variegated flowers attached to rope-like strands that draped down from the arbor. Miss Xuan whispered, "This flower is called *trang dai*."

In the gift shop, Miss Xuan placed a six-inch statuette in my hands with great care, like giving me charge over one of her young cashew starts. "Mr. Brian, this is for you," she said.

"*Cam on.* Thank you."

"She is Avalokitesvara or Quan Am, a Bodhisattva. She watches over you and listens to your prayers. And her right hand holds a vessel downward so the liquid, the water, will cleanse you of your sins and bad thoughts."

"*Cam on,*" I said again.

Today Quan Am sits in my office, high on a shelf, and looks over me as I compose these words.

TWENTY-SIX

The Soccer Team, 1966

Soccer isn't the same as Bach or Buddhism. But it is often more deeply felt than religion, and just as much a part of the community's fabric, a repository of traditions.

—From *How Soccer Explains the World: An Unlikely Theory of Globalization,* Franklin Foer

S TUDENTS KICKED A soccer ball around every afternoon at Hoa My School and most of them had excellent skills. One weekend a group of Marines next door to our motor pool played a soccer game and I recognized one of the men. When they stopped for a break I went up to him. "You're in MASS-2 aren't you?"

"Yes, sir."

He was tall, had some speed, and knew how to maneuver the ball. "You been playing soccer long?"

"I played as a kid. Haven't played much since I've been in the Marines."

"I would like to start a soccer program at this school where I teach English. You interested in coaching soccer?"

"Yes, sir. I can do that." A big smile formed on his face.

He and the students cleared rocks from the field in back of the school and erected two goal posts. The players were from Mr.

Hoan's sixth grade class and Mr. An's fifth grade class. The coach held practice twice a week for the twenty-two boys. They were experienced players with good skills, many with better skills than the coach. They divided into two teams for games.

My father-in-law, a builder in Seattle, donated T shirts for the team and my wife, Colleen, added letters and a number to two different sets of shirts. She and our daughter, Kaye, finished up the work and sent them to Vietnam. One set had black striped lines on the sleeves and red numbers. The other set had no stripes on the sleeves and yellow numbers. Both sets of shirts had the name of the school in red letters below the number: "HOA MY."

A month after the players started practices with their coach, the T-shirts arrived from the States. I took the box of shirts to the school during a practice and Mr. Hoan and I walked out to the field. For one drill the barefoot players kicked goals against a goalie who stood between two tall posts set deep in the ground. Since they didn't have a net behind the posts, the ball at times passed the goalie and rolled out into the weeds. A barefoot boy ran to retrieve the ball over rocks and stickers but never winced or jerked a foot up in pain due to the callused feet from years of going barefoot.

During a break in the action I asked the coach to call the team over. The players gathered around and I opened the box of T-shirts. Mr. Hoan and I each held up a shirt. "Tell them," I said to Mr. Hoan, "that my wife and daughter sewed these numbers and letters on the shirts."

When the boys received their shirts they held them up and shouted out their numbers to each other. One boy ran over to me and smiled and carefully held his shirt up for me to see. The shirt was way too big for the boy but he talked a blue streak to Mr. Hoan.

"He wants to thank Mrs. Brian for his shirt," Mr. Hoan said. "His lucky number is number 5."

They took off their own shirts and put the new ones on. A few exchanged shirts, yellow numbers for red ones because they wanted to be on the same team as a friend.

Mr. Hoan asked me to take a photo of the team, and every time I look at that photo of twenty-two boys with Mr. Hoan on one end and the coach on the other, I realize Hoa My School was a better place because of my work there. It wasn't a drastic transformation but for those boys, I remember a spark of energy and an intensity of physical effort when they played soccer. I was proud of my work then and I'm still proud of what I accomplished at Hoa My School from May 1966 to May 1967.

TWENTY-SEVEN

The Crabs of Vung Tau, 2001

maggie and milly and molly and may
went down to the beach (to play one day)

and maggie discovered a shell that sang
so sweetly she couldn't remember her troubles, and

milly befriended a stranded star
whose rays five languid fingers were;

and molly was chased by a horrible thing
which raced sideways while blowing bubbles: and

may came home with a smooth round stone
as small as a world and as large as alone.

For whatever we lose (like a you or a me)
it's always ourselves we find in the sea

—"maggie and milly and molly and may," E. E. Cummings

AFTER WE LEFT Miss Xuan's pagoda we continued toward Vung Tau on Highway 51 and the traffic immediately slowed as we merged into one lane for a tollbooth. Across the highway three women swept an entrance that led back to Ho Chi Minh City. Dirt and rocks from countless dump trucks covered the highway and all its entrances and exits.

The three women who stood a few meters apart wore conical hats, black pajama pants, tan jackets, and masks that covered their noses and mouths. They bent low to the ground and brushed the pavement with brooms that had a three-foot band of straw attached to the bottom. Their long-handled besoms swept in a semi-circular motion from the highway side of the entrance to the field side in a path of carefully choreographed motions and when they finished a section they raised their long broom plumes one after another, like dancers in a Las Vegas revue, and stepped forward in unison.

When a truck drove onto the entrance the three hoisted their brooms into the air like flagpoles and walked to the side of the road. Dust swirled around their masked faces while more dirt and rocks dropped to the pavement. But undeterred, they walked back out to their places and without rancor or animosity began where they left off, 5 – 6 – 7 – 8 and push.

At the tollbooth, our driver rolled down his window and handed some Vietnamese *dong* to a man outside a shack. That man gave our driver a ticket then handed the money to another man who handed it to another man who dropped it in a wooden box. We drove to the barricade a few meters away and our driver handed the ticket to the ticket-taker who gave it to another toll-booth employee who put it in another wooden box. Yet another tollbooth employee raised the wooden pole for us to pass. All this on the major highway from Ho Chi Minh City to the coast.

This may seem awkward to someone from America but what happened on the roads of Vietnam gave me a course in the Viet-namese psyche of patience and perseverance. That's how they won their American War. They would have carried it on as long as it took to wear us down—both the Americans in Vietnam and the Americans at home. It took almost a hundred years to defeat the French and we were in Vietnam "officially" less than ten years before we decided to leave.

We drove to the main bathing beach in Vung Tau called Bai Sau or "Back Beach." This beach faced the Eastern Sea, known as the South China Sea to countries other than Vietnam, where a hundred-foot statue of Jesus, built by U.S. soldiers in the early seventies, loomed over the bay from its perch atop Nghinh Phong Cape.

The sun reflected off Vung Tau's bathing beach of white sand with a mirror-like glare as Miss Xuan and I watched Miss Nguyet Cam and the two young girls take off their sandals and dash into the water. They screamed when ruffled waves, no higher than their ankles, chased them back up the beach where they giggled and twirled around with outstretched arms.

Then, as if on command, they froze in midstride and stared at the wet sand. Hundreds of crabs, no more than a half-inch across, appeared out of nowhere and scurried sideways indiscriminately all around us. The crabs were shaped, in all respects, like a Dungeness crab, with miniature crab legs and miniature claws but when Miss Nguyet Cam stomped her foot all the crabs, literally hundreds of them, disappeared in an instant. I stared in disbelief at the flat and empty granules of sand.

In a moment, the crabs popped up and covered the sand again with a jiggle and jerk dance movement as though nothing happened until I too, stomped my foot. Once again, the crabs disappeared.

There was no time between seeing hundreds, maybe thousands, of crabs crawling on the beach, and then seeing nothing but wet sand. There were no dimples, no remnant of an escape hole, no trace of life. Then, presto, the crabs covered the sand again and marched around the beach in a jiggling mass.

Suddenly, a much larger crab, three inches across, appeared out of nowhere and scampered among the throng of tiny crabs. The two girls screeched in delight and began chasing the larger crustacean around the beach. But the crab turned onto its side and whirled around the sand like an orange Frisbee in a windstorm.

The girls ran with the crabs and screamed while Miss Xuan and I bent at the waist to laugh. Miss Nguyet Cam and her mother laughed. They laughed out loud and had to hold onto each other to keep from falling down.

"*Con cong, con cong*! (small crab!)" yelled Miss Xuan.

A tornado of crab and child made us dizzy until all the crabs marched down the beach and out of sight.

* * * *

After dinner in Vung Tau, we drove to Bai Truoc, or Front Beach, and for the first time on my 2001 trip the evening sky was clear. When we walked on a sidewalk two meters above the rocky beach we stopped to look at the stars above the bay. I tried to find the Big Dipper.

"What do you look for?" said Miss Xuan.

"I want to show you the Big Dipper. It's a constellation of stars in the sky. It points to the North Star. When you find the Big Dipper, you can always find north. *Bac*."

Miss Xuan looked up. "What is a 'big dipper?'"

"It's a constellation. A group of stars. Seven, I think. They make a handle or form a handle that's curved. And a pot, a dipper, like you use for water." A young couple stopped and looked up to the sky. Miss Nguyet Cam explained that we were looking for the Big Dipper. They looked at me and smiled. Other people stopped and looked up.

Miss Nguyet Cam said, "This person tells me that what you look for is not in the southern sky." Miss Nguyet Cam pointed straight up to where I was looking. "He says that that star group is to the north. You cannot see it from this location. And you cannot see it during the months that follow October. Only summer and fall. So, you can see it at this season, but you must look to the north. That is where that star group lives. You are looking to the south."

"Ah, thank you. *Cam on*," I said to the gentleman. "The Big Dipper is in the northern sky. *Bac*."

The elderly gentleman nodded and smiled, "You are an American."

"Yes, American."

TWENTY-EIGHT

The Birth and My Hernia, 1966

There was only one catch and that was Catch-22, which specified that a concern for one's own safety in the face of dangers that were real and immediate was the process of a rational mind. Orr was crazy and could be grounded. All he had to do was ask; and as soon as he did, he would no longer be crazy and would have to fly more missions.

— From *Catch-22*, Joseph Heller

The Birth

C OLLEEN AND I were expecting a child on 10 November and I wanted to be sure I heard the news as soon as possible. It took two weeks for letters to arrive from the west coast so the best plan was to alert the Red Cross in Danang that an important message was coming from Seattle, Washington. Colleen's plan was to tell her parents to notify the Red Cross immediately after the baby was born.

The Military Affiliate Radio System, or MARS short wave radio, just down the hill from MASS-2, provided a way to speak to loved ones back in the States. We used head phones and sat at a table covered in green felt like a poker table. The MARS operator spoke over a microphone from a room in the dark area so I never saw him. Colleen knew the procedure well after many calls but sometimes

the static made it hard to hear. Other times it sounded like Colleen
sat across the table from me but the "over" part was awkward:

"Hello honey, how are you? *Over.*"

"I'm fine. I miss you. *Over.*"

"I miss you too. How is Kaye? *Over.*"

"She is fine. She's doing well in first grade. *Over.*"

As there were no cell phones in 1966, the MARS phone, that
opened at 1800 hours with a line forming immediately, was the
only option for personal contact with loved ones. It often rained
and there wasn't enough room in the sheltered area so we were
soaked by the time we made our call. I planned to use the MARS
phone on 12 November if I hadn't heard anything and again,
when I called, I learned she was still waiting.

I waited all the next week for a call from the Red Cross and
nothing. Late on Saturday night, 19 November, since I had not
heard from the Red Cross, I stood in the rain to call on the MARS
phone again. It was early morning in Seattle and I had a hunch
Colleen wouldn't be at home so I called my wife's parents and
my mother-in-law answered the phone.

She heard me and screamed, "It's Brian! He's on the phone!"

There's was a long pause.

"Oh, *over,*" she said.

"How's everything? *Over.*"

"You're a papa. *Over.*"

"The baby was born? *Over!*"

"Yes! *Over.*"

"What did we have? Over." There was a lot of static and my
mother-in-law started to fade out but she said enough for me to
realize I was now the father of a baby boy.

I took off the head phones, set them on the table, and heard,
"Congratulations, sir," from the voice in the dark.

"Thank you. Wow. A boy. I have a son. Born today. This morning. What's today?"

"Saturday, 19 November, sir. Twenty-three forty-five. Almost midnight."

"Wow. Thank you." I yelled my news to the Marines waiting in line and sprinted back to my hooch.

"I'm a father. A boy," I yelled but only heard groans from my sleeping bunk mates.

A letter from Colleen arrived a week-and-a-half later and I learned my wife's parents had just arrived home from the hospital when I called that night. Charles Colin Biggs entered this world at 1:09 a.m. on Saturday, 19 November 1966. I talked to my wife's mother eight hours after my son was born—great timing. Charlie weighed in at nine pounds, six ounces and measured twenty-one inches long. My mother-in-law had already called the Red Cross by the time I reached her on the short-wave radio but I didn't hear from them for a week. The following is Colleen's first letter after Charlie was born:

> *He's beautiful! Honey, you'd be so proud of us both— we had to work at it but he's here, healthy and wonderful. Honey, when they pulled him out and Dr. Carlson said, 'It's a boy,' I just poured tears. I was so happy and just cried and cried. Dr. Carlson said, 'That's fine, you cry all you want now.' Needless to say, I really wanted you there right then!*
> *All my love, Colleen*

My Hernia

After the birth of my son, Charlie, I felt proud and invincible. I walked around our motor pool with an air of machismo and helped change tires then stacked the old tires in back of the shop. We needed extra help anyway. Never enough mechanics.

However, a lump appeared on the left side of my groin that began to bother me. I decided to drive down to the field hospital where I took Mr. Hoan's daughter, Hien, and the doctor said I had a hernia.

A hernia! That's something my grandfather used to get. My dad had one and my older brother had two, one on each side. *How could this happen to me? I'm young and in great shape.*

The doctor gave me a note and told me to go to the Naval Hospital near Marble Mountain to schedule surgery and on Friday 2 December 1966 at 0900 I had a hernia operation. I could not get out of bed until late that evening and then just to take a leak.

The next day I couldn't straighten up. When I walked I was hunched over at the waist and shuffled my feet across the floor. The Red Cross nurse who visited our ward gave me Joseph Heller's *Catch-22* to read. The book kept me interested all day and well into the night. The ironic similarity with my situation was humorous: In a war zone hospital but in for a hernia operation.

Senator Henry "Scoop" Jackson, from Washington State, visited the hospital while I was there and asked to see all the men and women from his state. I was still stooped over but mostly recovered when the Senator came by. He had an entourage of high ranking Marine officers, someone from the press, and a nervous man in dark civilian clothes that stood in back of the group and swiveled his head back and forth like a metronome. I stepped out of my bed to greet the senator.

Senator Jackson is a short man with a big smile and high forehead. He looked me right in the eyes and grasped my hand real hard, "How are you feeling, Lieutenant?"

"Fine, sir," I said.

"What outfit are you with?"

"MASS-2, sir. I run the motor pool there."

"Motor transport, eh? Good work."

A Marine bird colonel asked, "What put you in the hospital, Lieutenant?"

"I have a hernia, sir."

He frowned and stepped back as if I were contagious. Some of the men took Senator Jackson by the arm and said they should move on.

"Well, Lieutenant," the Senator said, "you take care."

We shook hands again and he was gone. I didn't get to tell him I also graduated from the University of Washington, played football there, and that my mother-in-law thought he was the greatest thing that ever happened to the state of Washington. One of the bird colonels glared at me as though I were a disgrace to the uniform, which at the time happened to be a flimsy hospital no-back gown.

A few weeks later Colleen received a letter from Senator Jackson. She was happy to have been praised for "her bravery," but a little startled when she read: "When I visited your son in Vietnam he was in good spirits and looked well."

Also, after my return from the hospital, I returned to Hoa My School and asked Mr. Hoan about his daughter, Hein and he told me the specialist in Saigon was not able to correct her hearing.

TWENTY-NINE

Back to Miss Xuan's Farm, 2001

There's no place like home. —Dorothy, in *The Wizard of Oz*

AS OUR VAN neared Miss Xuan's farm, she looked out the window and began to shake. She put her hands on her face. Her fingers rubbed her cheeks. She turned to look out the other side of the van. She rocked back and forth on her seat and smiled. She had not been that far away from her farm in years.

She screamed and opened her eyes wide when we stopped at the tollbooth. She spoke in Vietnamese to Nguyet Cam and handed her some Vietnamese *dong*. She smiled and spoke to the workers as we drove through. She looked out the window like a small child on the Disneyland train and studied every farmhouse and the brick spires that surrounded them used for growing green beans. These spires were as tall as the house itself and looked like green ice cream cones turned upside down and smashed into the ground.

Nguyen Thi Thanh Xuan did not hold back her exuberance at returning home. Dorothy in *The Wizard of Oz* says, "There's no place like home." In Vietnam there is a proverb, "*Ta ve ta tam ao ta, du trong du duc ao nha van hon.*" Literally, "Let's go home to swim in our own pond. Clear or muddy, our pond is always better."

We finally reached Miss Xuan's home and the two of us sat down at our marble topped table in the corner for a last visit.

"Are you happy to be home?"

"Yes," she said.

"You like living and working on your farm?"

"It is a hard life. Very difficult. When the cashew season comes it is very hard work. In March and April." She looked back at me and smiled. "But I like it. I enjoy the peace of my farm."

"It is peaceful here."

Miss Xuan put her hand on my arm and said, "My sister wants me move to Than Pho Ho Chi Minh and live with she and Nguyet Cam."

"Would you consider moving in with them?"

She shook her head "no" and spoke in a high voice, "I don't want that. My farm is good."

"I will come back to visit you," I said. "Here or Ho Chi Minh City. Or Danang. I enjoyed my visit with you and your family. I hope your cashew harvest is good."

"Thank you. I enjoyed your visit to my house, Mr. Brian, and my pagoda, and Vung Tau."

I still had other questions but my struggle with the language prevented me from saying more. I could have called Miss Nguyet Cam in to help with the translation. I wanted to know more about Miss Xuan and her life after she lost the man she loved. I wanted to know more about the time she spent in the mountains to live with the Viet Cong. But I didn't want to pry. She was happy at her home. Back in her routine.

The van pulled up in front of the house and Miss Xuan walked me out to the road. I wanted to remember Miss Xuan's voice so I asked her to please say something into my tape recorder.

"In Vietnamese?"

"*Da, Tieng Viet.*"

Miss Xuan's translated farewell: "Mr. Brian, you were an enthusiastic and devoted teacher at Hoa My School. Thank you for your enthusiasm. We will continue to exchange letters to each other to understand more. I hope that our friendship is endless. I wish that you have a good trip back to America. Please give my love to your family. I hope they are happy and healthy."

THIRTY

Christmas, Bob Hope, and The VC Attack, 1966-1967

Thanks for the memories. —Bob Hope

Christmas

FOR CHRISTMAS DAY, Sunday, 25 December 1966, Mr. Hoan invited several MASS-2 Marines to a luncheon at Hoa My School. Our CO, XO (Executive Officer), and everyone at MASS-2 who worked at Hoa My School received an invitation to the Christmas party. Lieutenant Colonel Hunter couldn't make it but Major David Karcher, the no-nonsense XO came. Frank Markowski and Rich Vandiver, the two other officers who taught English classes with me, came. Ray King, the S-1, and Sergeant Gary Palmer from the motor pool also came.

We drove down to the school at noon on Christmas Day and parked the two jeeps. Children played in the school yard even though it was a Sunday. Mr. Hoan, Miss Xuan, and several other teachers greeted us in the yard.

"Happy Christmas," Mr. Hoan said. He was dressed in a white short sleeved shirt and dark tie.

Miss Xuan was dressed in her blue *ao dai*. She smiled and greeted everyone.

I thanked them for the invitation and introduced Major Karcher. "He is the Executive Officer of our squadron."

"Ah, number one boss," one of the teachers said.

"Number two boss," I said. "Our Commanding Officer is busy today and cannot make it to the lunch. Major Karcher is next in command of our squadron."

We walked into Miss Xuan's classroom where fourteen chairs sat around two long, narrow tables and the air smelled of those pungent bun bo spices: Vietnamese coriander, lemon grass, mint, cilantro, basil, and others. Young girls dressed in *ao dais*, set tea cups, bowls, and *dua* around the table and waved their delicate, doll-like hands at the flies.

"Please, sit down," Mr. Hoan said.

At Thanksgiving I gave a canned ham to each of the Hoa My teachers who took our English classes. On this day they reciprocated. Miss Xuan and her third-grade students filled bowls with all the *bun bo* condiments and then, with erect backs and steady hands, they carried each bowl to our place setting.

Meanwhile, Mr. Hoan brought out a large pot and laughed, saying, "I hope you are hungry."

"Starved," said the major.

Miss Xuan lit a small gas stove that sat at one end of the table. Blue flames hissed from the burner then flattened out when Mr. Hoan placed the pot of *Bun Bo* (beef noodle soup) on the stove.

Mr. Hoan stood at the end of the table and took out a small piece of paper to read.

"It is Christmas day. We are happy that you can visit with us on this special day. We are happy you can come to Hoa My School and join the teachers and the students in celebration. It is time for thanks. This small meal of *Bun Bo* is appreciation from us to say 'thank you.' Thank you for teaching us the language of

English. We are happy to learn your language. We appreciate what you are doing for us at Hoa My School.

"We appreciate that you come to Vietnam. You are friends and we welcome you to our country. We hope you will enjoy to return to the United States soon. Next Christmas we hope you can be with your family in the United States. Be at the home of your family. Thank you."

We clapped our hands and I said, "Mr. Hoan, we have a present for you." I handed Mr. Hoan a gift. He removed the ribbon and paper and took out a brown Vietnamese/English dictionary. "You can share that with the teachers who study English," I said.

"Thank you. Thank you for this gift of a dictionary. It is good for us to study the words of English."

"And Miss Xuan, I have a present for you and the students." I walked to the corner of the classroom and brought a package for Miss Xuan.

Miss Xuan put her hands to her mouth, "Thank you, Lieutenant Brian." She unwrapped the shiny paper with delicate precision, folded it twice and pressed the length of each edge against the table before setting it aside. She took the lid off a large box and stared at a set of scales with a black mat top and a raised dial with red numbers at the front.

"This is from all of us at MASS-2," I said. "Here, let me show you what to do." I lifted the scales out of the box and placed them on the floor. "Now, step on the scale. Step here."

"It is for my weight?" Miss Xuan said.

"Yes. Look at this arrow. It points to the pounds you weigh." I removed a chart from the box. "And this chart tells you the kilograms you weigh. This column is pounds. You weigh ninety-five pounds. And look, here, this column tells you in kilograms. You weigh forty-three kilograms."

"Ahhhhh!" Miss Xuan screamed.

Mr. Hoan wanted to weigh himself but Miss Xuan said, "We

must eat first. After the meal we can stand on the scale. Thank you for this gift, Lieutenant Brian and all of you."

"You're welcome," we said.

The *bun bo* was as good as it was at Miss Xuan's home. The other Marines shared my feelings about the Vietnamese food and seconds were served.

After lunch the students stood in line to step on the scales and check the chart to see what they weighed. They giggled at their weight and hugged while other children came in from the playground to weigh themselves.

We left Hoa My School in the early afternoon of Christmas day. Major Karcher watched the teachers and students wave goodbye. "They are a very generous people," he said.

"Yes, sir, very generous." *It was good*, I thought, *to have our Executive Officer down to see what we have accomplished at the school.*

Bob Hope

Bob Hope came to the Seabee Theatre below Hill 327 on 28 December 1966. This was the *big* show—the Bob Hope Christmas Special, with jokes and singers and dancers. I packed up my movie camera and four rolls of Super-8 film and left for the theater early but still had to sit half-way up the hill.

It rained most of the show. Not a hard rain, just a drizzle, but stagehands had to mop the stage between acts. I sat with a poncho over my head to cover the camera and I put my knees up to hold it steady. Joey Heatherton danced in a skimpy black dress, then Bob Hope joined her for a dance and definitely had the better moves.

After the show I hustled down front to watch Bob Hope board his helicopter. I pointed the camera and started shooting. He walked from the stage area to his helicopter and looked dapper in tan slacks, a blue shirt, and a navy-blue sport coat. He wore a short brimmed checkered hat to match his coat and carried a golf club over his right shoulder. He had books in his left hand and looked like a college professor. Someone next to me yelled down, "Hey, Mr. Hope. Can you swing that club?" Bob Hope stopped, looked directly at me with my camera, and took a beautiful one-handed swing into the crowd. He waved, boarded the chopper, and disappeared into the clouds.

The VC Attack

In late February 1967, the sound of explosions jerked me into my mosquito net at three in the morning. I jumped out of my rack, put on trousers and boots, grabbed my weapon, and ran to the door to see Marines running past my hooch. There was another explosion in the distance. And another one. I followed the Marines to our last hooch where a crowd stood in the dark. "The airbase is getting hit," someone said.

From our hill we could see the Danang airbase six kilometers away. Streams of white fire shot up from the airstrip but it took a moment for the sound to reach our ears. "The OD says there's no action on our perimeter," someone yelled. "It's just the airbase getting hit."

Most of the Marines walked back to their hooches but a few of us stayed for the excitement. We brought out lawn chairs and sat down to watch the fireworks. More bursts of phosphorescent light were followed by the distant sound of an explosion. And then there was a large burst of flame, thirty or forty meters in the air followed by an even louder explosion. "Wow! They must have hit an ammo dump," I said.

It didn't last long. We sat on the hill and watched the fires die down and the smoke dissipate from the airfield. The sky was clear, no clouds, just a crescent moon and stars. The lights on the ships in the Bay of Danang twinkled like Christmas lights. One of the larger ships, a floating hospital named the U.S.S. *Repose*, sat in the middle of a vast circle of U.S. Navy ships and cargo ships loaded with the implements and nourishments to feed the war.

We put our lawn chairs away and went back into our hooches to try to get some sleep. It was all the excitement we needed. Or wanted.

That attack on the Danang Airbase was executed on 27 February 1967 with precision by Viet Cong soldiers who were never seen. Eleven Americans and thirty-five Vietnamese were killed, seventeen U.S. aircraft were damaged, and a fire destroyed several structures in a Vietnamese village adjacent to the airbase.

Like the small crabs on the beach of Vung Tau, the Viet Cong could pop up from a camouflaged tunnel, set up their mortars, fire at an American position, and then disappear into the landscape without a trace.

THIRTY-ONE

Hoa Minh Secondary School, 2001

Kieu stands for Vietnam itself, a land well-endowed with natural and human resources, but too often doomed to see such riches gone to waste or destroyed. And yet, despite its grim details and sordid aspects, Kieu's story conveys a message of hope for both the individual and the country: if, like Kieu, the Vietnamese accept and endure with fortitude whatever happens to them, someday they will have paid the cost of their evil karma and will achieve both personal and national salvation.

—From Huynh Sanh Thong's introduction to *The Tale of Kieu*, by Nguyen Du

T HE DAY AFTER I arrived back in Danang from my visit with Miss Xuan, Mr. Hoan ordered a taxi to take us to the village of Hoa My. I had found the old MASS-2 headquarters area and I wanted to see the old Hoa My School location, now turned into a junior high school. Mr. Hoan's daughter, Mrs. Hanh, joined us as did her daughter Hanh Dung, whom I now called Dung (Yoom).

As our taxi drove up Highway 1, now paved and widened to four lanes, there were new restaurants and shops mixed with small groups of people squatted on the sidewalk around cook pots propped above charcoal fires. Young and old lifted bowls to their chins and maneuvered *dua* to their lips so fast not a particle of food fell to the ground. The spicy tamarind and basil aroma, still mixed with gasoline and raw sewage, permeated the air. That facet of Vietnam had not changed from the days in 1966 when this road was dusty and served the wishes of the U.S. Military.

These new shops and eateries that lined Highway 1 brought the young consumer-conscious Vietnamese out of the city, millennials who were interested in the latest fashion or techno gadget.

Merchants pushed racks of Western clothes onto the sidewalk and set out pottery, televisions, refrigerators, furniture, computers, and racks of CDs. An elderly woman dressed in black silk pants and matching blouse with a conical hat carried a long pole over one shoulder with the characteristic drooping baskets at each end. This iconic Vietnamese woman walked in front of two dozen television screens that changed images in unison.

After I saw the fence that boarded the old Hoa My Elementary School ahead of us on the left, our driver, without slowing down, jerked the vehicle into a U-turn that bounced us over a low divider strip in front of an oncoming car. My head hit the top of the taxi and the oncoming car missed us by just a few feet but our driver maneuvered onto the parking strip in front of the school and stopped with a force that bounced all of us forward. We were in front of what was now Hoa Minh Secondary School.

The school's playground had shrunk considerably because of a widened Highway 1. In 1967, when I left Vietnam, the fence in front of Hoa My Elementary School was fifteen meters from the school's *kien kien* tree. Now the fence was three meters from the same tree.

They demolished the old Hoa My Elementary School in 1993, including the two additional classrooms built by MASS-2 Marines and citizens from the village. The new Hoa Minh Secondary School, a modern two-story U-shaped building that surrounded a large courtyard, stood in its place.

Birds sang in the giant *kien kien* tree and the warm air felt good out there, away from the city. A young teacher walked toward us. He had the beginnings of a mustache but so sparse, with strands that began on either side his philtrum and curved around his upper lip, it could not yet be classified as one. A photo ID card hung from the pocket of his white open-collar shirt and the vertical wrinkles between his eyebrows gave him a worried look, exacerbated by the twitch of his mouth between a half smile and frown.

"Hello, Mr. Brian," he said as he put out his hand. His mouth went into a smile much too big and he sang his words in a staccato tempo. "I am Mr. Quang. Teacher of English. At Hoa Minh Secondary School. I will be the interpreter. For you on your visit."

"*Cam on*," I said.

Mr. Quang handed me a piece of paper and said, "We would like the answers to these questions: What is your full name? What is your age? What is your address? What is your telephone number? What is your children's ages?" Mr. Quang handed me a pencil.

The pencil and piece of paper were in my left hand. I had nowhere to put them. My right hand secured my backpack onto my right shoulder and there was neither a place to write the answers nor time to answer them if I had a place.

Mr. Quang took me by the hand, the one with the pencil and paper, to a waiting group of people. "This is our literature teacher at Hoa Minh School," said Mr. Quang.

"I'm very happy to meet you, Mr. Brian." She wore a dark gray *ao dai* over white *quan dai* (pants) and spoke perfect English. I set my backpack down so we could shake hands and she had a firm grip.

"Mr. Brian, this is our principal, Nguyen Van Thau."

The principal was in his forties, short and stocky and also wore a white open-collar shirt. His mustache was thick, unlike Mr. Quang's, and he spoke Vietnamese as though I understood every word. Mr. Quang translated but too slowly for the conversation. The principal shook my hand and kept talking and shaking my hand. He laughed at some humorous anecdote that no one translated, grabbed my arm with his other hand, and pumped my hand up and down like he was at a well. He laughed again and the others laughed right along with him. I smiled. Hanh Dung was too far away to help translate.

Mr. Quang sang, "We can go upstairs for the reception."

The literature teacher and I climbed the stairs together and to make conversation, I asked, "Have your students read *The Sorrow of War* by Bao Ninh?

She frowned and gave me a startled look, almost accusatory. "I do not know this book."

At the top of the stairs I asked Mr. Quang, "Do your students read *The Sorrow of War* by Bao Ninh?

"I do not know this author," he said and moved away. Then I remembered, Robert Templer warned me not to mention my military service but the Hoa Minh staff knew from Mr. Hoan that I was a Marine during the war.

The communist government was against publication of Bao Ninh's book in 1991 "...because of its nonheroic, non-ideological tone," according to the book's back cover, and only allowed it to be published under the name *The Fate of Love*, not *The Sorrow of War*. That's probably the reason the teachers did not know the book. Had I said, *The Fate of Love*, they most likely would have known the book.

Robert Templer mentioned in his book, *Shadows and Wind,* that Bao Ninh was monitored by the police after the book came out. My question had anti-government implications, and maybe did not go over well, but to this day, Bao Ninh still lives in Hanoi and works as an editor and writer.

We walked into a room for my "reception," a room without windows that looked like an interrogation room. It had a table and a few chairs and a red flag with a yellow star in the middle that took up half of one wall. It was the communist flag designed originally by Ho Chi Minh himself. There was a portrait of Uncle Ho with deep set eyes, whispy hair, and goatee. That piece of classroom décor, like the portrait of a rosy cheeked George Washington in American classrooms, could frighten the bejesus out of junior high students. Old George frightened me.

Mr. Quang put his hand on my shoulder, "Please, sit down here, Mr. Brian."

"*Cam on.*"

Dung sat down next to me. I could now answer the questions. My name, easy, "What is your telephone number?" I looked down at Dung but she only tugged on my arm hair. My telephone number would be of little use to anyone and in 2001 it was too expensive to call the United States. My work number or home number? I left it blank and went on to the next question. *Age*: Sixty. *Address*: Home or PO Box? *Why my address?* My PO Box was a safe answer. *Age of my children*: Forty-two, thirty-five, thirty-four.

By the time I finished four of the five questions a few other people were in the room and students served tea. Mr. Quang stood and said, "Mr. Brian, you are the first foreign person to visit Hoa Minh School. We are honored that you come to visit our school. It is a special day for Hoa Minh School. Thank you. Welcome."

I stood up and said, "I am very happy to be here. I have wanted to return for many years and I am thankful that you have welcomed me to your school. I look forward to visiting with the students and your faculty. I am also happy that Mr. Hoan, who I have known since 1966, is here with me today. And his daughter, Mrs. Hanh, who went to Hoa My School, and her daughter, Miss Dung."

Mr. Quang translated my words and the Hoa Minh staff smiled and nodded and said "*Duoc biet dai*" (welcome), and some patted Mr. Hoan on the shoulders.

I sat down. More tea. The teachers smiled and nodded their heads at me. Some raised their cup of tea in appreciation of my presence. This is not an *apparatchik* faculty of communist party members, but I should not have asked about Bao Ninh's book. *The Tale of Kieu* by Nguyen Du was the popular book every student read in school, not *The Sorrow of War*.

Mr. Quang brought out a black and white photocopy of the soccer team picture I sent to Mr. Hoan, the photo I framed and gave him at the hotel. Mr. Hoan was in the back row on the right and the soccer coach, a Marine from MASS-2, stood in the back row on the left. Twenty-two soccer players in those T-shirts made by my wife and daughter are grouped between them.

Mr. Quang passed the photo to the principal who stared at it and then spoke in Vietnamese to Mr. Quang. "My principal says that you look much different now."

"Oh, no," I said. "I am not in this picture, that's the coach. The soccer coach. He might have a resemblance, but I'm not in this picture." The group stared at me and huddled around the principal to look at the photo. They bent their bodies down to the table and wrinkled their foreheads then looked up at me as if to say, "You might be wrong there, Mister Brian, this sure looks like it could be you."

"We may look alike but it is not me," I said. Maybe I took the picture." I took out a new, color copy from my backpack and handed it to Mr. Quang. I pointed to the soccer coach, "This is not me."

I shared another photo from my Super 8 movies, the one of Miss Xuan, Mr. Hoan, and four other Hoa My teachers standing in front of the *kien kien* tree in 1966. The teachers and principal tried to remember the names of the four other Hoa My School instructors but could only come up with Mr. An and Mr. Thang, so I gave them the other two names.

Mr. Quang looked at his watch. "We must now visit classes of Hoa Minh School."

Dung and I stood up and followed our guide out the door. We were on the second floor and could see down into the empty courtyard in front of the school.

I heard students singing in a nearby classroom and recognized a few English words along with some laughter and hollering.

Mr. Quang said, "Mr. Brian, please look here." He guided me over to the end of a walkway that looked down to the yard behind the school. There were red tiled rooftops, treetops, and telephone poles. Mr. Quang held up the soccer team picture and pointed to the trees behind the school. "The old soccer field was there, this picture was taken from that spot."

The hills in the distance were the hills in the picture. The old soccer field and outhouse were long gone and replaced with several homes. Mr. Quang said, "We cannot take you to the spot of this picture, you cannot see mountains from down there."

"Thank you. *Cam on,*" I said. The hills and ridges in the distance were exactly the same as the ones in the photo. I smiled when I saw the similarities. "*Cam on*, Mr. Quang. That was very nice of you to show me that spot."

We walked toward the singing, now more raucous and exuberant than before, but when we entered this English class the students immediately stopped singing and said in unison, "Hello, Mr. Brian." The principal had a big grin on his face.

They knew my name and sang a song in English. I was impressed that the teacher would have her students learn a song in English, although I did not hear enough to recognize it. The teacher motioned for the students to sit and Mr. Quang introduced me to the class.

The thirty-five students were neatly dressed in white shirts, red bandannas around their collars, and dark pants. Some of the students had a blue patch on their left shoulder with "Hoa Minh Secondary School" written on it. All students in Vietnam wear a school uniform through grade twelve. The uniform varies slightly depending on the student's grade and gender.

"Can you answer questions from the class, Mr. Brian?" said Mr. Quang.

"Yes. I would be happy to answer questions."

The teacher told the students to raise their hands and said in perfect English to me, "You can call on students for the questions."

The first student asked, "Where do you come from?"

"Oregon, the state of Oregon. It's in the Western part of the United States located on the Pacific Coast."

"What is your address?" I told them my home address out loud then wrote it on the board. *Maybe they are going to write me a letter. What a treat.*

"What is your phone number?" asked a young girl. *They are determined to have my phone number.* I gave her my home phone number and she asked me to repeat it. I did and also wrote it on the board.

The next girl asked, "Can you take a picture of us?"

"Yes. I would love a picture of you." I reached into my bag and took out my camera.

"No. You be in the picture," she said. A young boy in the front row opened his eyes wide and tapped his finger on the chair next to him. I sat down in the chair and he smiled and looked up at me. The teacher brought her chair over then looked around at her class and smiled. Mr. Quang spoke to the class and took the picture with my Olympus 35 millimeter, OM10, then said, "We must go now to visit another class."

I asked the teacher, "May I hear the song?"

"I beg your pardon."

"Can we hear the song you were singing? The song you were working on when we came into the room?"

She looked toward her principal. "Yes. We can sing a little. Class." The students stood up and sang with such energy and volume that it sounded like they were in a concert choir. I hadn't realized how beautiful their voices were from outside the room. It was an a cappella version of "You are My Sunshine." Their harmony was beautiful and their English perfect. They sang with such gusto, without inhibition, that Ray Charles would have been proud. When they finished I clapped my hands with tears in my eyes, as there are now as I write this and recall that moment in time.

When I packed up to leave, the students said, "Goodbye, Mr. Brian."

"*Chao, sinh vien*," I said. There were some giggles from the students.

The teacher of literature whispered, "You must say, *Chao cac em*, Mr. Brian. *Sinh vien* is for college students. *Cac em* is said for younger students."

"*Chao cac em*," I said, extra loud.

The students clapped and laughed. "Goodbye, Mr. Brian."

"Thank you for the visit to us."

I wrote down my phone number in the blank spot on Mr. Quang's list of five questions and handed him the sheet.

We walked into a dark biology classroom that smelled of rubbing alcohol. A group of five students stood at the front of the class and listened to their instructor speak behind a tall lab table with a built-in sink at one end. The only light in the room came from a desk lamp that illuminated an animal organ about the size of a grapefruit. The organ, covered with fatty tissue, sat on a cafeteria tray. When the instructor finished her explanation, Mr. Quang introduced me to the group of students and said, "Mr. Brian, Miss Nhon's students, work on a pig heart. They must learn all the parts and operation of this heart.

"Your students are very attentive," I said.

"*Cam on*," she said without waiting for a translation. She spoke to her students and one volunteered to step up to the table and cut open the heart. He smiled at me when Miss Nhon handed him the scalpel and then pointed to a spot on the heart. He put the scalpel at that exact spot and cut the organ into two halves with the precision of a heart surgeon. Miss Nhon nodded in approval.

There were two chambers inside each half and the aorta artery poked up at the top of the heart. The left and right ventricles were visible on one half and the two atriums on the other half.

My finger stretched down to the left ventricle. "*Ten la gi?*" I said. Some giggles came from the students. The boy looked at Miss Nhon and then at me. He answered my question in Vietnamese. Miss Nhon nodded "yes."

Mr. Quang said, "Mr. Brian, the student answered correct to your question. He said 'the left ventricle.' Miss Nhon said this is the correct answer."

"What did I ask the student?" I said

"You asked the student, 'What is your name?' But he understood what question you meant because you pointed to the pig heart and not to himself."

Mr. Quang said, "Miss Nhon says to tell you that she was a student of Miss Xuan when she attended Hoa My Elementary School. That was many years in the past. She remembers her fondly. Now, Mr. Brian, please we must to go outside."

I shook hands with Miss Nhon, and looked at the students, "*Chao cac em.*" Then shook the hand of the student who cut open the pig heart. "Good job."

We walked outside and Mr. Quang told me he also attended Hoa My Elementary School and finished high school in Danang. "I then come to Hoa Minh Secondary School to teach."

"Did you attend a college or university?"

"No. I come to this school from high school in Danang.

The group paused next to the *kien kien* tree. "Mr. Hoan," I said. "Line up with the teachers and principal. I want to take your picture by the tree." This was the same spot where Mr. Hoan and Miss Xuan stood in 1966 to pose for my movie. I held up the picture I copied from that super-8 movie. The tree was twice the diameter and where the tree forked in 1966 was now ten feet higher.

Mr. Quang walked over to me, "Mr. Brian, my principal, Mr. Thau, would like to invite you to a meal of lunch."

"*Cam on*," I said and looked at my watch—11:30. "Mr. Hoan, can we eat lunch here?" I asked.

"Yes. We can eat lunch."

"Will we eat in the school cafeteria?"

"There is no cafeteria in our school," Mr. Quang said. "The morning students go home now, the afternoon students come to school at 1:30 p.m. Some of Hoa Minh teachers go to restaurants near the school to eat and some go home to eat. Please, you will go with my principal to eat just near the school. The food is good in this restaurant."

THIRTY-TWO

The Cerlist, 1967

Cerlist Diesel, Inc. was incorporated in North Carolina on 26 March1956 as the sole producer of loop-scavenged two-cycle diesel engines.The name Cerlist is a combination of names of the two men responsible for the company's formation: Mr. Peter H. Cerf (the founder) and Dr. Hans List (inventor of the loop-scavenged diesel engine).

—From *www.thefcconnection.com/cerlist_diesel.htm*

O UR NEW COMMANDING Officer, Lieutenant Colonel Harry Hunter, wore crisp, olive drab utilities, always starched and pressed, a belt buckle, always Brassoed to a golden sparkle that matched his shiny Aviator Wings pinned above his left breast pocket, and black boots, shined so he could see his reflection, should he glance down in that direction. His desk, like his military alignment, held a lamp, a calendar, a notepad and two boxes, one for "in" and one for "out."

Lieutenant Colonel Hunter had morning meetings three days a week. At each meeting, I had to explain the status of every generator and backup generator at the four MASS-2 locations. On the days when my report included news of a "down generator," I heard, "Lieutenant Biggs may I see you after the meeting?" Then I heard how important it was for generators to remain "up and running at all times," and how important it was for a young

officer to "foresee problems and execute proper maintenance pro-
cedures and instill in every NCO and driver and mechanic the
desire to fulfill his mission with utmost precision and scrutiny."

There was also the matter of Lieutenant Colonel Hunter's vehicle. When he arrived at MASS-2, he requested our smooth riding Cerlist Diesel, M676 Jeep. It was actually a pickup with a
canopy, and much more comfortable than the M38A1 Jeep.

Charlie Bond, my college roommate and also in the same Basic
School class with me at Quantico, was a platoon commander in
an infantry company near Hoi An. He came up to visit me on occasion and went with me to have the Cerlist washed for Lieutenant Colonel Hunter at one of the Vietnamese car washes.

Charlie Bond also played football with me at the University of
Washington and is my son Charlie's namesake. He was a tackle on
our football team and voted the most inspirational player the year
we went to the Rose Bowl. That was our senior year, and Charlie
and I made a pact that year to not get married until we were thirty.
We may have been drunk when we made the pact, I can't remember.
I was married within the year and Charlie Bond has never married.

We drove to the nearest "car wash" and pulled into a darkened
tent area where one side was graveled and set up to wash military
vehicles. These "car washes" also served as brothels. The back
area of the tent apparently had beds and offered, I assumed, all
manner of sexual favors. Charlie Bond said he was going to the
back room and would meet me out front after he was done.

I paid for a car wash and stood in the semi-dark, sweating from
the humidity and heat. The standup fans only circulated hot air
around the tent. A Vietnamese woman about my age, dressed in
black silk pajamas and a tan blouse walked up and said something
in Vietnamese that I didn't understand. She undid the buttons of
her blouse, smiled, and pulled her blouse apart to expose breasts
that seemed large for a Vietnamese woman.

This got me excited and as I stared at her breasts she put her hands on one of them and caressed it until milk started to squirt out of her nipple. I stepped back a bit and she laughed and said, "You like this?"

I had never seen milk come out of a woman's breast before. It wasn't white like regular milk but opaque and gray looking. I said something to her about having a baby but she started rubbing my penis which had grown considerably. She looked into my eyes as she undid my belt and then knelt down to undo each button of my fly. She took her time with this but when she finished she pulled down my trousers and underwear and began to masturbate me. It didn't take long.

It felt good, great in fact, but as she walked away I wondered about her. Did she have a husband who maybe worked at the car wash? And they now have a child?

Someone backed the Cerlist out of the tent and yelled, "Finished." I didn't know if I was supposed to pay extra or not. I decided that it wasn't necessary since it may have been an incentive to come back to this particular car wash, so I climbed into the Cerlist and drove around to pick up Charlie Bond.

The CO used his Cerlist daily to check on MASS-2 operations or attend various meetings at Headquarters, or shop at the 327 PX. Unfortunately, a month after he assumed command, the Cerlist went down. Off line. Dead. He wanted his Cerlist repaired immediately but we were waiting on parts."

A month later, during the morning briefing on 26 February 1967, Lieutenant Colonel Hunter asked about his Cerlist vehicle again: "Is my vehicle running yet?"

"No, sir," I said. "We're still waiting on those parts."

There was nothing else I could say. The parts weren't in and we didn't have an old Cerlist vehicle we could cannibalize to put the CO's vehicle back on line.

He looked at me and shook his head and looked around the room at the other officers. He grinned and said, "And?"

"Those parts should arrive any day now, sir."

"Is there a possibility the vehicle will be back on line before the end of my tour?"

"Oh, yes, sir," I said.

"I'll believe it when I see it."

"I do have some good news about our showers, sir," I said. "Sergeant Stuck rigged up a hot water heater to one of our generators and we've got hot water between 1600 and 1800."

"Outstanding, Lieutenant. You tell Sergeant Stuck to come by and see me. I want to personally thank him."

"I will, sir. He's a good Marine."

2001

Hanh Quyen & "Mr. Brian." Her purse is the gift from me.

Me with the English teacher and her class. They asked me to be in a photo with them.

My birthday cake with (*left to right*) Hanh Thy, Huong, and Hanh Dung. The only photo left from my 60th birthday party.

With Miss Xuan on her cashew farm in
Hac Dich.

Miss Xuan's sister, Miss Tam (*left*), and Miss
Xuan on her cashew farm.

Left to right: Miss Xuan, me, Thuong Toa Thich Quang Hanh, and Cam Nguyet visiting her monk at his monastery.

The group that visited the beach at Vung Tau where the children were surrounded by tiny crabs.

2004

The van load that visited Hoi An in 2004.

Phuc and his mother, Nghia.

The gravesite of Miss Hoai, Mr. Hoan's daughter. Her sister, Mrs. Hang, is praying while her husband, Mr. Thang, waits his turn. I was the next to pray.

A differrent view of Mr. Hoan's daughter's grave. MASS-2 was located in those hills in the background, off to the right.

Left to right: Miss Xuan, Co (Mr. Hoan's wife), Mr. Hoan, and me.

2006

Hanh Dung and Mr. Brian on the "Love Seat."

THIRTY-THREE

Lunch with the Principal, 2001

What is emerging in Vietnam is a complex, hybrid culture with a multitude of messages, some of which reinforce what the state sees as traditional values, others that seriously undermine them. The reality is that this process has been going on for centuries; there is no pure set of Vietnamese values to undermine. Popular culture will not erode Vietnamese identity, it will remake it and keep it in a state of constant flux.

—From *Shadows and Wind*, Robert Templer

THE PRINCIPAL TOOK us up Highway 1 to the restaurant. By this time the humidity had soaked my shirt so much it felt like I just pulled it out of a washing machine spin cycle. A water buffalo standing in a field stared at us through the heat waves that floated off the raised highway. The tall and narrow pagoda I visited in 1967 still stood across the highway with its tiled roofs, pink and orange walls, and ornate pots of flowers that lined a porch with only enough room for two columns. The pagoda's grounds had more trees and plants than in 1967.

We all walked without talking, maybe because of the heat, but we were quiet, like we were on a road in the desert until a lone motorbike puttered past. Then, that desert quiet again.

Even though Highway 1 was now paved, dust still covered the bushes and trees on the sides of the road. Dust like the dust deuce-and-a-half trucks stirred up during the war. Trucks filled with Marines and their rifles and ammo boxes and canteens, hunkered down under camo covered helmets. Going north.

How lucky, I thought, to be walking along this paved and peaceful highway at sixty years old. Marine friends of mine rode convoys of trucks with big 105 howitzers on this road, over Hai Van Pass and beyond.

Some of my Marines friends could only speak a few words about the battles at those northern destinations. Then they'd turn away, silent. Some can't remember anything of those battles because of PTSD. One friend told me, "At times everything comes back just like it was yesterday. This happened on 9/11. That day I could remember each person in my platoon. I knew their names and could see their faces. Now I have to struggle to remember just one."

The principal shouted, "Ah," and pointed to the restaurant, a room that looked like a double garage made into a rumpus room. A dark mahogany bar ran along the back wall, a wall with one picture hung in the middle. In fact, all three walls had one picture hung in the middle. Mahogany tables and chairs sat around the concrete floor and an oscillating fan rotated hot air around the restaurant. Still it felt good to sit down. Our party consisted of Mr. Hoan, Mrs. Hanh, Dung, the Hoa Minh principal, the vice principal, the literature teacher who had not heard of *The Sorrow of War*, and me. Mr. Quang went home for lunch.

"Mr. Brian, do you want a 7-Up?" said Dung.

"Yes, *cam on.*"

The principal, vice principal, Mr. Hoan, and the teacher of literature each ordered a beer. A much more relaxed school administration than those in the States.

The principal and Mr. Hoan agreed on what to order.

Dung said, "My grandfather told me that you like all the Vietnamese food."

"Well, I do. Yes. Most everything."

"The principal ordered for you, *banh trang* and *thit bo nuong*," said Mr. Hoan.

When the dish came Mrs. Hanh used her *dua* to lay strips of meat around a metal griddle attached to a propane stove and there was an instant sizzle sound. A teriyaki sauce and pepper aroma filled the air as the meat strips frizzled down in size. Mrs. Hanh put the cooked ones on a plate and filled each vacated slot with more meat strips.

The waiter brought beer and soft drinks and I held up my glass. "*Chuc suc khoe.*"

Everyone raised their glasses and shouted, "*Chuc suc khoe.*"

My 7-Up went down easy in the heat, I drank half the glass in one gulp. Dung layered my rice paper taco with several meat strips then added the *muoi ot* sauce and a squeeze of lime. "Here, Mr. Brian, this is called *thit bo nuong.*"

The rice paper texture was crunchy and the meat was spicy and tender, something like a teriyaki taco with Tabasco—but that doesn't come close to its description or flavor. "Mmmm," I said. "What is this meat?"

Dung translated the question to the group and Mr. Hoan immediately turned to me and said, "Dog."

As my reaction to this statement I picked up a good portion of meat strips, dangled them in the air with my *dua,* and then relished the bite. "Ahhhhh."

The group roared with laughter.

"No, Mr. Brian," said Dung, "It is not dog. It is beef. Beef from a cow."

"Well, it is excellent," I said.

The vice principal spoke to Dung. "Mr. Brian, he wants to ask you, what you do in your country, in an American school, when a student comes late to class?" Everyone heard the question in Vietnamese and knew what Dung asked me. They stopped eating, held onto their *duas,* and cocked their heads toward me for this bit of American educational wisdom.

I nodded my head, looked around the table at each of them. Then made a hawking sound while I slit my throat with the *dua.*

The vice principal's eyes opened wide and the principal slapped the table as they both laughed out loud.

"Dung, please ask the principal how many students there are at Hoa Minh School."

Dung translated Mr. Thau's answer. "He says there are four hundred students in the morning and four hundred students in the afternoon. Very crowded classrooms."

Then another question to Dung came from the vice principal. Dung turned to me, "He wants to know how you feel about your visit to Hoa Minh School? And also, did you learn *Tieng Viet* just to come to Vietnam?"

I put my hand on Mr. Hoan's shoulder, "Eighteen months ago I decided to visit Vietnam to find my friends from Hoa My School. Mr. Hoan and Miss Xuan." Dung translated and continued to translate as I spoke.

"I thought I should learn the language, as much as possible, in that short time period, so I took a beginning Vietnamese language class at a junior college and joined a Sunday school class full of young Vietnamese children who were learning to speak the language of their parents.

"Now, after learning some of the history of Vietnam and reading many books on your country and listening to many personal stories from my Vietnamese friends, I realize how much more there is to learn about your country and your culture.

"I have visited Mr. Hoan and Miss Xuan and their families and I know I want to return. My visit to Hoa Minh Secondary School fulfilled a dream I've had for many years." I tapped my *dua* on the plate of meat and waited for the catch in my throat to dissolve. "I loved my visit to your school after such a long period of time."

Mr. Hoan nodded his head. "I am happy you have this new building and new school," I continued, "and thankful that today I was able to witness the teachers and young students in the classroom.

"I spent twenty-nine years teaching in high school and I know how much work you do every single day. I know how important your work is and I know that these children are very lucky they have you for role models. Your influence, your every gesture and act of kindness will have a lasting impression on them. It is rewarding for me to be able to share this day with all of you. I wish you much success."

Dung finished translating and the group clapped their hands.

Mr. Hoan said, in his slow, melodic tone, "Thank you, Mr. Brian. You make a kind remark."

The principal paid the bill and we walked out to the highway. It was hot and bright standing next to the pavement. I shook hands with the principal and vice principal. "Thank you for opening your school to me. I enjoyed my visit and thank you for the lunch."

The literature teacher who did not know Bao Ninh's book said, "Mr. Brian, would you please come home with me?"

This seemed a bit strange, but it must have been a gesture of friendship, or possibly an opportunity for her to practice English but I replied, "I'm traveling with Mr. Hoan and his family today." I shook her hand. "Maybe I can come to your home some other time."

THIRTY-FOUR

Mr. Hoan's Addition, 1967

Habitat for Humanity began working in Vietnam in January 2001 with its first project in Danang City in the central coastal region. As of June 2014, Habitat has enabled more than 13,300 low income Vietnamese families to improve their living conditions through decent homes, clean water and safe sanitation.

—From the Habitat for Humanity website:
(http://www.habitat.org/where-we-build/vietnam)

A FTER TEACHING MY English class at Hoa My School I packed up the homework assignments and my lesson plans. Mr. Hoan waited by the door with his hands at his side.

"You did well today, Mr. Hoan, your English is very good now," I told him.

He stood erect with his shoulders back, as though he had some sad news but he didn't speak. "I must return to my base," I said.

"Lieutenant Brian," he finally said, "the students of Hoa My need a room to be built. Two more classrooms are needed at Hoa My School." Mr. Hoan took a step out the door and turned to look at the school yard. "Two more rooms must be added in the school yard."

"Do you have plans, construction drawings, for the rooms?"

"Yes."

"Do you need help building the rooms?"

"Yes."

"There are people at MASS-2 who would be happy to help you build it and we can get a work party to come down here I'm sure."

"We must have the...the..." Mr. Hoan shook his head. "In English you say the 'wood,' the 'cement.' We don't have these items. We don't know how to get this."

"Material? Supplies?"

"Yes, material. We would like to ask you to help Hoa My School have the material for two more classrooms. Wood, cement to build two room." Mr. Hoan laughed at his mistake. "Rooms," he corrected. "Two more rooms in the school yard."

"I think that can be arranged. Let me ask my CO and some of the people in our outfit. We might be able to scrounge the material. I can't say for sure. But let me try."

"Thank you." Mr. Hoan smiled. He took me by the hand and said, "Thank you Lieutenant Brian for your help with our new school rooms."

The schoolyard was quiet and the air smelled of flowering *phuong* blossoms. Mr. Hoan pointed to the left side of the yard, "We will put the new building there."

"Good," I said.

He walked north and knelt down to scratch the soil. "The corner of our new building is here." He rose and walked around the school yard and scratched a little crease in the soil at each corner of the proposed rectangular building, like his contact with the earth insured completion of the project.

The two proposed classrooms were a separate building from the existing school. The new building would sit perpendicular to the six-room building and form an "L-shaped" Hoa My School.

Mr. Hoan put his hand on my arm and looked at his empty schoolyard. Three six-by-six trucks headed north past the school on Highway 1. Diesel fumes replaced the smell of the *phuong* blossoms and the noise of truck tires on the rough road drowned out our conversation. The military made two deuce-and-a-half, six-by-six trucks when I ran a motor pool in Vietnam. The M35 and the M35 A1. The M35, 2 ½ ton truck, the ones we had, had four duel tires in the rear and two single tires in front. Ten tires. Each tire on the "six-by" was over three feet tall and eight inches wide. These trucks made a lot of noise on paved roads and when they drove by on the rough, mostly unpaved Highway 1, everyone in the playground had to wait until they passed to finish a conversation.

The noise faded as the trucks disappeared and the dust settled in the schoolyard. Mr. Hoan took out a white handkerchief, unfolded it, and wiped his lips. "Mr. Hoan, there are Marines who can look at your plans and decide how much lumber, cement and equipment you would need for the project," I said. "I will bring someone down here in the next couple of days."

* * * *

My work in the motor pool had not been up to Lieutenant Colonel Hunter's standards and this request to supply lumber and build the two new school rooms, if approved, could divert my attention away from vehicles and generators.

The outhouse project was simple as it took very little material and was completed in two days. This project was a major construction job that required coordination with the Tenth Engineer Battalion, MASS-2 volunteers, and the Vietnamese people from Hoa My village. Not to mention my time away from the motor pool.

Lieutenant Colonel Hunter leaned forward, put his elbows on his desk, and nestled his chin into the cup of his hands. He looked up at me and said nothing. Then he pushed his head up with his thumbs and said, "Go ahead with the project, Lieutenant Biggs. See if you can't scrounge the supplies from Tenth Engineers. Don't they owe you a favor?"

"Yes, sir. They do owe us a favor." They certainly did. Sergeant Wix often drove our 6000-pound forklift over to the Tenth Engineers chow hall to unload supplies.

"Well they should be willing to help with the project and come up with the material. Just don't spend so much time down there that our generators end up off line."

"No, sir."

"Any news on the repair of my Cerlist?"

"Nothing new, sir."

* * * *

Sergeant Wix arranged with Tenth Engineers to look over the plans and deliver the material to Hoa My School within two weeks, and there was no shortage of volunteers from MASS-2 to help build the two new classrooms. In early March 1967 MASS-2 Marines joined the Vietnamese construction workers from Hoa My Village and began work on the new building.

On the first day of the project I joined the crew to help carry material from Highway 1 to the construction site in the school-yard. Mr. Hoan and some of the Hoa My teachers stood near the gate and watched us carry lumber and concrete forms.

After several loads of lumber, I stopped in front of the group of teachers. "Mr. Hoan, why don't you help us carry this lumber?"

"We are not used to doing that work," Mr. Hoan said with no expression on his face.

I smiled at the group. "Well, if you do it for a while, you'll get used to it." Mr. Hoan looked at his colleagues and back at me. His mouth was closed and straight across. His eyes gave no hint of his contemplation.

Marines from MASS-2 went down to Hoa My School after work for several weeks. I helped out on occasion but didn't work on the project too much because the English classes took enough of my time and we did not need a generator off-line while I worked on the addition to Hoa My School.

I remember watching the foundation forms go into place, the

arrival of cement trucks, and how the new building took shape as the two-by-four studs enclosed each room. This was a major accomplishment for these teachers, MASS-2, and me. Even though I never saw them completed, I was proud of facilitating the construction of those two classrooms.

THIRTY-FIVE

Mr. Chau's Gift, 2001

A picture is worth a thousand words.
—From a 1918 newspaper advertisement in the *San Antonio Light*

A FTER LUNCH WITH the principal, Mr. Hoan and I visited the pagoda across Highway 1, then walked past Hoa Minh School to the house of Mr. Chau. His daughter, Mrs. Hanh, and Dung were there waiting at what appeared to be an outdoor café with two tables, each covered with a red checkered plastic table-cloth. Mr. Chau and Mrs. Hanh were classmates in Mr. Hoan's sixth grade class.

We sat down and heard children laughing and screaming off in the distance. Mr. Chau's house had a screened-in porch with a large soft drink dispensing machine that flashed "7-Up" on and off. A cabinet that also acted as a counter, had items for sale—convenience store items, miniature water buffalos, Buddhas made of marble, bags of jellybeans, postcards, and Vietnamese flags, red with a yellow star.

A husky man in a white polo shirt came out of the house with a tray of tea. "Ah, this is Mr. Chau," said Mr. Hoan.

I stood up to greet Mr. Chau, and he was impressed with the Vietnamese I knew. Mr. Chau and Mr. Hoan shook hands and Mr. Chau laughed as he shared some remembrance of his old teacher and laughed again as he patted Mr. Hoan on the upper arm, then poured our tea.

"Mr. Chau," I said. "Is this café your business?"

Dung translated. "He said this is his house. His wife works in this small restaurant and store and he is a maker of *bonsai* plants. You know the *bonsai* plant?"

"Yes. I know the *bonsai* plant. I've seen a bonsai plant."

Mr. Chau jumped up and disappeared into his house for a moment then came out with a small plant he held with both hands. His lips curved into a smile and his eyebrows arched well up on his forehead as he set the vase containing an eight-inch tree into my hands.

A brown rough-barked tree-trunk angled up from the small pot at forty-five-degrees until limbs covered with green feather-like needles curved back above the trunk with a wind-blown look. The tree resembled a sailor leaning forward in a sou'wester looking out to sea. I set the plant down on our table. "It's a beautiful piece of art."

Mr. Chau nodded his head up and down while he showed me a booklet filled with *bonsai* plants that he sold all over the world. He opened his eyes wide and began talking very fast. He gestured with his long arms and pointed up Highway 1 toward the school.

Dung translated: "Mr. Chau says that he sends a letter to all the students, how do you say, he organizes a reunion of all Hoa My students at the end of each year. To come back to Hoa My village. Students from many years ago. My grandfather went to the reunion also. Mr. Chau, my mother, my aunt. All go to the reunion of Hoa My School."

Mr. Chau ran into his house.

"Mrs. Hanh," I said to Dung's mother, "were you ever in Miss Xuan's class?"

Dung translated and said, "Yes, my mother was in the class of Miss Xuan when she was in grade three."

"Can you ask your mother if she has a story about Miss Xuan?"

Dung spoke to her mother. "My mother said she will tell the story into a tape and give it to you before you go back to your country."

I held up my small tape recorder and said, "Tell her 'thank you.' I will let her use my tape recorder."

"She does not need your recorder. My mother has a tape recorder just the same. She will give you a tape with a story of Miss Xuan."

Mr. Chau jogged back to his chair and handed me some pictures in plastic holders. "Mr. Chau," said Dung, "tells you he took these pictures at many reunion celebrations."

"Were these reunions held at the school?"

"Yes," Mr. Hoan said. "At Hoa My School. Then at the new school. Hoa Minh School. After the old school was taken down, destroyed. The reunions, brought many students who attended Hoa My School. They met for many years but it does not happen for three or four years now. No more."

There were several pictures in the plastic holders. All of them in front of Hoa My School. "This photo," I said, "was taken in front of the *kien kien* tree. And the old Hoa My School is in the background. Look at this."

"Yes," said Mr. Hoan. "The old school."

"And this photo is in front of the two additional classrooms we had built in 1967."

"Yes. That is school rooms that you build."

"I never saw that building. I never saw that building completed. It was not completed when I left in 1967. What year was this reunion?"

Dung asked Mr. Chau. "Mr. Chau says the picture you hold was taken in 1993. The next year the old school came down and the new one was built."

I held the pictures up in the light. The shutters on the doors and windows were green. They were brown in 1966, brown in my movies. The *kien kien* tree in the picture had large letters carved in the bark, *Lop BA* (grade three). Mr. Chau was in both pictures but younger then. The picture in front of the two additional classrooms that I had built showed the porch and its yellow stucco pillars with green mold around the bottom of each pillar.

Mr. Chau spoke to me and tapped the picture with his finger. Dung looked at the pictures. "Mr. Chau says that the former students who come to that reunion, the reunion of 1993, were sad to learn that the old school is to be destroyed," Dung said. "Former students went into their classroom to stare at the desks where they sat. They looked for their mark on desks and told old tales and adventure from their days attending Hoa My School.

"We do the same thing in America."

Mr. Hoan looked over at me. "The students at these reunions like to remember old friends."

"Yes," I said, "we all do." I stacked the plastic holders back in order. "*Cam on*, Mr. Chau. These are good photos."

Mr. Chau took his stack of photos and shuffled through them. He pulled out the two 1993 photos and handed them to me.

They are of the old Hoa My School. "*Cam on*, Mr. Chau. I will have them copied and send the originals back to you."

Dung translated this to Mr. Chau and he shook his head "no" and spoke in Vietnamese as he reached over to hold my hand. "Mr. Chau wants you to keep them," Dung said. "He doesn't want them. He said, 'Please, you keep the photos of the classrooms you built.'"

"Thank you. *Cam on*. You are very generous." I opened my backpack and placed the pictures in a book, safe from damage.

This was my last day on this trip to Vietnam and this gesture from Mr. Chau, this gift, gave me something I thought I would never have: photographs of the two classrooms I had built, my biggest and most successful project in the village of Hoa My. I don't think I have ever experienced a gesture as generous and meaningful to me as this.

THIRTY-SIX

Eric Barnes in Vietnam, 1967

I count myself in nothing else so happy
As in a soul remembering my good friends.

—Bolingbroke in *Richard II, Act 2, scene 3*, William Shakespeare

I N FEBRUARY 1967 I left the motor pool just after the sun went down and drove the two kilometers up to my hooch. Once I turned onto the road to the MASS-2 Headquarters area I saw a Marine two-hundred meters ahead of my jeep. At Basic School in Quantico, our platoon commander, Captain Hancock, told us, "A good platoon leader should recognize each one of his men at dusk, walking away from him at a hundred meters." I mastered that feat before I left Basic School. I'm lucky to have better night vision than most due to the number of rod cells in my peripheral retina. This Marine, now silhouetted a-hundred-and-fifty meters in front of the jeep, looked familiar. Broad shoulders and walking at a quick pace up the hill. He wore camouflage utilities and canvas jungle boots—something I hadn't seen many of.

One hundred and twenty-five meters: His sleeves were rolled up and he looked like one squared away Marine. *One hundred meters*: Over a football field away, his boots were bloused in a perfect tuck. From the back he looked like Eric Barnes. He swung his arms back the way Eric did.

At the fork in the road, where it either went down into the old French Fort or up to the MASS-2 area halfway up the hill, I pulled even with the Marine. "Eric. Eric Barnes. Wow! What are you doing?" I parked the jeep and jumped out. "Man, it's good to see you. You look great. Where're you going?" Eric and I shook hands. There was no sweat on his face, he wasn't even breathing hard. He smiled at me with that big Eric Barnes smile and laughed. He had stories to tell.

"Biggs. It's good to see you. I heard you were up here. I'm down at the airbase waiting for my flight to Hawaii in the morning. So I hitched a ride to the bottom of your hill."

His arms were all muscle. We were both in Captain Hancock's platoon at Basic School and Eric Barnes was at the top of our platoon. He had the best time on the "O" Course and led the platoon in almost every category.

"Hawaii. That's right," I said. "Colleen wrote me about your trip. She wrote that Noreen was going to meet you there. Fantastic! Gees it's good to see you. You look fit, man. Strong. Where're you located?"

"Out at Hill 55, with 1/26."

"Can you spend the night? I've got an extra bunk in my hooch and we've got great chow. When's your flight out?"

Eric slapped me on the shoulder. "Early in the morning. I'll eat and stay awhile but I can't spend the night. I don't want to miss that flight." Eric looked out toward the Bay of Danang, took off his cover (hat) and put his hands on his hips. "Look at this view. You live up here?"

"Yeah. I work down in the valley. You can see my motor pool just off to the left there. And the Vietnamese village where I work in out there on Highway 1."

He looked out to the east, "That's what they call Monkey Mountain?"

"Yes," I said. "Full of monkeys, I guess. I've never been over there. And that's Hai Van Pass up there."

"Beautiful," Eric said. "There is a lot of beauty in Vietnam."

I let Eric stare out to the bay as the evening darkened until he turned back to me, "Let's get some chow, I'm starved."

We hopped in my jeep and drove up the road to MASS-2. "I'm going to run into the club and get some beer. I'll be right back."

The club wasn't busy. "*Hoa,*" I said to our Vietnamese waitress, "I'll take two bottles of Budweiser."

"Lieutenant Biggs, where're you off to in such a hurry?" It was Lieutenant Len Tygart, the tall, lanky former warrant officer who ran our supply building and lived two hooches below mine.

"I'll be back, Len. A buddy from Basic School came in from Hill 55." I grabbed my beer and left some pink piasters on the bar. "*Cam on, Hoa.*"

"Eric, let's walk down to my hooch and cool off with a beer."

"A beer sounds good."

"This is where I live." Eric opened my cabinet with the burning light bulb and picked up the movie camera. He held it up to his eye and looked through the viewfinder. "You take many movies?"

"Yeah, a lot." A box of Colleen's letters sat on my desk. I found the one about Noreen's trip to Hawaii and grabbed some pictures of my son Charlie. "Let's sit outside."

Out on my deck we opened our beer. We could see the mountain ridge to the west just black against an amber sky.

Eric raised his bottle and tapped it against mine, "Bri, it's good to see you."

The ice-cold Budweiser sent a cool sensation all the way down to my stomach. "Ahhh. That first sip of beer is the best."

Eric held his beer up to the fading light. "There's nothing better."

"R & R in Hawaii. Wow, that's great. Listen to Colleen's letter. 'Snowed yesterday. Kaye likes school. House OK, but plumbing problem in kitchen,' bla, bla, bla. Here, 'Noreen will spend the week with Eric in Hawaii and then spend a night with me on her way home. I'm anxious for Noreen to see Charlie. He's so big now even at three months. And, of course it will be fun for Noreen to see Kaye again.'"

"Here's a picture of my son, Charlie." I pulled out a worn Polaroid photo of little Charles Colin Biggs dressed in a white pair of pajamas. His cheeks were fat and rosy against the white terry cloth and his black hair flopped over his forehead. "Look at that. He's about three weeks old in that shot."

"Congratulations, Bri. You've got a son." Eric held up the picture to the light of my hooch. "Lots of hair."

"Yeah. There's some of it here, in the envelope. Look." I gave Eric a curled-up chunk of black hair.

Eric took the lock of hair in the palm of his hand and held it. He looked at it for a moment, like it was a bug from the garden about to crawl away. Then he rubbed it between his thumb and finger to see what it felt like. "A son, Bri. Just like me. Congratulations." When he handed back the lock of hair, a dynamite blast went off in the rock quarry.

"What the hell was that? Blasting?" He knew that sound.

"There's a rock quarry right below us. It goes on all the time. They drill a hole for hours then a blast of dynamite. You get used to it. Let's go eat."

"Good."

We finished our beer and walked to the chow hall. Eric stopped at a grassy viewpoint and looked out to the Bay of Danang again. The evening sky and sea blended together with that twinkle of lights from the massive fleet of ships in the harbor. Then he looked east to the lights on the Danang runway six kilometers away.

After dinner we walked to Club Vagabond in the light rain. It was smoky and crowded and several Marines were at the bar. The Marines at Len Tygart's table stood up to leave and Len just finished his steak dinner. "I forgot the club was barbequing steaks tonight," I said. We sat down with Len and I ordered more beer. "How was the steak?"

Len, with a mouth full, managed to say, "Delicious."

"Len Tygart, this is Eric Barnes. We were in Basic School together, same platoon. I think I told you I got married halfway through Basic School and my wife and daughter and I moved into married officer's quarters right next door to Eric and his wife and son. We were also neighbors at Camp Lejeune.

"Glad to meet you Lieutenant. Brian says you're out at Hill 55."

"Yes, with 1/26."

"Who were you with in Lejeune?" Len, a West Virginian, spoke in a melodic, slow drawl. He gave his syllables an extra beat at times and when he said the word "can't"—it rhymed with "paint"—and "bekuz" was always "be cause." His big hand grabbed the pitcher of beer and he poured three glasses.

"3/8. I was a platoon commander," Eric said. "Partied hard with Lieutenant Biggs."

"Lots of wild parties at Lejeune," I said.

"I can't imagine you at wild parties, Brian."

"Eric was the wild one." I said.

"Not me."

Len smiled and looked at Eric.

"What about the time you were under that blanket?" I said.

Eric looked around and pretended not to remember the incident. "When was that?

"Len, we had a bunch of friends over and the women made us play this game where someone had to sit in the middle of the living room with a blanket over their head."

"I sat in the middle of this group with a blanket over my head," Eric said. "Then they tell me to take off something."

"Something you don't need," I said.

"Yeah. So, I took off my shoes and threw them out from under the blanket. Then everyone said, 'No, not your shoes.' I took off my socks. Then my shirt." Eric mimed taking off his shirt. "'No, not your shirt.'"

"Eric you were crazy."

Len had a big grin on his face. He finished his glass of beer. "How far'd you go?"

"He got down to his skivvies. Then his wife yelled, 'The blanket, Eric, the blanket!'"

"Who would think of the blanket?"

"Eric, the blanket was obvious. How could you not know it was the blanket? Man, I laughed my head off that night."

Eric leaned forward, "You don't think of the blanket. You think of your clothes."

"Let me get another round," Len said.

"No thanks," Eric said. "I better get down to the airbase. I don't want to miss my flight." Eric reached for his cover on the back of a chair.

"It doesn't take any time at all to get to the airbase," I said. "My jeep's parked at S-1. We can have one more beer. Tell Noreen we had a few beers before you left."

"What the hell." He threw his cover on the table. "One more. Thanks, Len."

Henry Lee's guitar case leaned up against the wall. In the evenings I sat outside my hooch and heard either Henry Lee or Len strumin' away. Len came back with the beer. "Len," I said, "that's Henry Lee's guitar isn't it?"

"Yep."

"Can Eric borrow it? I haven't heard him sing since we were at Lejeune."

"Sure." Len set the pitcher of beer on the table and took Henry Lee's guitar out of the case. Real careful, like it was a newborn baby. "Here, Eric."

"Eric, what was the name of your band at Tufts?" I said.

"The Barnstormers."

"Yeah, that was it. 'Eric Barnes and the Barnstormers.'" Eric tuned the guitar and started off with "Hey, sweet truckin' mama, trucking all my blues away." Marines at the club clapped and yelled and gathered around our table. Eric stood up and put his foot on a chair for "Plastic Jesus on the Dashboard of My Car." He rocked back and forth and stamped his foot on the chair. At the end of the song there was more applause and shouts for this song or that.

"I've really got to get going," Eric said.

"One more," came from the crowd.

"All right, one more." Eric sang "Folsom Prison Blues" with some references switched to Vietnam.

By this time MASS-2 Marines had packed the Club and when Eric finished someone shouted above the clapping, "Buy that Marine another beer."

But Eric handed the guitar to Len and yelled, "I've got to get down to the airbase. R & R tomorrow in Hawaii!"

"Yee haaaaah," erupted from the crowd. (This was years before "OOH-RAH" became the Marine Corps chant of choice.)

When we got in my jeep I told Eric that I saw Johnny Cash give a concert.

"Where?" Eric asked

"He was at the Dream Bowl in Vallejo. Must have been '60 or '61.

"He's the best. Johnny Cash."

It was still raining when I parked my jeep at the airbase.

"It was great to see you, Eric. Stop by when you get back. Give me a call and I'll come pick you up."

"I will."

"Say hello to Noreen."

Eric jogged to the airbase terminal with that long stride of his. Head tilted back a bit, chest forward. His jungle boots splashed in the puddles, his shoulders were hunched up and his elbows high on each determined stride. His jog was so fluid it looked like he was in slow motion. When he reached the hanger door he stopped, turned to look back at me and waved in the dim light a hundred meters away. Then he ducked out of sight.

THIRTY-SEVEN

Don't Panic, 2001

The art of losing isn't hard to master;
so many things seem filled with the intent
to be lost that their loss is no disaster.

Lose something every day. Accept the fluster
of lost door keys, the hour badly spent.
The art of losing isn't hard to master.

—From "One Art," Elizabeth Bishop

P ACKING UP TO leave Vietnam in 2001 had its difficulties. Several presents and souvenirs were on the bed next to my large suitcase, among them a pearl bracelet for my wife, Vicki. I undid the red ribbon on the sturdy box and picked up the bracelet. It weighed nothing. An eighteen-karat gold chain of tiny horseshoes and pearls. A pearl, two horseshoes back to back, another pearl, two horseshoes back to back. Ten pearls altogether. I lay the bracelet back in its cotton nest.

I bought a box of nine miniature figurines in ethnic dress that represented nine ethnic groups of Vietnam. There were six boxes in a set each with nine figurines to represent the fifty-four ethnic groups. I bought box number six that contained eight women figurines, one man, and one house each about an inch-and-a-half high. The house, labeled "Bana, Vietnam" had a thatched roof.

In 1965, during a Recon class at Basic School in Quantico, Virginia, the instructor ran through a slide show of Vietnam. One slide pictured three huts in a Vietnamese village, each with a thatched roof, like the "Bana, Vietnam' figurine. A red and white barber pole stuck into the ground just outside one hut looked a little odd. The instructor said, "Gentlemen, what is unusual about this slide?" No one raised their hand. There had to be others that thought the barber pole was unusual for Vietnam but no one said anything.

The instructor said, "Look at this slide. What is unusual, gentlemen?" He asked one more time and then blew up, "YOU ARE A BUNCH OF IGNORANT SONS-OF-BITCHES WHO ARE GOING TO GET YOUR ASSES BLOWN OFF THE FIRST DAY YOU'RE IN VIETNAM, AND YOU WILL BE IN VIETNAM!"

The red and white pole, he explained, was not a barber pole but a pole painted red and white for easy vision and used with another pole just like it to calibrate mortar rounds when firing at the enemy. "Gentlemen," he said, "this village is obviously full of VC."

Any Marine in that Recon class who spoke up about the red and white barber poll being unusual could have had a direct path to a reconnaissance unit and snuck through the jungle near a village "full of VC." Most Marines would have loved that, to spy like what the students and teachers at Hoa My School thought I did. But no one spoke up.

I wrapped the box of figurines in a T shirt. I counted the rolls of film I took on this trip and made sure they were in my camera bag for the plane. I did have a picture of Miss Xuan but I didn't give it to the Saigon government, I kept it for myself.

The one large and one medium suitcase sat in the corner. Locked. My camera bag and carry-on pack sat on top of them. I put a tea bag in the teapot and poured hot water from the hotel thermos and sat down to relax. The blue fishing fleet returned to the docks on the River Han. The five peaks of Marble Mountain were visible in the distance and my tea was hot and musky. I opened the flap on my carry-on backpack to check my passport.

It was not there. I set the backpack on the bed and opened the secret compartment where I kept important documents. The passport wasn't there either. The desk drawer was empty except for brochures and some stationery. My bed stand drawer was empty. My passport was in a safe place, I put it somewhere that would be safe because I needed it to board the plane.

There was nothing under the bed. I re-checked the papers in the desk drawer. It wasn't in the closet or in any of my pockets so I hoisted my large suitcase onto the bed again and checked the outside pockets. Not there. I unlocked the suitcase and checked the small compartments. I rummaged through the clothes. Nothing. I locked the suitcase and set it back in the corner.

I brought up my medium sized suitcase and unlocked it to check all the pockets. I took out a few of the clothes. It was not there. I locked it again and set it on top of the large suitcase.

Miss Hong had put it in the hotel safe for a period of time with my extra money and the pearl bracelet. I took the passport out of the safe at one point. *Or did I? My valuables and money are here. The passport must be in the safe.*

I went down to the desk to check if, for some reason, my passport was left in the safe. No, not there. Back in my room I checked the camera case and my backpack. No passport.

The phone rang. *Aha! Miss Hong found it.* No. It was a teacher. *Which teacher? One from Hoa Minh School?* Miss Hong said he wanted to see Mr. Hoan's daughter, Miss Hao. Mr. Hoan told me Miss Hao would stop by my hotel to drop off some Vietnamese coffee for me to take home. She hadn't arrived and this man wanted to visit her. I did not understand who he was. I did not understand his name nor did I understand where we met, so I politely said I was busy and had to get back to my work. I hung up the phone and continued to look for my passport.

My large suitcase went back up on the bed. I unlocked the suitcase again and heard a knock at the door. The Bell Captain stood there with Mr. Chot, the English teacher from Mr. Son's school.

"Hello Mr. Brian. I am Mr. Chot. Friend of Mr. Son. I came to see Miss Hao."

"I am very sorry. I apologize for not recognizing you on the phone." I remembered, Mr. Chot taught English at Mr. Son's school.

"That is no problem, Mr. Brian. I understand. I will wait for Miss Hao."

"Okay," I said. "I'm sorry, I'm looking for a very important paper. I must look in my suitcase."

"Yes, yes," he said. "I will not bother."

I opened the outside pockets of the suitcase. Nothing again. I opened the main compartment and took out some presents, books, clothes. "No passport," I said.

"Please let me help you look for your passport, Mr. Brian."

I sat down at the desk. "Please sit down, Mr. Chot. No, thank you. That is not necessary. I just need to search both my suitcases for a second time. I'm sure the passport is in one of them." Another knock at the door, it was Mr. Hoan's daughter, Miss Hao.

"*Chao co,* Miss Hao. Please come in."

Mr. Chot said, "Miss Hao gives you this Vietnamese coffee."

"*Cam on.*"

Miss Hao and Mr. Chot excused themselves and left the room. Mr. Chot did not want to "see" Miss Hao, Mr. Son had asked him to come over to translate for her. Mr. Chot drove all the way over to my hotel from China Beach just to translate one sentence for Miss Hao. And yes, Miss Hao would have been embarrassed not to speak English and yes, I was not good company. But then, I was an American.

I poked around in the large suitcase, took out the presents, and did the same with the medium suitcase—but still no passport.

I called the airport to check if I could use a copy of my passport to board the plane. There was a message in English that said, "If you would like to speak to an airport agent, please press zero now." I pressed "0" and heard, "If you would like to speak to an airport agent, please press zero now."

I hung up the phone and it rang almost immediately. It was Mr. Hoan. "My daughter, Miss Hao, said you are upset and have lost your passport. You must call police in this case."

"Thank you, Mr. Hoan. I will call you when I find my passport."

I knew I had put the passport in a safe place. I took everything out of my carry-on backpack again. I opened the suitcases for a third time and took everything out this time. I opened my dirty clothes bag and picked up the waist pouch I used on the flight over here. Something inside the center pocket of my waist pouch felt hard, about the size of a passport. I unzipped the pocket. And there, with its shiny gold emblem on a blue cover, my passport sat in a safe place!

I took it out and held it in my hand, all the pages intact, my picture on page two; everything still in order, a bit wrinkled but still in order.

Ah, I remember. Yes. I put the passport in the waist pouch because I knew I would wear it on the plane. But later I decided not to wear it on the way home. It was uncomfortable and I had no valuables or money to take home. So, it went in with the dirty clothes. The passport tucked inside the middle pocket.

I stretched out my legs, held on to my passport, and took a deep breath, 9:30 p.m. I laughed with my crinkled blue passport in hand and took a sip of cold tea.

THIRTY-EIGHT

The CO's Cerlist, 1967

"The best thing for being sad," replied Merlin, beginning to puff and blow, "is to learn something."

—From *The Once and Future King*, T.H. White

IN MID-MARCH 1967, Lieutenant Colonel Hunter's Cerlist vehicle was finally back on-line and running smoothly. The morning after we had it fixed I drove it up from the motor pool and parked below the supply building next to the generator shed and walked along the wooden planks toward the colonel's office with a smile on my face.

"Is my vehicle running yet?" the colonel said in a matter-of-fact, "checked-off that item," tone. An obligatory comment made at the start of every meeting.

"Yes, sir," I said. "Up and running and parked over by the generator shed."

There was a hush in the room. The officers looked up from their notes and stuck their necks out like turtles and craned their heads first toward me and then over to Lieutenant Colonel Hunter. The officers clapped their hands and hollered. Colonel Hunter beamed. "That's a good job, Lieutenant Biggs. How many weeks has it been?"

"It's been a while, sir. But it's fixed. Here are the keys."

After the meeting Sergeant Stuck picked me up and drove me back to the motor pool. When I arrived at my office the dispatcher said, "Lieutenant Tygart's on the horn, sir."

"Hello, Len," I said.

"Brian, you need to come on up to supply. I've got something to show you."

When I drove up, Len Tygart was outside the supply Butler building.

"Hi Len, wha-da-ya-got?"

He walked over to the edge of the road and looked down the hill. A gentle slope ran down to the area above the old French Fort. The Cerlist vehicle was in elephant grass tilted on its side.

The scene troubled me. It was like the appearance, in a dream, of disjointed and distorted bits of random incidents from one's past, diluted, morphed, and dropped into a grotesque image that only lasts a millisecond. But this image stayed.

There it sat. The newly repaired Cerlist vehicle twenty meters down a rocky embankment, rolled over in the elephant grass.

"What happened?"

"Well," Len Tygart began, "I was walking back from the colonel's meeting on that wooden walkway just coming up past the shower when, out of the corner of my eye, I notice the Cerlist roll back a few inches. I kept on walking but pretty soon the vehicle just started rolling down that incline away from the generator shed toward the main road. I ran to the vehicle and got the door open but it was gaining so much speed that I couldn't get inside and I couldn't reach the brake. So I let go of the door and the old Cerlist rolled across the road and over the embankment and ended up right there just as you see it."

I shook my head, "I hope it doesn't go back on deadline."

But it of course it did. Body work. Sprung door hinges. Front tire blown. Canopy bent out of shape. Oil pan broken.

My job now was to inform Lieutenant Colonel Hunter and have the vehicle winched up the embankment and towed to the shop. The Cerlist went off-line again. Down. Parts on order. Hence, his comment on my Fitness Report at the end of my tour of duty in Vietnam:

Lt. Biggs is a sincere, well-mannered individual. He was not as effective as the MTO [Motor Transport Officer] where organizing and supervisory ability as well as technical knowledge are necessary as he has been in his Legal and Civic Action roles where there is more interpersonal action involved. He relates well with people and conveys a genuine interest in them thereby making him effective in this type of assignment. His growth potential as a Marine Officer is about average.

—H. Hunter, Jr., Lt. Colonel, Commanding Officer, MASS-2

THIRTY-NINE

Hanh Quyen and Hanh Thy

A friend is a gift you give yourself.
—Author unknown

A FTER I WENT down to the front desk to tell Miss Hong I found my passport, I called Mr. Hoan and told him. He told me it was good to have found the passport, and just as he hung up I heard another knock on my door. Hanh Quyen and her younger sister, Hanh Thy, stood in the doorway with a big smile on their faces.

"Come in. Sit down. How are you? It is good to see you."

The two young women walked into my room. "We have a present for you, Mr. Brian."

They each sat at the foot of the bed and Young Thy had to scooch up on the bed so she wouldn't fall off.

Hanh Quyen handed me a present wrapped in white tissue paper. "For you, Mr. Brian."

I unwrapped a Vietnamese doll about eighteen inches high that portrayed a young woman in a white *ao dai*, white slacks, and white shoes. The doll, made of rubber the color of Vietnamese skin, wore a conical hat on her head that covered her long, black hair. "*Cam on.* She is beautiful."

Earlier in the week I asked Hanh Quyen what she wore to school. When she said she wore the white *ao dai* uniform I told her I would like to see her in her dress. She waited for me one morning dressed for school in her *ao dai* but I didn't arrive at her house until late that day. Hanh Quyen had to leave before I arrived. She was sad I was not able to see her in the *ao dai* so she gave me the doll.

She also gave me an intricate white origami swan and young Thy gave me two boxes of Vietnamese candy and dried papaya. "*Cam on.* These gifts are wonderful."

When it was time for the sisters to leave, Hanh Quyen's lower eyelids puffed up with tears.

"Why are you sad?" I said.

"I don't want you to go."

Hanh Thy looked at me and smiled and leaned her head on her sister's shoulder.

"I will be back. I will write you both and you can write me."

Hanh Quyen raised her head and tears rolled down her cheeks. "My mom cannot go to the airport tomorrow to see you leave because she cries more than I do. But she made this tape for you tonight." Hanh Quyen reached into the purple bag I brought her from the States and handed me a miniature cassette tape. I forgot that I had asked Mrs. Hanh for a story about Miss Xuan yesterday when we visited the home of Mr. Chau.

"She has a message for you on this tape," Hanh Quyen said.

I handed her a tissue from the desk and held her hand. Hanh Quyen wiped the tears away and looked at her sister, "We must go now."

As they gathered up their belongings I thought about asking Hanh Quyen to translate her mother's words but it was not a good time. Tears were still on her cheek. I didn't know what to say. I got all wobbly with her crying.

We walked down the stairs to the lobby and out to the front porch to say goodbye. I hugged both of them. They didn't mind the hug.

FORTY

Eric Barnes, 1967

I hear the train a comin' / It's rollin' round the bend
And I ain't seen the sunshine / Since I don't know when
I'm stuck in Southeast Asia / And time keeps draggin' on
But that train keeps a-rollin' / On down to old Quang Nam.

—From *Folsom Prison Blues*, Johnny Cash
(With modifications by Eric Barnes)

I N EARLY APRIL 1967 I picked up my mail, one letter from Colleen, and sat at my desk. The sun had just dropped behind the hills to give a golden tone to the clouds that hung in the Western sky. A warm breeze blew through the window screen as I opened Colleen's envelope with my miniature Mameluke sword letter opener. It was an exact replica of the real Mameluke sword every Marine Corps officer must purchase when he or she is commissioned. The letter opener is just eight-and-a-half inches long with a gold drag on the bottom of the scabbard and two gold rings for a tiny, black leather strap.

The letter, written in Colleen's cursive script, was on heavy brown paper. Each line ran straight across the page.

Dearest Brian,
I heard from Noreen Barnes yesterday and I'm

*very sorry to write that on March 25th Eric was killed
on a patrol.*

That sentence numbed my world. Clouds above the hills to the
west swirled in the sunset that Eric and I watched just five weeks
ago. I read the rest of the letter in the shadowed light. Colleen
wrote careful phrases. Hand written words about Eric Barnes,
"...a wonderful father. I know you will miss him as much as I
will." Colleen wrote words of friendship and humor, of love and
life, and death.

The twilight faded from partial light to black as I sat at my desk
and smelled the must of damp wood on my desktop, damp from
the humidity. It smelled like the blue mold that forms under a
damp cardboard box. The hills across the valley turned from sil-
houettes against the solitude of night to just the black of night.

Eric did not call or stop by after he returned from Hawaii and there
would be no other visits from Eric Barnes. Not in Vietnam, not back
in the States. Not years later when our children were grown.

At twenty-five years of age, only my grandfather and grandmother had died. None of my friends. No cousins, at least none
of the ones I knew. No teachers, coaches or principals, and up to
that point, no Marines. Eric Barnes was gone and I could not
imagine all of the implications.

My hooch was empty. Quiet. Everyone was either on duty or
at Club Vagabond. No drilling or quarry explosions. The darkness closed in on the valley below my hooch. The twenty-five
watt light bulb in my closet created a fuzz of light through the
crack in the door but I could barely see Colleen's brown envelope
on my desk or the letter in my hand. A pain on my left side felt
like a fist-sized branding iron sliced inside the stomach lining.
Tears wanted out of my eyes but couldn't find their way. Eric
had just sang in our club.

The paper of Colleen's letter stuck to my hands from sweat

and I finally folded it the way it came and slid it back into the envelope. My fingers ran back and forth across the slit in the envelope to seal the opening made by my miniature Mameluke sword letter opener but the slit of course wouldn't seal. If it could seal, I thought, maybe the news would be different, ordinary news about Charlie or Kaye.

Eric helped me with my daughter Kaye's first bicycle. We laughed ourselves silly at how complicated we made the simple task of attaching training wheels. He reassured Kaye when she was tentative about the new experience of riding a bike. He told me not to worry after Kaye crashed into the garbage cans because I forgot to tell her how to use the brakes.

On those hot August nights when Eric sang on our screened-in North Carolina porch, neighbors and friends clapped and shouted for more. He said the bugs clung thick to the screen just to hear him sing.

Eric Barnes worked hard to be number one on the "O" course or rifle range and personified *Semper Fidelis*. He made captain shortly before he died. Many of us who graduated from Basic School in June of 1965 were still first lieutenants.

Two weeks after I received the news of Eric's death, John Danko stopped by to visit. John Danko was also in Captain Hancock's Basic School platoon and stationed with Eric and me in North Carolina. He also went on a few patrols in Eric's outfit in Vietnam.

"John, you wanna go down to the club for a beer?"

"Yeah."

I grabbed the letter that Colleen wrote and brought it to the club. "I got a letter from my wife a couple weeks ago when she heard from Noreen Barnes. Told me about Eric."

"Yeah. Some men in his company came by my outfit to tell me about him. That kind of news, that's the kind of news that makes it...that news makes it hard." John Danko came from Tennessee and talked with a slow, melodic lilt. His "hard" stretched into two syllables, "haw-ured," and became a softer word. John Danko was a stocky man. Strong with big shoulders. He stared at me with deep set eyes and rolled his thin lips between his teeth. "That's the kind of news that makes this hard."

"It is," I said.

"That fool could run circles around all of us on the obstacle course. And sing." John Danko leaned back on his chair. "Whewie! He could sing like a bird. Those Johnny Cash songs were as good as Johnny Cash. And the parties in Lejeune were sumthin' else."

Hoa set two glasses of beer on our table and John Danko nodded and said, "*Cam on.*"

"He was fun at those parties," I said. "I never laughed so hard. The stuff he said and did was crazy."

John said, "You remember at the end of my weddin' when you guys pulled your swords out for Ina and me to walk under?"

"Yeah."

"And the guy next to you, Corbett I think it was, pulled his sword out of the scabbard and accidently stabbed Jim Greene in the arm?"

"I remember that. You and I looked at each other and didn't know whether to laugh or call a medic."

"Yeah, well Barnes got to snickerin' down there just off the porch. I thought he was gonna split a gut. We had good times in Lejeune."

"Good times." I finished my beer. "John, did you hear how Eric died?" I opened the letter from Colleen and looked at the sentence about Eric's death. "I haven't heard anything except what Colleen wrote in this letter: 'Eric was killed on a patrol.' I know he was with 1/26."

"He transferred out of 1/26 in January. Went over to First Force Recon after he returned from R&R in Hawaii. He was on a patrol when he got killed. He and a sergeant were killed when they det-onated a mine that was booby-trapped. Hooked up to a home-made device of some kind. That patrol was to be his last patrol 'cause he'd made captain. That's about all I know."

John Danko picked up his glass of beer and watched the bub-bles rise to the foam on top. He held his glass up to the light like he hadn't ever noticed those bubbles before. "It's hard," he said to the glass.

"Here's to Eric Barnes," I said.

"To Eric Barnes. He was a real friend. Those two Marines from his unit told me Eric was loved and admired by his men. I can believe that. What a loss."

FORTY-ONE

Co Hong's Translation, 2001

[Mr. Brian] we will be sad tomorrow. It may take a long time for us to get back the normal atmosphere that we had before you came.

—Mrs. Hanh

C O HONG READ a book at her desk since the hotel lobby was empty.

"I'm sorry about my passport mix-up," I said.

"It was good you found your passport, Mr. Bigg." She smiled. She looked fresh in her *ao dai* even though it was late at night. "It was nice for you to receive presents from the two girls."

"They are very special friends," I said. Miss Hong did not look busy behind the counter. "How much longer do you have to work?"

"I waited for my fellow worker to come in but the one who was supposed to work does not come in. So, I called another worker. He said he cannot come because of his family. So, I stay even though I arrived early this morning. And there is not much to do at this time of night. So, I study my Chinese lesson."

"You are learning to speak Chinese?"

"Yes, we have many Chinese guests at the hotel."

"Could you translate a small tape recording for me? The mother of the two girls sent me tape tonight and it's in Vietnamese."

"Yes, Mr. Bigg, I would be happy to do this for you."

I put Mrs. Hanh's tape in my small recorder and handed it to Miss Hong.

She turned it on and listened to several sentences. Then said, "She say you are leaving Vietnam tomorrow and she wants to tell you something. She says she wishes you and your family have good health and good luck."

Miss Hong listens to more of the tape. Translating, she related the following from Mrs. Hanh:

Honestly. My father, teacher Hoan, told you, Mr. Brian, that you might be the person who took pictures of Miss Xuan. In fact, no one could blame you about what you have done because your responsibility was to do so when you were in Vietnam at that time. You should not be sad about this because the problem was resolved.

I wrote the words down as fast as I could. Miss Hong looked at me and smiled while Mrs. Hanh's voice continued on my recorder. Miss Hong continued:

One of Miss Xuan's relatives told me long ago that Miss Xuan was a person who was suspected to be Viet Cong. There was a picture of her in her files. After that, there was an event before she was arrested. Teacher Hoan gave her a ride to hide in an area of people who revolted from the country.

I saw her in 1975. At this moment, she was member working for Communism. She told me stories about the time she had to leave our city. She had to live on the mountain. She had to live in a place where lack of living supplies and conditions. The more I listened to what she told, the more I loved her. Miss Xuan did not work anymore because she did not feel well.

Miss Hong played the rest of the tape. She looked at the recorder on her desk like it was a person talking to her and continued translating:

My daughters, Hanh Dung, Hanh Quyen, Hanh Thy, love you and consider you like a member in our family. Hanh Quyen wants to be your spiritual daughter. We are willing to do that. It will be very sad to say goodbye to you tomorrow. Hanh Quyen considers you as a friend.

Tomorrow, Hanh Quyen, Hanh Dung, and Hanh Thy will go to school, so they cannot accompany you to the airport. We will be sad tomorrow. It may take a long time for us to get back the normal atmosphere that we had before you came. I wish that you, your wife, and your children will have a chance to visit Vietnam. We would be glad to welcome all of you.

FORTY-TWO

The New Addition, 1967

so much depends
upon

a red wheel
barrow

glazed with rain
water

beside the white
chickens.

—"The Red Wheelbarrow," William Carlos Williams

B Y EARLY MAY, 1967, we had the foundation poured for the new classrooms and walls were framed but no roof yet. I stood under the porch of the main building to watch the crew of U.S. Marines and Vietnamese work together in the light rain.

Future and past are disguised in the maze of framed up two-by-four walls. One could see a window in the front and back of each classroom, recognized by the open space in the two-by-fours and the thick header on top of that opening. A doorway, also recognizable on the nascent structure, stood at the center of each classroom's front wall. The porch, covered with specks of sand and miscellaneous tools, had two steps down to the playground.

Concrete forms, removed from the foundation and grayed with dried concrete, lay on the ground and at the far end of the building, near Highway 1. A lone shovel poked up from a pile of dirt near an empty wheelbarrow where chickens pecked at playground pebbles.

"Your project is well on the way to completion," I said to Mr. Hoan.

Mr. Hoan looked at me and pushed his lips together for a moment. Then he said, "The day of starting work on these classrooms, you said to me, 'If you help to carry, you will get used to it.' I felt very ashamed about what you said."

"I did not mean to..."

Mr. Hoan put his hand on my arm, "I must tell you. What you say to me is true. After that time, I wrote an article to our teachers." His eyebrows came together to force some forehead wrinkles.

"I told the story of what you said to me, about working for our school. In this article, I called upon teachers for a need to work and to 'train' and to 'educate' students to love work. We will learn to be used to doing this type of work."

I didn't know what to say to Mr. Hoan. This moved me almost to tears. I was sorry for telling him he needed to "get used to doing work." But maybe it helped him and his fellow teachers; helped them by giving an example to the students. I hoped that was it.

With his hand still on my arm, I put my hand on his and said, "Well, if your students learn to love work, physical labor, learn it from the example you and your fellow teachers show them, I think that is a good sign, Mr. Hoan."

FORTY-THREE

My Last Day, 2001

You've changed me forever. And I'll never forget you.
—From *The Elite*, Kiera Cass

T HE SOUND OF a fog horn woke me early on my last day in Vietnam. I was about to begin the journey home to Portland, Oregon. What I thought was a fog horn was actually a blast from the large cargo ship docked across from my hotel. I sat down to breakfast on the top floor of the hotel just in time to see the VINASHIP pull away from the dock and sail straight down the River Han toward the Bay of Danang.

Small fishing boats sped from the huge ship's path and bounced up and down in its wake. The VINASHIP sailed down river toward Monkey Mountain and took a hard left at the river's mouth to enter the Bay of Danang. Once in the bay it turned right and sailed straight out to the South China Sea.

Mr. Thang arrived at 7:00 a.m. to make sure I had a ride to the airport but the hotel provided a taxi at no charge. When I arrived at the airport both Mr. Hoan and Mr. Thang were standing on the sidewalk.

Mr. Hoan said, "Your wife, Vicki, must come with you next time you visit Vietnam."

"She would like to come. Yes, we will see if that is possible. Thank you for everything. It was a wonderful visit with your family."

Mr. Hoan held out a small manila envelope. "A letter for you, Mr. Brian."

"Thank you." I took the envelope and saw my name on the front, *Mr. Brian*, written in Mr. Hoan's handwriting. I put it in my carry on backpack.

Mr. Thang and I shook hands and he smiled that huge smile. "*Cam on* for driving me all around Danang, I appreciate that," I said.

Mr. Hoan and Mr. Thang could not enter the airport, it was October 2001, just seven weeks after 9/11, so they watched from the window next to the terminal door. I put my luggage on the conveyor belt to be scanned and watched an attendant lift one of my suitcases off the belt. Two bottles of *nuoc mam* showed up on the x-ray screen. Fish sauce for my sons Charlie and Andrew, both chefs in Portland. The bottles were confiscated.

I walked up to the attendant at the conveyor belt and pointed to the terminal door. "May I take the bottles to my friends standing at the window?" Mr. Hoan stood with his hands pressed to the glass and cupped around his eyes.

The attendant motioned toward the door and nodded her head. I picked up the two bottles, "Mr. Hoan, they won't let me take these on the plane. Here, you have them." We shook hands again. "Goodbye. Give one to Mr. Thang."

I walked toward the passenger waiting area with my carry on luggage. Mr. Hoan and Mr. Thang were still at the window. Mr. Thang held the two bottles in his hands and Mr. Hoan's eyes were still pressed to the glass with his hands cupped around them. I waved. He raised his right hand and gave it a slight twist.

FORTY-FOUR

My Last Class, 1967

Food is our common ground, a universal experience.
—James Beard

O N MY LAST class, Mr. Hoan helped me pass out the stories written in English by the teachers. "Miss Xuan is not in class today?" I said.

"She is not able to come to class." Said Mr. Hoan.

"Will she be here later?"

"Miss Xuan cannot be here today."

"Well," I said, "I can drive down tomorrow to say goodbye and give her this paper." Miss Xuan's paper, written about a Vietnamese king named Quang Trung, received a B+. She told the story of a war with China in 1789. China sent two-hundred thousand troops into Northern Vietnam. The Vietnamese king led an army of one-hundred thousand soldiers and two hundred elephants from Hue to Hanoi. In three days, King Quang Trung killed "…most enemy generals with their soldiers and the rest ran away." I put Miss Xuan's paper in my folder.

After the day's lesson I told my friends, "Teaching this class has been rewarding for me. I have learned a lot and I know you have improved your English. You have been good students and have worked hard. *Cam on.* I am returning to the United States tomorrow and I wish all of you the best."

Then Mr. Hoan stood up straight and said with almost a scowl of seriousness, "Lieutenant Brian, the others in class, Mr. An, Mr. Me, Mr. Thang, Miss Cam Tu, Miss Xuan, and me, say we enjoy your teaching English to us. And we learn from you how to speak English."

"*Cam on.*"

"Lieutenant Brian, we want you to enjoy some lunch with us."

"Now?"

"Yes."

"I would love lunch." It was 5:00 p.m. and time for dinner but I could not miss this meal.

Mr. Hoan took me in to the classroom next door. The smell of spicy soup filled the room when I walked in but this aroma was different than the beef and pepper aroma of bun bo. This was more like the smell of barbecued chicken with lots of pepper and garlic. The classroom desks became tables set for lunch. Students brought out dishes of condiments: basil leaves, sliced green onions, bean sprouts, limes, and slices of hot green peppers. The familiar blackened pot sat in the middle of the desk with the lid off so steam floated into the classroom air.

"Please you sit down, Lieutenant Brian."

"*Cam on.*"

"We offer you *bun ga on* your last day of teaching at Hoa My School. *Bun ga* is chicken noodle soup."

"Ah, *cam on.*"

My bowl was filled with bun, chopped chives, and strips of cooked chicken. Miss Cam Tu poured the thick stock into my bowl and passed it down to me. There was a pepper and lemon aroma.

Mr. Hoan swatted at the flies around my bowl and said, "You squeeze lime into the bowl."

I did, and then I held my *dua* and spoon-holder spoon at the ready. The others added sprouts, leaves of basil, and hot green peppers to their bowl and I copied their actions. My mouth watered.

"Please, eat *bun ga*," said Mr. Hoan.

My *dua* dipped into the bowl and pinched a piece of chicken that had an unusual flavor. I could taste the oregano and basil but the other spices baffled me. "This is wonderful!"

"*Bun ga* is chicken noodle soup," Mr. Hoan said again.

I used the spoon-holder spoon to scoop up some broth. It had the same flavor as the chicken, a buttery flavor and was better than the beef noodle soup. "This is great soup. *Cam on.*"

After the meal, Mr. Hoan poured tea, a dark tea, into those cups without handles. Mr. Hoan handed me a small red and yellow can with a white ribbon around it. "This is for you from Miss Xuan. She wants you to remember her and to remember Hoa My School."

"*Cam on.*" A Vietnamese woman on the can washed clothes in a lake and Vietnamese words printed on one side of the can indicated a Danang address.

"This is a gift of tea," Mr. Hoan said. "*Xuong Che.* Vietnamese tea."

"Thank you. Please tell Miss Xuan thank you for me." I put the can of tea in my box of books and papers.

Mr. Hoan motioned for me to walk down the front steps to the schoolyard. Children giggled on the teeter-totters or squatted in that flat-footed position on the playground to play *O an Quan,* a game with a diagram of squares in the dirt.

The unfinished building stood to our left. Mr. Hoan raised his arm and pointed to the new building. "The new classrooms are almost complete."

"Yes." I said. "It will be nice for you to have the additional classrooms." A red tile roof covered the building and there were six pillars on the porch but the walls were still two-by-four studs.

The structure was weeks away from completion and my departure from Vietnam did not allow me to see it finished. "I'm sorry Miss Xuan could not be here today."

Mr. Hoan put his hand on my arm and held tight. He gave his hand a shake. "Lieutenant Brian, we enjoyed how much you taught us at Hoa My School. Thank you for your dedication to Hoa My School. Miss Xuan says this also."

I started to speak but a lump formed deep in my throat and stopped any sound from coming out or any saliva from going down. I put my hand to my nose and pretended to cough and waited for the lump to dissolve but it didn't. Mr. Hoan shook my arm again and after a while I was able to say, "*Cam on.*"

I set the box of books and papers on the new porch. "Mr. Hoan," I said, "it has been a wonderful experience for me. If I don't see Miss Xuan, please tell her how much I enjoyed my time here at your school. I will not forget this experience. Maybe I can return someday to visit you and Miss Xuan."

"Yes," Mr. Hoan said. "That would be good. We would like to see you again."

I took his hand and held it with both hands. "*Cam on* for the dinner of *bun ga.* It tasted delicious. Thank you for everything."

Mr. Hoan looked at me a long time with his hand in my grasp.

FORTY-FIVE

The Flight Home, 2001

Thank you very much for your interest about us,
who are your best friends. —Mr. Hoan

T HE MAN ON the plane next to me was from Australia. He spent a week with his relatives in Danang and told me that the economy in Vietnam was doing well. "Two point one billion dollars comes into Vietnam each year from the Viet Kieu (those Vietnamese living outside Vietnam.)" That was in 2001. The figure peaked at 7.2 billion U.S. dollars in 2008 and now it's leveled off to about 6.8 billion dollars a year.

Mr. Hoan's manila envelope sat on my lap and somewhere over the Pacific Ocean I decided to read it.

Dear Mr. Brian,

We do not mind that you were CIA and reported to Saigon police about the arrest of Miss Xuan. She must run to communist area and hide there. We absolutely did not blame you about that because it was the responsibility of a magnificent military man. You had to commit what your supervisor delivered to you. If we were upset or blamed you, we would not have been happy and welcome you when we heard you intended to go to Vietnam. We received gifts and

*letters you sent to us. We are very glad. I do not know what
to say but thank you very much for your interest about us,
who are your best friends.*

*Many unforgettable memories have been left when you
come to visit us. I hope that the years will pass quickly so
I'll see you again and your wife Vicki.*

Sincerely, Hoan

Mr. Hoan thought I was "a magnificent military man." I was
not a magnificent military man. Nor was I a spy. *How can he accept the fact that I spied on the teachers and students at Hoa My
School and then welcome me into his home as a trusted friend?*
Both Mr. Hoan and his daughter, Mrs. Hanh, said they didn't
blame me for turning a photo of Miss Xuan over to the Saigon
police. But Miss Xuan barely escaped arrest and needed a ride
from Mr. Hoan to a Viet Cong Base in the mountains. I could not
live with the knowledge that they thought I was responsible for
Miss Xuan's trouble with the Saigon police.

I read Mr. Hoan's letter again and one line stood out: "Many
unforgettable memories have been left when you come to visit."
That was very true, but Mr. Son still thought I was a spy who
worked for the CIA. They thanked me for my interest in them
who were my best friends. I would have to digest all this information and return to Vietnam. Or maybe I just needed to take
Phuc's advice: "Don't mourn for the past, nor worry about the
future, but live in the present moment."

FORTY-SIX

End of Tour, May 1967

I have seen the mysterious shores, the still water, the lands of brown nations, where a stealthy Nemesis lies in wait, pursues, overtakes so many of the conquering race, who are proud of their wisdom, of their knowledge, of their strength. But for me all the East is contained in that vision of my youth. It is all in that moment when I opened my young eyes on it. I came upon it from a tussle with the sea—and I was young—and I saw it looking at me. And that is all that is left of it! Only a moment. —From *Youth*, Joseph Conrad

O N THE DAY I left MASS-2, Sunday, 14 May 1967, it occurred to me that I may not see my friends from Hoa My School again. I sat for a long time at my empty desk. The closet was empty, my shelves were empty—ready for a new occupant. My sea bag sat in the corner with most of my gear. I would not go back to Hoa My School. Miss Xuan's paper on King Quang Trung was in the red Vietnamese lesson book, deep inside my sea bag. The larger items were shipped home: portable Royal typewriter, movie projector, editing equipment, books. I doled out, my other gear. Len Tygart, Scott Bannister, Leonard T. Clark, and Henry Lee all received something they could use in their hooches. Twelve months of accumulation: fans, light bulbs, extension cords, hot plate.

My jeep now sat in the motor pool waiting for the next motor transport officer. Sergeant Greene and Sergeant Wix had rotated back to the States months before.

Lieutenant Colonel Hunter walked around his desk to shake my hand. His white hair in a well-trimmed crew cut. "Good luck to you, Lieutenant Biggs."

As far as I know, his Cerlist vehicle never went back on line.

* * * *

The transient facility was a Quonset hut next to the tarmac. Quonset huts were half-round corrugated buildings, eighteen feet high at the peak, twenty feet across the front at ground level, and forty-eight feet long. They took their name from the town of Quonset, Rhode Island, where they were designed and produced at the beginning of World War II.

This one was filled with cots where Marines sat and read or slept or talked. F-4 Phantom jets took off every ten minutes. Two months earlier we sat on our hill and watched this airstrip take incoming from a VC mortar attack that killed eleven Americans. When I checked in, someone told me a Marine tried to take a grenade home from Vietnam to impress his girlfriend. It was hidden in his sea bag but they discovered it before he boarded the plane. It was not comforting for me to spend my last night in this Quonset hut.

Early in the morning of Monday, 15 May 1967, the sky was clear when we walked out to a commercial Boeing 707. A stewardess with blond hair that curved up at her shoulders stood at the top of the portable stairs. She had a white band wrapped around the top of her head and I could smell Tabu perfume when I passed her on the platform.

I sat in an aisle seat. It felt like ants were crawling inside my stomach. A smile formed on my lips. I was on the wrong side of the plane to see Danang but I could see houses and the intersection of Highway 1 and Dogpatch.

The pilot spoke to us. The engines started to whine. I smiled at the noise. Then chuckled. Dust swirled up behind the jet's engines. The plane pitched forward and started to roll toward the main runway. I nodded to the Marine next to me. When we were at the end of the runway facing the South China Sea I was tense. Please no malfunction, no engine problems. The plane sat on the runway. I saw Hill 327 out the window. My hands began to sweat.

My orders sat in an open manila folder on my lap. On the cover page of my orders a stamped black arrow pointed downward to *1st Lt Biggs B M* and my next duty station, the Marine Corps Base at Twentynine Palms, California.

The whine increased, the wings shook, and the plane started to move down the runway toward the open sea. As we moved down the runway, I could see the shacks in Dogpatch with their walls and roofs still spotted with Pepsi Cola, Budweiser, and Jim Beam signs. We gained speed as we rolled down the runway. We passed homes along Highway 1 and the large open hangers, and then the plane tilted upward, bumped, and thrust me back into my seat. I left the soil of Vietnam.

The pilot took off almost straight up and banked to the left. A strip of khaki-colored sand curved around the Bay of Danang and ended at the rocks below Hai Van Pass. I saw Highway 1 with trucks and motorbikes driving north and south, and then I caught a glimpse of Hoa My Elementary School just before we left Vietnam. My feet and legs helped lift the huge aircraft into the air until we leveled off over the South China Sea. Then I relaxed and melted into my seat.

FORTY-SEVEN

Second Trip to Vietnam, January 2004

Out from the plunging
orchard limbs, out of hoed rows,
away from the family taking an hour's ease in shade,
Turkey is the one who
walks toward you,
a tongue-tied stranger. Both hands
curved together in a bowl,
Turkey says, Here, share
tiny water-green pears, palest apricots,
that small hard village fruit
suited to rough going—Take these,
go smiling with a gift
resistant to bruise, sweet beyond
expectation or deserving.

—From *Blood Silk*, Paulann Petersen

Arrival

T HE PEOPLE THAT gathered next to the glass door of the Danang airport in 2004 wore sweaters and coats due to the cold January weather in Central Vietnam. I didn't bring a coat. My memory bank from 1966 did not contain the recollection of cold weather in Danang. Mr. Hoan appeared right away and I wrapped my hands around his and held tight. There were familiar faces around Mr. Hoan but my eyes landed on the dark and focused eyes of Miss Xuan. She now lived in Danang with the family of her brother, Mr. Phap.

She smiled, unmindful of her missing front teeth, and held out both hands to greet me. Her smooth complexion and black hair gave the impression of a much younger woman.

Hanh Quyen, Hanh Thy, and Hanh Dung, the three sisters, smiled and shook my hand and Hanh Quyen gave me a bouquet of red roses. "For my spirit father, she said."

I put my arm around Hanh Quyen and smiled, "My spirit daughter."

Mr. Hoan suggested we go to dinner and as we sat down he ordered a beer for me and Miss Xuan and himself and all the others around the table. "We must celebrate Mr. Brian's arrival for the Tet Celebration," he said in perfect English.

Ancestors

On my first morning, Mr. Hoan drove me to the gravesite of his daughter, Miss Hoai, the teacher who died of cancer at the age of thirty-one. Because of the Tet holiday Highway 1 was crowded with all manner of transportation. Bicycles, motorbikes, cyclos, taxis, and trucks vied for space on the narrow lanes.

We turned off Highway 1 onto a road that ended in a field covered with sepulchers: small ones, large ones, new ones painted white, and old ones yellowed and covered in black mold. They were all above ground. Some had headstones attached to the vault, some were only a blackened stucco box, and a few were elaborate structures that looked like miniature pagodas.

Mr. Hoan parked in the grass next to a row of vaults, each the size of a small child, and his family drove up on their motorbikes or piled out of a taxi. Two cows lay in the grass and worked their jaws on a second helping of cud while one bull stood in the corner of the cemetery and stared at our commotion.

I could see the MASS-2 headquarters area on the hill less than two kilometers away from this ancient graveyard but during the war I did not know it existed. Mr. Hoan's daughters and granddaughters moved everything from the taxi to Miss Hoai's marble sepulcher: plastic bags filled with envelopes and paper money, jars of cut flowers, and several objects that looked like Mexican piñatas.

Miss Hoai's vault stood on a marble slab with swirls of tan and brown. The headstone stood in front of the sepulcher with her name, the name of her parents, the year she was born, 1968, and the date she died, December 21, 1999.

Dung pulled weeds around her aunt's grave and Hanh Quyen put a jar of pink gladiolas to the right of the headstone and placed a jar of the yellow flowered *cay mai* branches to the left. Then both sisters took envelopes and paper money out of the plastic bags and set them next the gravestone. Mr. Hoan's daughter, Mrs. Hang, placed joss sticks into a ceramic vase full of sand and lit about half of them.

Mrs. Hang threw candy and confetti onto the grass around the grave, then picked up a bundle of the burning incense and stood facing her sister's headstone. She held the sticks in her hands, pressed flat together in front of her face, and bowed her head to pray. Smoke drifted up from the incense.

When Mrs. Hang finished her prayer, she offered the joss sticks to me. I was honored to be included in this ceremony and stood in front of the headstone, as Mrs. Hang had done, and placed my hands flat together in front of my face with the incense pointed up and burning. I told Miss Hoai that I was sorry I did not meet her, that her family was special to me, that she must have been a special person and a good teacher, and it was an honor for me to be at her gravesite on this eve of Tet.

Like the elephant who visits the burial grounds of loved ones and spends time touching the bones with its trunk and moving the earth around as if to reminisce about the life they had together, the Vietnamese converged on their cemeteries with above-ground sepulchers to spend time with their loved ones and give them letters and speak to them in full anticipation of communication.

Miss Hao, another daughter of Mr. Hoan, also prayed in front of her sister's grave, and then she and Dung took the rest of the paper from the plastic bags. The "piñatas" were actually a collection of colorful hats and boxes wrapped like Christmas presents. They moved all the paper items away from the grave and placed them in two piles—all the poems written to Miss Hoai, all the paper money, letters, hats, boxes, and booklets— and set them on fire. The paper flared up and burned and then smoldered for a long time. Miss Hao and Hanh Dung pushed and poked at the charred piles of paper so they could flare up again and burn.

All the epistles and money now ashes, blackened and weightless, floated up to the mountain, up to MASS-2 and the location of my old hooch. I thought of my work with Mr. Hoan during the war and how our friendship developed over that period of twelve months. The decision to go back to Vietnam and renew that friendship, and to be included in family gatherings and celebrations as if I were a member, gave me, like the birth of a child, a new universe to explore and enjoy and love.

Fireworks

On the eve of Tet, Hanh Quyen and her younger sister, Hanh Thy, rang my doorbell at 10:30 p.m. and headed straight for the balcony. They announced it was a perfect place to watch the fireworks. My hotel room faced the River Han Bridge and did provide the perfect spot for viewing, but I wasn't sure if I could stay awake that long. Besides, it was cold and windy on my balcony. But Hanh Quyen assured me it was a "perfect watching place."

The bridge, lit up with its strings of lights that made it look like a golden pyramid, closed down for the night so people of all ages could pack the pavement from railing to railing. The revelers shouted and whooped and hugged and looked down at the river. We came back inside and talked. Hanh Thy, now in the seventh grade, lay on my bed and practiced English: "How are you, Mr. Brian? Do you go to work today? Is your home on a block? Is your meal on the table?"

Before long Hanh Thy fell sound asleep so Hanh Quyen and I talked about her year in college, her classes, and if my corrections on her English papers helped her with the language. Hanh Quyen's cell phone rang an odd clatter of bells and chimes, a Beatles song maybe. "Ah LOW," she said. It surprised me to hear an almost English greeting, but it was actually the French word, *allo* used for answering the phone. A friend wanted Hanh Quyen to pick her up and bring her over to my balcony to watch the midnight fireworks display.

As Hanh Quyen put on her coat and gathered up her purse she said that her college year went well and her grades were very good.

The Beatles song again. "Allo." Her friend could not come. Hanh Quyen told me she moved into her grandfather's home because he had an extra room. She enjoyed living next door to her cousins, Bia and Bo.

My eyelids drooped in a half-sleep but the Beatles song woke me up. "Allo." Her sister, Hanh Dung, asked to be picked up so she could view the fireworks from my balcony. Hanh Quyen left and I sat down with a book and read the same word a dozen times before I gave up and dozed in my chair while young Hanh Thy slept on my bed.

At a quarter to twelve Hanh Quyen and her sister arrived. Hanh Dung, always full of energy, yelled, "Hello, Mr. Brian! We come to your balcony to watch the fireworks." She tickled her sister's feet, "Thy, wake up, it is almost time for the Tet celebration." Hanh Thy opened one eye, looked at her sister, and wiggled her feet away from the annoying tickle. Hanh Quyen, Hanh Dung, and I went out to the balcony. Hanh Thy struggled to her feet and joined us just in time.

The city of Danang put on a fireworks display like no other I have seen. There were "oohs" and "ahs" from the crowd on the bridge throughout the half-hour show and when the fireworks climaxed with multiple bursts of blue, red, and phosphorescent white circles that exploded into stars that burst again into dots that whistled and darted about the night sky in a mad flight to oblivion, the crowd erupted with cheers and applause. The cannons were loud and the air was foul but the crowd loved it. They cheered again when the bright sky finally faded to a gray cloud of smoke illuminated only by the lights that resembled a golden pyramid.

The Actual Day of Tet, The Year of the Monkey

On the morning of Tet, the Year of the Monkey, I took a taxi to Mrs. Hanh's home and arrived at 7:00 a.m. so I could be the first visitor of the New Year. Hanh Quyen asked me to do this since the first person who visits the home on New Year's Day gives influence or their character to that family for the coming year.

It was also customary to bring gifts. I brought the almond flavored *thang long* with its pink skin and green dragon-like spikes that gave it the nickname "Dragon Fruit." The fruit of *thang long* is white and dotted with black sesame-like seeds that reminded me of a tick. A bite of *thang long* provided a cool sensation with a sugar burst from each crunch of the tiny tick seeds.

I also brought some of the small bananas for Mr. Hoan's altar honoring Miss Hoai, a bottle of wine, and several red envelopes called *li xi* (lee see). These red envelopes, a little larger than a driver's license and decorated with gold writing, are filled with Vietnamese coins and given to children at Tet.

Mrs. Hanh stood in her open doorway and smiled when I walked up. Her daughters, Hanh Dung, Hanh Quyen, and Hanh Thy, came running downstairs and I gave them their red envelopes. They huddled in a corner to peek inside.

Mrs. Hanh poured my tea and offered cookies. An older woman in sandals, black pajamas, a large sweater, and a scarf over her head walked past the open front door. Her wrinkled face, stooped shoulders, and a thick, brown cigarette between her lips gave me the impression of a homeless person who begged for money. She walked past the wide doorway and stopped to look at the front of Mrs. Hanh's home for a moment. Then she turned back and walked up to where we sat. She could see that I was an American, I thought, and she'll ask me for money.

She spoke to Mrs. Hanh for several minutes. They shared some story about an animal and they both laughed out loud. Then the woman smiled a toothless smile, nodded at me, and continued on her way.

"What did the woman say to your mother?" I asked.

Hanh Dung explained: "The woman said she saw my mother's monkey at the zoo. She was worried for many days when she did not see this monkey outside our home. But she was happy when she saw the monkey at the zoo. That was the story she told my mom. My mother must give our monkey to the zoo because we can no longer keep him."

"How did the woman know it was your mother's monkey?"

"My mother's monkey has only one hand."

After my visit with Mrs. Hanh, Hanh Quyen drove me to the home of Mr. Hoan and told me to walk in the open front door. *You will be the first person to visit in the New Year and that is important.*

When I walked through the open front door of Mr. Hoan's home both he and his wife stood up from their wooden bench, the love seat, and greeted me. I asked how they were and they said they were "normal." Mrs. Co poured tea and I told Mr. Hoan about the fireworks show the night before and how his granddaughters watched from my balcony.

He knew about the fireworks show: "Yes, our granddaughter told us this." And Mr. Hoan told me he was glad I was the first guest in his home for the New Year. There was a *cay mai* tree in the corner of the room filled with yellow blossoms. I asked about the kumquat tree and Mr. Hoan showed me its place in the dining room. The *cay mai* and kumquat trees are brought into the Vietnamese homes in a pot during Tet and the *cay mai* tree is decorated like our Christmas tree is decorated.

"Mr. Hoan," I said. "I want you to know that I did not turn a photo of Miss Xuan over to the Saigon Government."

"That is okay, Mr. Brian, we don't worry about that. That is long past and forgotten. This is a time of celebration and we don't worry about that at this time."

Mr. Hoan had already told me the Vietnamese never talk about business or serious matters when they first greet each other. There is a long period of pleasantries and insignificant stories with tea before anything serious can be discussed.

Why can't I let that business go, I wondered. It was a mistake and rude, especially on the first day of the New Year. I did not want bad karma to befall Mr. Hoan and his family.

Tet Celebration with Miss Xuan's Family

Sometime after my 2001 visit, Miss Xuan moved from her cashew farm in Hac Dich to Danang to live with her brother. Her nephew, Phuc, picked me up at my hotel on the day after Tet for a motorbike ride to his mother and father's home near the beach.

We drove along the bay front where two-story and three-story homes were painted in Easter egg pastels: aqua, turquoise, pink, and peach. We turned into an alley only wide enough for one motorbike and drove past homes built so close to each other they reminded me of the row houses built on the streets of San Francisco.

Phuc stopped outside a gated courtyard and Miss Xuan walked out the backdoor to greet me with outstretched arms. She wore a turtleneck sweater and coat. "January is cold in Danang," she said.

Miss Xuan and I sat in her kitchen with Phuc to help translate. I told her I was glad she moved back to Danang so I could spend more time with her and she said she missed her farm, her two cats, and her friends in Hac Dich. She complained of the cold weather and said she was "practicing" to live in Danang but she may move back to Hac Dich. She didn't like the four seasons and city life was too busy.

Miss Xuan brought out a dish of dried apricots that were orange, sweet, and covered with hair. She put one in her mouth and chewed for a bit, then spit out the seed. To me it tasted more like an apple than an apricot. And the dried apple I ate looked like a prune but tasted like a date.

Miss Xuan suggested we visit her sister's home, Mrs. Nga, who was seventy-eight and lived three houses down. She was bigger boned than Miss Xuan with the same smooth face as her sister but her hair was almost white versus the raven colored hair on Miss Xuan.

Mrs. Nga invited us into her home and told me her husband was not well so we could not go to the back room. He was blind now and only spoke of the past, the war mostly, she said. Mrs. Nga and her husband were officers in the North Vietnamese Army.

Miss Xuan took me upstairs to the family altar decorated with flowers and photos of Miss Xuan's mother and father and her oldest sister who died of cancer in 1978. There were two picture frames on the wall that held military medals. One frame belonged to the husband and one belonged to Mrs. Nga. The medals were dusty and looked like the Marine medals I received for serving in Vietnam. A medal with a faded red ribbon above a silver bar hung in each frame. The bar was inscribed with the word "*Su Dac Thang*" (Victory) and the date, "30-4-1975" (April 30, 1975)—the day North Vietnamese troops took Saigon. The majority of U.S. troops were long gone by then.

It was time for lunch so I thanked Mrs. Nga for allowing me into her home and upstairs to see her shrines and medals. We drove a kilometer down the same road to the home of Miss Xuan's oldest brother, Mr. Loi. The three-story, brick and stucco home had a wide terracotta tiled porch with two peach colored columns on either side of a double mahogany door. There were six tables set up for lunch in a spotless garage with tiled walls of beige above a leather wainscot. Tables were also set up in the dining room and patio. There must have been fifty guests in the home. A kumquat tree with orange kumquats stood at one end of the living room and a potted cay Mai tree sat at the other end. A wooden staircase and banister curved down to the middle of the room.

Mr. Loi's son, Mr. Linh, who worked as an engineer in Danang designed the home for his father. Miss Xuan's brothers and sisters celebrated their mother every year on the day after Tet and this particular year, the Year of the Monkey, it was the actual anniversary of the death of Miss Xuan's mother. All Miss Xuan's brothers and sisters, nephews and nieces, and friends gathered to pay tribute to the matriarch of the family.

Phuc invited me upstairs. He told me he and his aunt needed to pay respects to their ancestors and that shrines in Vietnamese homes were always on the highest floor.

Several guests walked down the staircase, children dashed around, and people walked into one room and out another. On the third floor we walked into a room with a rug in front of a mahogany dresser. The dresser doors were engraved with antlered deer, long necked roosters, and forest fairies.

A glass case on top of the dresser had a twelve-inch statue of a woman in a white shawl that held her left hand up with the middle finger touching the thumb and her right hand pointed down holding on to a vase. This statue resembled the Bodhisattva Miss Xuan bought me at her pagoda, except a light rotated behind this woman's head. There were also candles, smoldering incense, bowls of fresh fruit, and pictures of the mother and father and the sister who died of cancer.

Phuc knelt in front of the dresser, aligned his body, and kowtowed with his forehead flat on the floor for many seconds. Then he stood up and faced the shrine with his hands pressed flat together in front of his face. He moved his arms up and down three times and then prayed several minutes to his aunt and grandparents.

Miss Xuan whispered, "That is the picture of my mother and father."

"Yes," I said. "I met them in 1966."

She tilted her head up, wrinkled her forehead, looked at the picture again then smiled. "Yes, you did, Mr. Brian." She walked to the shrine after Phuc finished his prayer.

I had a minute to myself and wandered over to the large open rooftop with a panoramic view of the bay. The ritual at the grave of Mr. Hoan's daughter and the ritual here on the highest floor of Mr. Loi's home made me think of my father who died of cancer in 1991 and my mother who died several years later.

Neither my mother nor father wanted a funeral, they wanted to be cremated. Their ashes are in a mausoleum in Berkeley, California, behind two small doors, high on a wall of small doors, in a narrow alcove with shrubbery and soft music. I miss my mother and father. I have visited them once.

FORTY-EIGHT

Third Trip to Vietnam, May 2006

That howl, the howl first heard in this damned Screaming Souls Jungle right by this same stream in the rainy season last year, the last rainy season of the war. The howl from the valley on the other side of the mountain, echoing down to us. Some said it was mountain ghosts, but Kien knew it was love's lament.

—From *The Sorrow Of War*, Bao Ninh

MASS-2

I N 2006, ON my last trip to Vietnam, Phuc drove me up to the old MASS-2 Headquarters area again. This time I wanted to find the location of my old hooch and also find the location of my motor pool down in the valley. We passed through the same guard station we went through in 2001 and the guard again just waved us through.

Phuc parked at the MASS-2 Headquarters area and a man walked down the road toward us. He didn't look military, more like a farmer, and Phuc greeted him. They talked and pointed to various spots on the hillside and Phuc said, "This man works up here to plant eucalyptus trees for the government. He knows this was a military area in 1966 and now he lives in a tent up at that high point."

"Why does he live here?" I asked.

The two men talked and then Phuc turned to me and said, "He must protect the young eucalyptus trees from ghosts."

The man smiled and waved and walked back up the road toward his tent. A question flashed in my brain about the ghosts but I only said, "Does he live with anyone?"

"Yes. His wife is there."

We walked across the road to look for the location of my hooch and stepped over a row of eight-inch eucalyptus trees planted parallel to the road. The spot where my hooch stood was now just palm fronds and overgrown bushes. I pointed to a bush, "My hooch was here."

"What is a hooch?" Phuc said.

"A hooch is a cabin, it's what we lived in. It's a Japanese word for 'dwelling' or where one lives. My hooch was a substantial structure that I shared with five other Marines. It had a corrugated metal roof and screened windows all around." Phuc took my picture with The Bay of Danang in the background.

We drove back down the hill to find my old motor pool in the valley but we couldn't find it and I haven't found it to this day. That entire end of the valley is now ground up into a rock quarry.

Phuc and I drove back toward Danang on the same road that Mr. Hoan and I took in 2001, the one with so many pot holes and the rivulet we had to ford. But the pot holes were gone and we didn't see a rivulet. The military base must have been dismantled because there were no barracks or buildings of any kind.

When Phuc came around a bend I recognized the hillside to our right as the large Seabee amphitheater area where the USO shows were held. "*Dung lai!*" I yelled. Phuc pulled over and stopped. During the war the hill above the old USO stage was covered with benches so we could sit and look down at the stage like spectators at an ancient Greek theater. The hill was now covered with manzanita and palm fronds.

We watched the Bob Hope Christmas show in the rain with

Joey Heatherton and Phyllis Diller. Bob Hope took off in a helicopter parked about where I stood. The slopped hill was perfect for a theater. There must have been three thousand Marines in the audience on that rainy day, maybe more.

This amphitheater, built by Navy Seabees (C.B. for Construction Battalion) wasn't the site of an historic battle or an area of great significance during the Vietnam War, but the theater kept my dream alive, the dream of working in theater or in film, acting or directing, it didn't matter.

I turned back toward Phuc and waved. I walked toward the area that would have been the stage. The hill above me was quiet.

"If we shadows have offended, think but this and all is mended: That you have but slumb'red here, while these visions did appear. And this weak and idle theme, No more yielding but a dream."

A Midsummer Night's Dream, my favorite play. I've directed it twice, acted in it three times, and saw Bert Lahr play Bottom in a San Francisco production.

Back at Phuc's motorbike he asked, "What is this place?"

"A theater. For entertaining the troops. I watched Bob Hope here one Christmas. Do you know of Bob Hope?"

"Yes, I have heard of Bob Hope. A comedian, yes?

"Yes."

"Brian, do you see many famous people?"

"Well, not up close. From a distance like when I saw Bob Hope I was way up in the audience. A few movie stars came into our classrooms at the Performing Arts High School where I ran the Theatre Program. Danny Glover was one."

"Have you seen any U.S. Presidents?"

"Ah, real close. President Kennedy, JFK. Do you know of that president?"

"Yes. I know of him. Did you see him?"

"Yes. He gave a speech at the University of Washington when I was a junior in the fall of 1962. He used our football locker room as a dressing room or a green room for relaxing before and after his speech. But a buddy of mine and I came a little early for practice and needed to get into our locker room. We didn't know anything about Kennedy's speech and our regular door to Hec Edmondson Pavilion was locked so we walked around to the stadium side and went in that door. When I put my hand out to open the locker room door it opened and President Kennedy almost bumped into me on his way out. We stood face to face, inches apart. I finally recognized him and smiled but by then some of the audience could see him and they started clapping. So I clapped too, right in his face and it startled him a bit. But he smiled at me and waved to the audience and walked past us and out of the pavilion."

"No autograph?"

"No. I didn't even shake his hand."

The Pagoda

The Principal of Hoa Minh School wrote a letter to me after my visit in 2001 and asked for money to pay for computers because they only had one computer in the entire school. I wrote to the Gates Foundation and explained the situation but did not receive any funds. Then I promised myself to give the school some of my earnings from writing this story and wanted Phuc to see where the school was so he could deliver the check.

(When I won $350 from *Crab Orchard Review* for a non-fiction contest I entered with a piece titled, "The Crabs of Vung Tau," I sent $150 to the school to help purchase computers.)

Phuc and I drove up Highway 1 and I pointed out Hoa Minh School on the left. Phuc saw the pagoda across the street and said, "Have you been to this pagoda, Brian?"

"Yes, I visited it during the war and also in 2001 with Mr. Hoan."

"Would you like to visit the pagoda again?"

"Yes."

Phuc drove his motorbike into the front garden and parked. The pagoda looked less cared for now than in the scenes of my movies. But there were still large pots with *cam chuong* (carnations) and fruit trees and flowering frangipani. We sat in a quiet place and the sun came out to warm us.

After a while I said, "Phuc, I'm still worried that Mr. Hoan and Miss Xuan believe I spied on them during the war because I always took movies when I came down to their school. And I came down maybe three days a week so I took lots of movies. The VHS one you saw and put on a DVD for me is only a fourth of the movies I took.

"Both Miss Xuan and Mr. Hoan believe I gave a photograph of your aunt to the Saigon police. She had to escape to the mountains to avoid being arrested. I would never teach someone English and go to their house for dinner and then turn them in to be arrested. I can't convince Mr. Hoan that I did not spy on them during the war. Nor can I convince him that I was not the one who gave a photograph of your aunt to the Saigon police."

"Brian, I spend most of my time to stay with some monks and I feel very happy to have the same point of view as them. I do not care much about the normal world, the world that I used to live before. I live the same way the Buddha lives so I am enjoying my life very much. You should read some works of the Monk, Thich Nhat Hanh.

"*Cam on*, I have read books by this monk."

Phuc pointed down the Highway to Hoa Minh School. "Please forgive all the teachers there. The Buddha taught me like this: You should not return to your past and you should not imagine your future because your past is gone and your future is not here yet. You must spend your precious time to live with your wonderful reality.

"I hope the Buddha's teaching will help you much, I know it is not easy to practice what the Buddha has taught. It takes time but if you work hard on it you will see the magic. If you take a good care of your breaths and your thoughts you will absolutely have very good health."

"I don't know about this but I will try," I said. "You have studied hard Phuc. I appreciate your knowledge and your guidance. *Cam on.*"

Resolution, 2006

Think of no one as "them"
Honor everyone's Holidays
Imagine other cultures through their poetry and novels
Listen to music you don't understand –
Dance to it

—From *How to Build a Global Community*,
written by the staff of Syracuse Cultural Workers

AFTER DINNER, MISS Xuan and I sat at her kitchen table with Phuc there to translate. The fruit bowl on the table was filled with *nhan*, the fruit similar to longan, and eaten by biting into its skin and sucking out the meat.

A television on the counter had a talk show on with the Vietnamese host dressed in a suit much the same as an American talk show host.

Miss Xuan wore a soft floppy stocking hat and a tan cardigan sweater. A Dry Erase board hung on the wall next to our table. Its white surface had a green dragonfly with big buggy eyes that Phuc's seven-year old daughter drew before dinner.

This was my last night in Vietnam and after several cups of tea, I figured enough time had passed so I could ask some questions that needed an answer. "Miss Xuan," I said, "Can you tell me why you left Danang in April 1967?"

She laughed and shook her head "no." "That was a long time ago."

"I'm curious about that story," I said. "I know it was a long time ago but I'm just curious what happened."

"I don't know."

"In Hac Dich, you told me you left Danang in April 1967."

"Yes. In 1967 I was, what do you say?" She looked at her nephew and spoke in Vietnamese.

"Watched," he said.

"I was watched by the CIA and SG."

"SG. What is that?"

"My aunt said 'SG,' which means Saigon government."

"But I did not know I was watched," Miss Xuan said, "until a friend of my family who worked for the CIA, informed me that I was watched through a photo that someone gave to the Saigon government." Miss Xuan raised her eyebrows to emphasize the point. "Two months after, a confidential policemen of the SG came to arrest me at my home."

"You were arrested?"

"Yes." She sang the word and held the "s" a long time. "I was, what do you call?" She looked at her nephew again, then without pause, said, "Lucky. I was lucky. I escaped through the fence in my backyard."

She stood up and looked at the Dry Erase board and paused for a moment, as if it were the first time she noticed the dragonfly. She walked to a sideboard and picked up a teapot, then said, "I ran to Mr. Hoan's home and asked him to take me to the mountains." She held the teapot next to her chest. "A decree from the SG about my," she paused, "activity, my demonstration against the war, was spread through the whole central region, so I had to go to a mountain base to be sheltered. That is the reason why I left Danang City." She returned to our table with the teapot.

"Were you sad to leave Danang?"

She set the teapot down and said nothing. The host on the television talk show stood to greet another guest. Phuc was interested and watched the show when he was not involved in our conversation. Miss Xuan walked back for three celadon cups that matched the teapot and put them on our table. She sat down in her chair and pulled the cups near the teapot. She smiled, took off her hat, folded it in half, and pressed it flat to the table.

"If I were arrested by SG government," she said, "they would think I was VC and I would be tortured. My life would be in danger of savage actions. My health was weak and my friends were dead." She nodded her head and opened her eyes wide, "Dead, or in prison. Or crippled".

When she took off her hat tufts of hair poked up in odd directions. She looked at me and tilted her head to the right. She was silent for a long time then poured tea into the three cups and pushed one to her nephew and one to me.

"*Cam on,*" I said. I remembered the story she told me in Hac Dich of her father's torture in the island prison.

"Vietnamese people," said Miss Xuan, "are good-natured, good-hearted, but can never accept to be a slave and never surrender. Many times I take to the street and demonstrate against the war. I love peace and I demonstrate against war." She spoke to Phuc in Vietnamese and he left the room.

"Do you think I had something to do with you being suspected by the Saigon government?"

Miss Xuan raised the small celadon cup to her lips and sipped her tea. "No. I don't think this. No. I am sad because Mr. Hoan said that you watched the teachers of Hoa My School and gave my photo to someone. I went to the mountains to avoid danger. I think, Mr. Hoan misunderstood, in fact, I don't suspect anybody."

Miss Xuan's fingers wrapped around her cup, "I don't regress and worry about anything. I always think that you are my best friend."

"*Cam on.*"

"You were enthusiastic and a devoted teacher at Hoa My

School. We thank you for your enthusiasm. After your visit in Hac Dich, I believe what you say is true. You're a good-hearted person, so didn't give my photo to someone to harm me and in fact, I don't care about this thing. To me, all of those things went by. Now I live in the present moment and this is the important thing. Is it right?"

I nodded at Miss Xuan. "Yes. Your poem, the one you sent to me that says, 'If your mind isn't clouded by unnecessary things this is the best season of your life.' I enjoyed that poem. I won't cloud my mind with these unnecessary things again."

"Yes." Miss Xuan laughed a high-pitched laugh and nodded her head up and down. "You're a good friend. You passed a long stretch of road to visit us, Mr. Hoan, my sister, and my niece and nephew. They love you very much, because you are a faithful friend."

The card that my wife, Vicki, sent to Mr. Hoan's house for my sixtieth birthday, read "Life can be found only in the present moment." Those words were written by Thich Nhat Hanh and had I paid attention to them and understood their significance, the fact that my Vietnamese friends thought I was a spy during the war would not have bothered me. It bothered me in 2001 and 2004, but on that visit in 2006 I was able to let it go.

Miss Xuan's message and stories that evening made sense to me. And Mr. Hoan's explanations of how it didn't matter what I did during the war, plus Phuc's belief that we must live in the present moment, has changed not only my way of thinking but the way I live my life. I'm not a Buddhist but I try to live in the present moment and not worry about the past or think too much about the future.

I'm lucky to call Mr. Hoan and Miss Xuan my friends. These two former teachers, half-a-world-away, small in stature, huge in heart, changed my way of looking at the world. What they thought my duties were during that long-ago war didn't matter. The fact that Mr. Hoan and Miss Xuan and their families invited me into their homes, trusted me, and appreciated my company, even though they believed I spied on them during the war, gave me a lesson in humanity and an appreciation of other cultures and beliefs. I have my flaws like everyone else and if my character is misconstrued or imagined to be something other than it is or was, so be it.

Phuc walked back into the kitchen and set a tray on the table. It was filled with narrow, white strips that looked like dried fruit.

"This candy is ginger," he said.

"Ginger is good for your digestions," said Miss Xuan.

"Thank you. *Cam on.*" The ginger was spicy and tasted like a ginger cookie. It weighed almost nothing and had the texture of a jellybean. I took another one.

"Phuc," I said, "when you told me the man on the mountain who planted the eucalyptus trees stayed up there to guard those new trees from ghosts, what did he mean by that?"

"Not ghosts," Phuc said. "Goats. He guarded the young trees from goats."

When I laughed at myself, Phuc laughed along with me. It was a misunderstanding of words. It was windy in those hills that day but in the meantime my brain concocted an elaborate Vietnamese myth that ghosts from the war wandered those hills near my old MASS-2 site like the "Screaming Souls" of Bao Ninh's *The Sorrow of War*. But I could not make a logical connection between ghosts and eucalyptus trees. There was none. Just as there was no connection between Miss Xuan's belief that I gave a picture of her to the Saigon police and the friendship we've developed over a period of almost fifty years.

"Miss Xuan," I said. "Would you mind telling me about the time you had to jump off the bridge to escape the bombs of U.S. planes? I am curious about that incident."

"Yes, I can tell you about that day. I was with women friends in the Que Son Mountains. After we attended a conference we walked on the Ky Lam Bridge and heard planes that came closer and closer. We saw that they were American planes, and in just a quick burst, the bridge was covered with fire. Napalm fire came from the planes, so we had no choice but to jump off the bridge. When I landed in the river my hat flew off my head and floated away in the current. A plane came toward the hat and shot many times. The bullets were meant for me but only my hat was destroyed. I was not scared because I must pull on some of my friends who could not swim. I dragged a friend to the bank and returned to the river for another friend. Then the planes were gone. We watched the fire destroy the bridge and soon it fell into the river.

Miss Xuan's hands lay flat on the table. I covered her hands with mine, "Thank you for sharing that story. I'm sorry that happened to you and happy you were able to escape and save your friends." Miss Xuan smiled. "I appreciate the invitation into your home and to meet your family again."

"We want you to enjoy Vietnam," she said. "I hope the people all over the world understand and love one another. You and me and the people are ready to forgive and wipe out all enemies and resentment. To live ourselves in peace and the immense love."

She slipped her hands out of mine and reached for my empty teacup and filled it from the teapot.

"*Cam on.*" I held the small cup with both hands and warmed my fingers, then raised it to my mouth. The steam and spicy jasmine aroma washed over my face as I took a sip.

ACKNOWLEDGMENTS

VICKI L. BIGGS, for reading every word of every draft and telling me over and over to keep my own voice. Joanna Rose, who was there in 2000 to tell me to love my objects. Larry Colton, for untold hours of guidance. Robert Templer, for writing *Shadows and Wind: A View of Modern Vietnam* and advising me in May of 2000 to send a photo of Mr. Hoan and Miss Xuan to Hoa My Elementary School. Father Tran Van Doan, a priest in Danang who found Mr. Hoan because of that photo and told him I wanted to contact him; Father Tran Van Doan's niece, Hoa Tran, who sent the letter and photo to her uncle. John Balaban for his inspiring work in Vietnam, his books, and his confidence. Charlie Barnes, Eric's brother, for his knowledge, our discussions, and his friendship, Laura Stanfill, for advice and coffee. Jackie Shannon Hollis, for her support and advice. And Miss Xuan and Mr. Hoan and their families who were happy to send information whenever I asked.

George K. Myrus for his company on the ship and his knowledge and friendship. George Rodowsky, for bringing us all together. Jim Moran, Harry Stockton, Dick Amos, Charlie Bond, Tom Dieter, Steve Hurney, John Danko, Arthur Vandiver, John Dicheira, Dinh Dinh, Leonard D. Tygart, Bob Wix, Leonard T. Clark, Leon J. Bochenski, Jr, and Colin R. "Collie" Biggs, my dad, who taught me how to walk through the forest. *Semper Fi* to all of you.

My mom, Jean Biggs, for supporting my interest in the arts. Bob Biggs, my brother, for his friendship, his service, and his knowledge of cars. Bob Anderson, for information on Dong Ha and reading many chapters. Stevan Allred, Joanna Rose, and the Pinewood Table Writers Group for listening to all my chapters with a careful ear. Andrea Davis for advice; Colleen L. Biggs for the valuable information in my letters; Bob and JoAnn Mansfield; Steve and Danielle Tee; Kristin Firth, Mia Matasou; Jim Eaton, Bobby Campo, David Kelly, David Biespiel, Wendy Willis, Karen Karbo, Lee Montgomery, Debra Gwartney, Tom Larson, Gardner Mein, Ty Boespflug, Hoang Minh Tran, Thu Thuy Tran, and Amit Vishwas; Jeff Bechthold, Director of Athletic Communications at the University of Washington; Carter Henderson, UW Associate Athletic Director; John W. Croy of AVP Media; Doug Siegfried from the Tailhook Association; Bodhipaksa for info on Avalokitesvara; Dr. Neill S. Cowles and David Schor, members of the Barnstormers Band; Frank King at Ross Island Sand and Gravel; Mike Pacey, Butler Manufacturing Company for info on the Butler Building; Gert Almind, for info on Cinebox; Bob Orlowsky, for info on Scopitone; Leonard Gorelick of Antelope Valley Equipment and Truck Parts, for info on grease points; Pat Ware, for info on the Cerlist Vehicle; and Jeff Morton, the bug man in Jacksonville, North Carolina.

ABOUT THE AUTHOR

B RIAN M. BIGGS attended the University of Washington on a football scholarship (this included a trip to the 1964 Rose Bowl) and majored in Theatre. He ran the Theatre Program at Franklin High School and Jefferson Performing Arts High School, both in Portland, Oregon. He was also Executive Director of Young Musicians & Artists for twenty-two years, a performing and visual arts resident summer program held at Willamette University, now in its fifty-fourth year. His stories, poems, essays, and photographs are published in *Crab Orchard Review, Perfume River Poetry, Brave on the Page, Oberon Poetry Magazine*, and *Stone Path Review*, among others. He lives with his wife, Vicki, in Oregon City, Oregon, on five acres. Vicki tends to her two horses; Brian writes and tends to his garden. They both love on their black lab, Boo.

www.hellgatepress.com

CPSIA information can be obtained
at www.ICGtesting.com
Printed in the USA
FSHW011302130819
61006FS

9 781555 719524